STATE IN INDIA, PAKISTAN, RUSSIA AND CENTRAL ASIA

STATE IN INDIA, PAKISTAN, RUSSIA AND CENTRAL ASIA

Rakesh Gupta

Publications
KALPAZ PUBLICATIONS
Delhi-110 052

State in India, Pakistan, Russia and Central Asia
(International Relation)

ISBN: 81-7835-263-X

Published in 2004 in India by
Kalpaz Publications
C-30, Satyawati Nagar
Delhi-110052
E-mail : Kalpaz@hotmail.com

Laser Type Setting by: Varsha Graphics, Delhi
Printed by: Mehra Offset Press, Delhi

For

Kaushal and Debjani

enjoying critical mass

Contents

Preface

This book is a product of writing on these various cases over a period of five years. These writings were a product of my teaching interests. I have rarely had an opportunity of discussing these in their finished form with any one. Part of one of these chapters were presented in brief and different versions in seminars in the last five to seven years, especially on Central Asia and Russia. I must confess that there was no felicity of discussions owing to the nature of these hurried though significant seminars. The chapters on India and Pakistan have not been presented before.

The rationale for bringing these together is that since the end of the cold war and the onset of the new hegemony of globalisation patterns of constructing the economy and polity in the new states of Russia and Central Asia, though unprecedented in history, follow a similar trajectory. It is a transition with common features of authoritarian structures and extended accumulation. These, secondly follow similar patterns with transformations with states like Pakistan, which transited from colonial to peripheral imperative. In that sense they go to prove that transitional Third World States that do not have a democratic revolution land up with authoritarian governments. The difference between Pakistan and these new developing States is that there is a lack of militarism and religious sectarian strife in the erstwhile Soviet Central Asia, though they may be on their way of being caught in the peripheral imperative and cultural dynamic of sectarian segmentation. They are in any case with Russia in the CIS (Commonwealth of Independent States). In case of Russia though it will be too early to claim that it has a peripheral status, there is no doubt that it has anarcho-capitalism. Further there is no denying the fact that the democratic institutionalisation is weak and the State is authoritarian, under a plutocracy and a market, that implies mafiaisation. Currently Putin is engaged in expelling some of the Plutocrats and the Courts are registering cases against some of them who are in power. The absence of rule of law was ignored by the West since it benefitted the Western companies. Its economy collapsed in 1998. It is owing to the oil prices that in 2000 the economy had picked up a little bit to four percent. Standing tall, despite its weak status as a borderline case of middle income country and threatened democratic culture, is India. It has had its weak moments of the Emergency (1975-77) where democratic rights were suspended, and, now when it is being threatened by the RSS through its surrogate BJP to become an authoritarian State. It's status as a democratic polity, despite the RSS shadow, is in sharp contrast to all the other cases.

Both India and Pakistan are different in matters of globalisation from the other cases we compare. We notice that the Russian and Central Asian States are the products of the globalisation drive that also imposes democracy and market. In case of Pakistan the impact of globalisation is severe. This could be only on a periphery. It has always been a part of the World Bank and IMF thinking. It has been twice a 'Frontline State' in the US strategic thinking in the region, especially with reference to the Muslim world, former Soviet Union and Afghanistan. This has happened during the period of three military dictators, Ayub, Zia and Musharaff, 1956-68, 1977-88 and 1999 till date. On the three occasions Pakistan's economy was in the doldrums. India's globalisation began in 1991, though it gained nothing by devaluing its rupee, under pressure from the World Bank and IMF, in the late 1960s. The policy of liberalisation followed since 1991 and pursued haltingly since 1995 needed no World Bank and IMF prescriptions on democracy, pluralism, human rights and free press that it had prescribed for Africa. For Russia the European Development Bank for Russia's reconstruction had desired it to be a democracy. This did not happen. We notice that India's second phase of reforms is witnessing a threat to its democratic credentials. The programme slowed down since India did not benefit in FDI, as did China. The comparable figures of the two are appaling: it rose in India from $0.17 billion to 2.59 billion during 1985-96. For China the comparable figures are

2.65 billion to 42.3 billion. It is suggested that the slow down is also related to the pressures from the social sector and the BJP's Hindutva is to throttle that resistance. In Pakistan the bilateral and multilateral aid under globalisation has come during the period of Musharraf, who is occupying, like Zia, the post of the Army Commander and the civilian post of the President. Globalisation therefore has no links with democracy as the 19th century version of the liberal agenda had no genetic links with it. In order to hold on to the neo-liberal agenda in the Third World, the World Bank Report, 1997, talks about 'embedded autonomy'. The theme of autonomy is touched upon in the section on India as a case of functional flexibility independent of embedded autonomy. In all these case studies one notices that the ruling elites are able to insulate themselves from class pressures and pressures of groups in crisis situations as any technical intelligence is supposed to do. The manner in which Central Asian managers, the Russian plutocracy, Indian middle classes, Pakistan's military and civilian bureaucrats have handled change in the pre- and post-liberal phase does not call for 'embedded autonomy'.

They enjoyed autonomy before and after 1996. This raises a significant issue. Traditional wisdom has it that developmental states need the State while marketisation does not. This is untrue. The creation of free market is as much dependent on the State as creation of infrastructure or industrial enterprises. In fact the State is very much needed for market failures, if Great Depression is a case to remind us of it. The collapse of the banks and State intervention therein shows how they matter today even in the phase of post-Washington consensus. The State in the classical home of laiss'ez faire, the USA has not vanished. In the wake of the Japanese nationalisation of their largest bank (The Long Term Credit Bank), the New York Federal Reserve officials called all the CEOs of the Wall Street's leading firms and told them they would not be allowed to leave the room until they had agreed to take over the insolvent hedgefund, Long Term Management Fund. This was a tremendous assertion of the State in the USA. State in our case studies have not vanished and manage finance as much as political crisis. The autonomy of the State is a Weberian truism that operates in both developmental as well as market oriented societies. It operates in peripheral economies as well as those that pursue self-reliant economy. The Marxian truism would be with the refrain of Poulantzas who would attach to the present US State the title of Imperial State. Otherwise, it gets drowned in the din of euphemism like globalisation implying deregulation, liberalisation, privatisation, marketisation, etc. Today in India the consumer items are under licensed production as the defence equipment was earlier on. It needs to be watched for it may slide into the peripheral imperative under the present regime of Vajpayee. Today the Pakistani State manages popular revolt by the use of the military as it did yesterday. The Russian State is pushing for its Eurasian identity as it was pursuing Westernisation in the earlier period. The Central Asian States today are resisting Islamisation as they were doing earlier. Today the State there has to deal with much stronger competition in strategic terms than it had to earlier from the US.

This is to acknowledge the help of the staffs of the library of Institute of Defense Studies and Analyses, Amita, and the library staff of the JNU. My thanks also go to the innumerable students for a variety of help they gave me over these years. To my family special thanks are due for bearing my swings of mood and ailments. To Sunanda for being under constant pressure of mood and ailments (without reprieve) what shall I say! Last but not the least, I thank my father and my relentless teacher-critic, Prof. N. L. Gupta, for going through the chapter on India in its earlier smaller version. Both of us have looked at India in similar fashion- he with a broader vision and insightful depth. Further I hope both Debi and Kaushal do not mind my taking liberties with their names.

The weaknesses of the work are mine and none other bears that responsibility.

This is to acknowledge that parts of the chapters on Russia and Central Asia were pubished in Strategic Analysis, IDSA, New Delhi. The book in its present form has not been published earlier. I record my thanks to Dr. B.M. Chengappa, Dr. Arun Kumar Jana and Dr. Bhupen Sarma. I am thankful to Nitish for computerising a part of a chapter. I am also thankful to Mr. B.P. Garg and Mr. Amit Garg for publishing the manuscript.

Rakesh Gupta
New Delhi

1

State in India

The 13 day government of Vajpayee in 1998, the subsequent elections under it as a caretaker government, since the Congress could not form an alternative government, the making of the NDA government in 1999, the RSS' bloody flourish in 2002 in Gujarat, the testing of the nuclear weapon and the emerging nuclear deterrence, pale the destruction of the Babri Masjid in 1992 as a mild signal for the things to come. The destruction of Babri Masjid preceded by the Rath Yatra were stronger assertions of the communalisation of the political space that had begun as communal riot in Jabalpur in Nehru's last year of existence. Similarly, Bhabha's foresight about the nuclear issue and the Chinese going nuclear in 1964 were miles apart from a young Third World State joining the nuclear issue with China in 1974. Pakistan played the nuclear card since 1971 as against which India practised recessed deterrence. BJP attempted unsuccessfully a jingoist twist in the wake of a Pokharan-II in 1998. The State in India was increasingly coming under the shadow of arms twisting abroad and communal destabilisation within, punctuated by the regime of liberalisation and its attendant pros and cons of contracting social base, poverty percentage remaining constant and expenditure on the social sector declining.

Threat

The Gujarat carnage of 2002, the post-election announcement, by Vajpayee and Advani, that this was the pointer to the future Indian polity makes any one with commitment to the project of modernity with which India began its journey of independence sit up. At a discursive level is the State's march in India going to be of the RSS men in uniform? Is the cultural space going to have mahants as dramatis personae? Is the nationalist discourse in India taking the shape of the Kumbh mela? Is the search for the 'Mata' be the only search for identity in the women's discourse? Is the political message of politics going to be that politics in this country will be with 'trishul'? These powerful images generated by the present regime can easily be conveyed through the media. Is the extreme right wing ruse, called the BJP's five years completion going to be succeeded by authoritarian assertions of the RSS polity? In contrast to V. P. Singh's cap the BJP angwastram is far more serious a joke and needs to be taken much more seriously before the secular-liberal project becomes a mere laughing stock. There is a swell of mass support for the secular-liberal agenda that all parties need to support. Whether India follows Washington consensus (a prescription for Latin America originally) or not it needs to defend its democracy and prevent the RSS from turning India to authoritarianism. This would be a sad climax to a liberal democratic polity that has practised social development, much before the author of Washington Consensus, Williamson included it in his 1998 revisit to it.

Theatre

At a discursive level the State in independent India is like theatre. It has its tragedies, tragic comedies, comedies and farces. This is more so if one looks at the behaviour of elements of political class in relation to different regimes. Some regimes also have indulged in theatrical performances. We make a distinction between regimes and State forms. Poulantzas made the distinction thus

" ...forms of State must however be distinguished from forms of regime (a term we shall retain in place of the ambiguous term ' forms of government".

By forms of government he referred to presidential and parliamentary forms of government as being part of the process of maturation of the same social formation. We do not use this distinction[1] .We distinguish between different types of regimes on the basis of parties and the ideological orientation to the maturation process of capitalism in India and distinguish between the rightwing, leftwing and the centrist regimes. The Congress regimes have generally been regarded as the Centrist, the Janata regimes as right of the Centre and the BJP coalitions as extreme right. The changes in regimes are related to the changes in the electoral fortunes of the Congress Party which has also implied ideological change. The splits in the Congress have led to emergence of left of the centre politics of the Congress for a brief period (1969 - 75). The opposition mix of the right and the left in coalition experiments brought in right of the centre governments of Morarji Desai and V.P. Singh (1977 - 79, 1989 - 91). The latter came up with the middle caste radicalism of Lohiaism. All these regimes have been very different from the one that Nehru presided over and offered their own theatre.

These regimes have pursued capitalism with different set of policies and ideological orientation. The latter has some times threatened to under cut the path of independent development, though ironically, in its name. They have also represented different strategies of development, though very often their commitment to the goals of the Constitution have been farcical, if not tragic or tragic comic. Values of secularism, democracy, nationalism and the welfare State have been mocked on the basis of these very values being declared. Their goals have represented different stages in development strategy as also different set of development goals. Nehru's regime pursued mixed economy with an industrial policy that limited big capital, benefitted larger deprived segment and allowed for small scale sector to grow. This, Kothari calls, pursuit of happiness and the economists call the phase of accumulation of capital. Mrs. Indira Gandhi's first very long tenure, but especially during 1971 and 1977 was marked by pursuit of power at home and abroad. This happened after she witnessed the devaluation of the rupee under pressure of international finance institutions and an attack on her leadership from the rightwing elements from within her own party during 1966 and 1969. Her policies of Green Revolution, of defiance of the USA, of liberation of Bangladesh, nationalisation of the Banks, abolition of the Privy Purses, take over of the whole sale trade, strengthening of the public distribution system, peaceful nuclear explosion in 1974, *pattas* to the agricultural poor and the fact of having the maximum number of scheduled caste and Muslims in her government aimed at building up power with social justice. Her Emergency excesses brought in the Desai Government with a right wing tinge and the goal of defending democracy. It brought in the vision of Charan Singh's bullock capitalism. It implied agro-based industries and rolling plan that was considered as a plan holiday. The Government, though voted on the basis of massive rejection of Mrs. Gandhi, the Congress Party and the emergency, disintegrated on issues of personality clashes. That was a tragedy. Its farce being bringing in of a short-lived Charan Singh Government with the support of the Congress Party. The government of V.P. Singh in 1989 came with the tragic comedy of the BJP and CPI(M) support. The V. P. Singh Government, out of realpolitik, tragically started the jenny of caste and communal violence after he announced the implementation of the Mandal Commission in the name of caste-based social equity. The left parties got academically involved in discussing equity's class and caste dimensions while as the BJP unleashed the bloody tragedy of communalising the struggle for its chances to come to power. Then the three moments of liberalisation for arriving at prosperity during Mrs. Gandhi, Rajiv Gandhi and P.V. Narasimha's Prime Ministership arrived. Subsequent decade has witnessed the second phase of the reforms till 2002 crisis is the world.

This is also the time of farces. Piloo Modi paraded outside the Parliament that he was a CIA agent in the 1970s. Charan Singh declared that he would make the nuclear bomb from the ramparts of the Red Fort during his extremely short-lived Prime Ministership in which he never faced the Parliament. Raj Narain wanted to give to ministries a rural look by having a village like décor in his office. V. P. Singh's cap became a laughing stock. Dewe Goda was reported to be sleeping during his meetings. Atal Bihari Vajpayee formed his first government, knowing that it will not last. Yet, he said during the confidence vote that he was bound to loose, that he was not after power. He did not even wait for the Parliament to decide anything on the motion. In 1998 elections he formed the Government again with the support of the NDA and remained in office for a full term, even though this was the BJP Government. At one stage the BJP had announced that it will go it alone. Today it is claiming NDA stability.

The tragedies with ironic twist are quite a few. Pandit Nehru's view that development would mean an end to strife, particularly communal ones, did not. His quest for Panch Sheel, for no fault of his, got a rude shock at the hands of the Chinese who were known to practice realpolitik. Mrs. Gandhi's quest for power witnessed the beginnings of terrorist violence[2] and by 1979 opposition terrorist activities came to the fore in Punjab and her assassination by her own bodyguards. Rajiv Gandhi's quest for helping the Sri Lankan's by sending the Indian Peace Keeping Force had its tragic other in his assassination through a conspiracy by the LTTE. Morarji Desai's search for Gandhian version of moral values combined with a stress on his personal and political fads, led not to democracy's enrichment. It led to instability and anger in the north- east, particularly at a time when negotiations were on to reign in insurgency there. V. P. Singh's desire for social equity led to self-immolation on behalf of the students. The second regime of Atal Behari Vajpayee and RSS parivar's Hindutva has led to the tragedy of assassinations of the Scheduled Castes, Muslims and the Christians. Communal violence has been the tragedy that this regime has witnessed beginning with the Rath Yatra[3]. This was followed by the demolition of the Babri Masjid that saw a nation weeping together and in fragments. It then meant a decline in the moral stature of the office of the Prime Minister since P.V. Narasimha Rao could not prevent the destruction though he had information that this was being done. In 2002 Gujarat witnessed a version of the RSS polity through the carnage bordering on ethnic cleansing since the ruling BJP had started loosing votes in the local elections to the Congress.

The theatre has not been of the Brechtian variety. It did not, except in case of a miniscule minority, did not lead to political alienation from the system, nor even from the one dominant party except for two brief interludes till the beginning of the 1990s. After the assassination of Mrs. Gandhi there was an unprecedented mandate from the electorate for the Rajiv Gandhi Congress. It is only in the 1990s, particularly after Narasimha Rao's Government that the Congress has vacated the political space that it had occupied. The attempt on the part of the BJP to fill it up has not succeeded despite the divisions in the anti-BJP votes. The voter still is aligned with the original values of liberal democratic constitution and the development strategy that focuses on developing capitalism on a welfare path. The electoral pattern has shown an ever increasing voter turnout, both male and female.[4] In the elections in Gujarat after the communal carnage the Congress got 45 per cent votes and is identified with the poor of the State. At Panchmani it has openly declared to be the party of the poor.

Mythical Tool

Many strategies were adopted to harness voter support at the ideological level, especially through the audio-visual media, particularly conventional cinema which replaced theatre. This has been a very popular medium through which the messages of the Indian State and the regimes that occupied it have been filtered to the nook and corner of the Indian citizens' psyche in the urban and rural sectors. This has been done through interpolation and representation through conventional and political cinema. Distancing of the masses is possible through peoples' cinema which has not been popular cinema. In fact conventional cinema itself has a political package.[5] Contrary to this cinema it is the people's cinema that actually exposes the people's alienation from political practice of the State. But this is very ineffective. The mass appeal of populist cinema makes actors like N. T. Rama Rao, Ramachandran, Amitabh Bachchan, Rajesh Khanna, Rajni Kanth, Jaya Pradha, Jaya Lalitha, Vyjantimala, Dilip Kumar, Vinod Khanna, Raj Babbar, Hema Malini, Shabana Azmi, Shatrughan Singha and others win elections or get them nominations to the Rajya Sabha, National Integration Council and other public posts as Ministers. Appealing to mass culture conventional cinema performs the ideological role of the State in the society.[5] State and cinema's close identity has been there since the freedom struggle. They help in creating icons on the basis of myths, culture, identity of the self and the other, idioms of political practice and policy. Some views are in order here.

"Phalke's mythological enjoyed immense popularity not only in Bombay but also in other urban centres of India. Their success convinced some Indian industrialists of the profitability of investing in films."[6]

Sunita Chakravarty shows that the films in independent India articulated the dominant themes of Indian politics.[7] Very rarely did they offer a view into smaller cultural narratives away from the dominant narratives of the regimes in power. Partition, hunger, pursuit of happiness and early period of development construction and generally the Gandhi-Nehruvian model was supportively portrayed. Abnormal times of wars were similarly portrayed. The next phase of politics under Mrs. Gandhi with its mix of power and emerging violence was subjected to the camera's gaze. This produced the Bachchan icon. It became an icon since conflict was resolved through mother love, search for family and domestication of the woman. Lalit Vachani says of this.

The antagonistic relationship between the State and industry should not obscure the fact that the Hindi film performs a significant function in extending the hegemony of the ethical - moral State...' which '... broke the linguistic barriers that impeded communication in India and in inscribing the spectator - subject in a complex nationalism.'[8]

With the advent of political leaders into reins of power, like Laloo and Mulayam Singh Yadav, the representation of the middle castes finds their icons. Phoolan Devi became Bandit Queen with social sanction and applause.[9] With the BJP regime coming to power Hindutva is sought to be constructed through the audio - visual media. This is done through '... television production, videos and by the body metaphors of India being shown as a woman's body or through Murli Manohar Joshi's Ekta Yatra being represented as Ekatmata Yajna staged by the VHP in 1983.'[10]

Lastly the NRI phenomena, the phase of liberalisation and the images of plentitude portrayed through deep focus is represented by the roaring success of films like Hum Apke Hein Kaun and Dilwale Dulhania Lye Jayeinge. We have taken this detour into cinema since it reflects the myth of political practice of the State and that has a mass appeal which turns into voting behaviour. In any case the ideological reformulation of social needs backs up the discourse of the State.[11] Films that are partially in the fold, ones that attack the dominant ideology, and, avowedly political films have a binding thread: dominant nuances of politics in each regime type. The overtly political films in independent India since Neecha Nagar to Dil Se and Sarfarosh are critically or fully supportive of the State, sometimes at the cost of misrepresenting pluralities of India and smaller and micro narratives, especially the narrative of the Muslims, dalits and the poor.

To look at the Indian State as theatre or cinema is not to trivialize it but to lay bare the reach of the State in its construction of a social formation. It is in this fashion that Amiya Kumar Bagchi has noted the colonial rule. He said of it

' ...some theatre is more awesome than others, and some theatre involves more pomp and circumstances than others. The theatre of rule also involves careful management of the distance between the watchers and actors. The British administrators who came to India habituated as they were to the ways of 'gentlemanly capitalism', and as agents of a mercantile organisation owing its birth to the same compromise that legitimised the same landlord oligarchy of the 18th century, were well used to the nuances of theatricality of public rule.' Bagchi recognises the theatricality of the democratic rule as well.[12] In case of the Indian State the Brechtian distance between the actor and the watcher is very little despite the existence of poverty, ennui and alienation in certain pockets. The middle class that mans the State and carries forward its business creates a sense of nationhood by engaging in the drama of managing class alliances for transition to capitalism as a dominant mode of production. This is as well portrayed in the cinema.

Centrality

As a category of analysis the middle class is relevant in the Marxist and non-Marxist social science. Marx and Engels' writings on the German State, on Eighteenth Brummaire, on Hegel's Philosophy of Right, in the Communist Manifesto in the fourth volume of Capital and their correspondence they refer to the middle class.[13] In the Capital they refer to the growing number of the middle class that stands between the workman on the one hand and the capitalist and landlord on the other. This class is not the owner of capital or land but mans the tertiary sector and has diverse origins and episteme positions. In the context of the State, Verma refers to the acquisitive role of this middle class without looking at its diverse background and potential.[14]

The centrality of the State cannot be minimized. Whether a plug board, an arbitrator or protector its inevitable interventionist role in a Third World country cannot be ignored. We focus on it as a protector. In Mills' theory for achieving a society of 'free and equal individuals' the State played a Minimalist role in the political economy of capitalism. Marx interpreted the argument of Mill as one for a Maximalist State. Marx himself opted for a Maximalist State. So did some of the leaders of the Third World after completion of the liberation movements. The history of the liberal State in the West has evolved from being a facilitator to regulator to developer and interventionist. A very brief period is marked by the State allowing the market to pursue its course and that also after the State had done its spade work. This has not led to a society of free and equal individuals. Macpherson has criticised the Western State for the lack of opportunity to participate owing to its links with the market.[15] That ideal is now sought to be achieved by going beyond the confines of the liberal and the Marxist framework.[16]

In the European context the centrality of the State raises a further question of the relationship between the State and Civil Society. Quite a few viewpoints are available. John Locke views the society not only as anti State and democratic but also prior to State. Montesquieu ,unlike Locke, does not consider it as pre-political. He considers the State as coeval with society. Rousseau's view is society centric and finds the creation of the Civil Society as a guarantee of democracy. Habermas gives us the concept of the public sphere in which he excludes the women and the plebeians. The civil society includes economic activities and associational life that leads to communicative action. This realm is constituted of public opinion, debates in the coffee houses, saloons, popular literature, newspapers and so on. Not only does this articulate a defense of society against State, in engaging the historically unprecedented public use of reason, it introduces a rational critical discourse on public matters. In Germany the theorising on the issue was State centric in the hands of Hegel. Positing of a Civil Society in a modern setting is possible with the liquidation of pre-modern social solidarities. In the Third World countries that are witnessing a mix of the modern and the pre-modern, it is difficult to adopt this approach. It can be done sectorally and not universally, given the ascriptive social order, and neo patrimonial culture. Civil society may support the State.

Society Simultaneity

There is the dynamic question of the agency of the State as an agent of modernisation and democracy. Is it possible to look at the State as an agency of modernisation and democracy? According to John Keane

"Sovereign State power is as indispensable condition of the democratisation of 'civil society.' And concludes that a more democratic order cannot be built through State power and it cannot be built without State power."

In the context of India, history offers us *simultaneity* of the processes of the State and the Society. There is their ascendance of the one over the other at different points of time in histories of specific States. The inter-action of the State with social formations in terms of ideology, social solidarities, family lineages and extension of real State Sovereignty from the nuclear areas to the far flung regions is noted both by Chattopadhyaya and Thapar in the historical antecedents of the Indian State.[17] The dependence of the State and Society has been mutual. A look at the debate on the State-Society relationship in feudal and late feudal India shows up the dominance of the State in terms of social change and autonomy of various social institutions. The theorists of the traditional polity or feudal State have not been able to deny the relevance of the State for the purposes of protection and development. It has had a significant presence.[18] The theories of Segmentary and Patrimonial State (with analytical lineages from Africa and Weberian Sultanism) have acknowleged the significance of the State over Society in the nuclear areas. The Segmentary State theorisation refutes political centredness and regards the State's sovereignty as ritual and not as real especially if one goes beyond the nuclear to the peripheral territory.[19] It is real in nuclear and ritual sovereignty in far flung areas. To quote Stein

"...such lineage based regimes never displaced the control of high caste, corporate assemblies in the river-valley cores of the Chola kingdom, but only in the dry upland parts of southern peninsula that were gradually opened."[20]

Once the Chola State expanded the same logic could not be applied. The State did become independent of the religious institutions that had earlier played an autonomous role. A similar argument of the dominance of the society is built for the colonial period with reference to the portfolio capitalists.

The high noon of the feudal and the pre-colonial State showed that the State remained central to economic and societal processes. In the Colonial State this happened with a dose of racism and exploitation. We are currently not looking at the debate on the exogenous or indigenous sources of the Colonial State. We note its centrality in pre-colonial and colonial periods. In the post-independence period that centrality continues for the purposes of development, as noted by Bardhan, in an argument against the society-centred positions of contemporary contrary theorisations. The central role of the State, as a material base,[21] filled an institutional vacuum and its continued relevance in the wake of threat from local Bonapartes in the social structure at the local village level, absence of economic rationality at the local level, the need to extend the market production and exchange and for removal of regional imbalances between well endowed and poor State units. Given the presence of imperialism the need for nascent capitalist State to assert against the practices of the multinational corporations and predatory and savage practices of the predatory States[22] and predatory policies of international lending institutions has been underlined by the State intervention in India.

We assume the centrality of the State, recognise its role as a protector, and focus on the centrality of the middle class in the management of its social alliances to extend the national agenda of development with welfare as also its role in the phase of globalisation. We look at its ontos - not in historical and metaphysical but social terms. We look at the State Society processes as simultaneous with a State centredness as an independent variable. This helps the penetration of the market into the pre-capitalist zones of economy and change feudal relations to wage relations of production. It is the State that through its legislations puts forward the scenario of fighting the institutions of feudal labour practices like *begari,* forced and unpaid labour and if the local high caste landlords inflict injuries for refusal to perform this, the State, with all its halting intervention, comes to protect the victims. For this chapter we use the category of State-Society simultaneity as suggested by Chattopadhyaya. Salient features of this are; he delves for its conceptualisation into the 11th century. He suggests that State and private interests developed simultaneously and in terms of one another to enhance the territoriality of the State-Society from the nuclear regions to the periphery through ideological legitimisation (religious), administrative hierarchies and social rankings. All this led to the State structures penetrating resource base. This was the integrative process then. Ignoring the intermediate stages of State and social formation we opine that the State-Society relationship is very much similar given the modern context of transition to capitalism, the ideology of unity in diversity, democratic legitimisation process with its subsets of caste, cultural, regional and class dynamics for the integration of the peripheral to the nuclear regions through capital in market relations. At the core of this process is the middle class with functional flexibility, as an extension of the Weberian technical intelligence that he posits in the bureaucracy and modernisation.

We assume that western concepts of power were modified to bring in the Indian dimension to it. Power has been variously defined to imply the appropriation of the labour of others for one's own rational satisfaction. Its articulation is classically provided by Jeremy Bentham.[23] The Indian concept of power would have an added dimension of protection/ service. Chattopadhyaya says, temporal power meant that the State was to give protection. For him it would be too narrow a view of protection to take it simply to mean the physical protection of subjects. Protection related to ideal social order as defined by the guardians of the sacred domain. The ideal social order was defined. The King was recognised to preserve social order, he was at the same time enjoined to allow the disparate dharmas of regions, guilds and associations and social groups to continue. The territorial spread of the State-society required the cutting through the tangle of disparate *dharmas* by ensuring the territorial spread of the *brahmanas* and of institutions representing a uniform norm or other caste became the vehicle of spread for it the structure. In the religious process local cults were integrated.[24] In case of Nehru the extension under unity in diversity meant a national unity in plural composite terms through scientific temper and not Hindutva, welfarist economics and democratic polity. In the 11th century the wielding of the 'danda', was accompanied by two constraints. They were that the structure of the nuclear region and the need of that structure to recognise different social rankings in local identities (polities) and their accommodation in the integrative process. Accommodation became the condition of the process of integration. Coercive use of power had its other in accommodation for the purposes of integration. In the democratic process the strategies of coercive use of the State needed to be accompanied by processes and strategies of conciliation in conflict situations with national integration and not Hindutva assimilation as the watch-word.

If expansion meant the more developed region performing the expansion, then integration of the newer regions lead to the development of the newer regions. For R.S. Sharma, who uses Marxist categories of analysis of the feudal State, this expansion of the developed region into the periphery or the less developed region marked the predominance of the State in the more developed iron age of the upper Ganga region in contrast to the less developed iron age region of the mid Ganga.[25] The analysis of the process is society centric here as different from Chattopadhyaya, who emphasizes the simultaneity of the State and Society's processes. The function of the State in R. S. Sharma is to uphold of family more importantly the hierarchical relations involved in the Varna system. We assume the simultaneous process with interchangeable importance of the State and Society to be a more useful understanding of reality as it evolved then and as it evolves now. Nordlinger's prioritisation if the State-Society significance does not deny the autonomy of the State over society.[26] Apart from the function of protection we discover the ideas of fair play and justice related to the high noon of the feudal State, particularly during Akbar's time. *Ain-I-Akbari* says of Akbar.

"He showed, besides, no partiality to the Muhammedans: and when in straits of money, would even plunder the mosque to equip his cavalry." [27]

On issues of fair play and controlling the rapacity of the traders the document notes,

" Many people are desirous of building houses; but honesty and conscientiousness are rare, especially among traders. His majesty has carefully inquired into their profits and losses, and has fixed the prices of articles in such a manner, that both parties are satisfied."[28]

In his time Akbar had humanised the *mansabdari* system which meant dealing strictly with the officers of the State. *Ain-I-Akbari* notes,

"...Sabdars had been guilty of bribery and dishonest practices. He therefore appointed, at the recommendation of near friends ...when His Majesty discovered that qazis were in the habit of taking bribes from the grant holders, he resolved... to place no further reliance on these men...who are bad at heart...and fall short in sense...and dismissed all qazis."[29]

On the functioning of the *bazaars* the State functioned as a regulator. Success in statecraft, i.e., advancement of agriculture, order in the household, the readiness of the champions of the empire and the discipline of the army was

"...connected with the exercise of the proper care on the part of the monarch, his love for the people, and with an intelligent management of the revenues and the public expenditure. It is only when cared for, that the inhabitants of the towns and those of the rural districts, are able to satisfy their wants, and to enjoy prosperity. Hence it is incumbent on just kings, to care for the former, and to protect the latter class of men."

This idea of protection is found in Chattopadhyaya's analysis of the State in the 11th century.

The current culturalist discourse available in the writings of Bailey, Sanjay Subramaniam and Stein[30] focuses on the autonomous role of the bazaars, economic dynamics in the society (portfolio capitalists) and other merchant industrial entrepreneurs. They regarded the State to be detrimental to the society. Marxist writers like Irfan Habib and Satish Chandra focus on the extraction of the revenue by the State for helping the activity of commerce. The former find the commercial activity of the social groups as anti-Statist and democratic while the latter group regards the collection of the revenue as helpful to the commercial activity within the feudal paradigm. They suggest that it is the progressive urges of the society which provide the basis of the subsequent Colonial State. Whether this means autonomous democratic urges of the society independent of the State will be discussed later when we deal with approaches to the study of the State in India, particularly when we deal with Rajni Kothari's theorisation of the State as being against Society in India's history.

In line with Chattopadhyaya's Society-State Simultaneity we reiterate that the political and the social had a more dynamic functional fusion and flexibility. The State policy intervened now with force and then with accommodation for both integration and to help the merchant, the merchant entrepreneur and the merchant manufacturer. The dynamic was now Society centric then State centric depending on the stage of the evolution of the polity. At the heart of this functionality lay the issue of the ontos or essence of the State. Whatever the ontos of the State, and, the

State-society social compact, its functional flexibility depended on the State. Bureaucracy has ignored any religious or any cultural biases and prejudices except the interests of the State and Society.

We want to stress that the independent State of India, under the Nehru-Gandhi model of development, had more in common with the Indian concepts of power, protection and service built into the modern notions of polity. It had its consent and coercion elements. It had its danda, dharma and development. The analyses of the Constituent Assembly show that it was the Nehruvian model that was the dominant one and the Gandhian frills were added to it.[31] The State in India is seen as representing the nation's aspirations with the least gap between the State and the Civil Society since it is able to manage the coalition of classes that forms its ontos and the popular support of the electoral majorities by changing the complexion of those coalitions by incorporating newer and newer groups as and when the need arose. It has expressed a *functional flexibility owing to its middle class technical intelligence* that has practised different liberal models of State intervention since Independence till the end of the 1990s.We focus on the middle class and the distributive function of the State. In the next section we go into a review of the literature on the State in India in order to justify our examination. We have a modest claim that the two dimensions of the State, i.e., it, middle class character and its distributive function need a sharp focus not given to it in the theories about it so far. The distribution function is under threat today.

Middle Class

Before going into the review we would like to get into our category of the middle class in the functional sense since we have already noticed above that it is a relevant category in the Marxist and liberal writings. It is a heterogeneous class with plural lineages. It has no single epistemology. Its view of the public sphere and the private sphere may be contradictory. It may have a secular view of the public sphere but a culturalist view of the private domain. It may view the State as a secular institution but practice mobilization strategies on the basis of caste and communalism or on other ethnic and cultural grounds. It may have democratic, communal and fascistic tendencies and within the democratic it may have a neo-liberal or liberal welfare view of development strategies.

In Europe its duality has been noticed, particularly with its lower sections. Carsten highlights this duality with reference to fascism in Germany. He says,

"In Germany as well as in Italy some social groups were more inclined to follow the fascist appeal than others; this applied in particular to the old and the new Mittelstand, the self employed, white collar workers, lower grade officials, as well as to students and members of some of the professions, such as teachers and doctors." [32]

In the Indian case, Bipan Chandra takes a similar position about their dual role. He says,

'... they used the very conditions of unemployment, economic stagnation, underdevelopment and the atmosphere of frustration to arouse anti-imperialist movement' as well as 'petty bourgeois identity and ego got tied up with the cow or peepal tree protection and music before mosques that caused communal riots.' [33]

Historically speaking in India the middle class was split by the end of the 19th century. The one with the Congress was committed to articulating the demands for representative institutions. The other section was for revivalist identity. B.B. Mishra says of the split,

'The rise of the religious revivalism and the beginning of a split in the ranks of the middle classes formed yet another characteristic feature of the period to 1905....'

The signs of this split were available in the 1890s. It was basically due to two different reactions to the western influences which were of the reformist or the revivalist character.[34] The reformist middle class clamoured for social reforms, representative institutions and the protection of the Indian industry. The revivalist middle class, originating in lower middle class, receiving pre-university education in English and unemployed, appealed to tradition of all communities and defended the interests of the Indian industry. After 1905 the revivalist section engaged in communal riots.

The middle classes in India need to be distinguished from the intermediate and auxiliary classes in the peripheral States and Societies in South Asia and the Middle East that Aijaz Ahmed analyses. He includes small landowners, rich and middle peasants, the merchants of rural and semi rural townships, small scale manufacturers, retailers and so on in the category of the intermediate and auxiliary classes. He underlines the ruling caste thus,

"The professional petty bourgeoisie has arisen mainly from these classes and shares many of the same interests and attitudes, whether of the populist or of the revolutionary kind. The intermediate and auxiliary classes on the periphery occupy a strategic field in the economy and politics of their countries, thus obtaining powers and initiatives which make it possible for them to struggle for political dominance over other classes, including the bourgeoisie. Thus, elements drawn from these classes play a clear role in the construction of political reaction as well as in the process of radicalization and revolution." [35]

He excludes India from this category since India obtained a fully capitalist class during the colonial period itself, large fractions of which participated in the anti-colonial movement, and which emerged as the ruling class after independence, and although immensely powerful in its own right, civil bureaucracy in India has accepted the supremacy of Parliament and the highest judiciary, while the military bureaucracy has a remarkable record of obeying constitutional authority. In contrast in other peripheral societies despite their other differences a governing caste developed. In majority of the countries the Army is the predominant part of the State apparatus. Coercive minority regimes were established as a result and the State became absolutist and predatory. Against this the so called 'middle class' in combination with the landed elements leads the cultural ethnic national movements. In contrast to this analysis of Ahmed the Indian middle class is committed to the democratic institutions, the Army to the civilian supremacy, sections of the middle class emerging from the developmental model in different regions and communities assume their leadership to enhance their bargaining power within the system on the basis of secular or religious symbols.

Protectionist

We regard the State in India as independent and not post-colonial primarily for this reason. The expression used for peripheral States-post-colonial-devalues the more developed maturation of social classes - bourgeoisie, industrial labour, middle classes, heterogeneous peasantry - as also their role in the anti-imperialist struggle. It ignores the comparison of the Indian State with other peripheral States of the region. It ignores the development of the industrial capacities unique to India. The textile, tea, sugar cane, metallurgical and engineering industries had developed and the value of their output together as in 1949 was Rs. 4,986 million. According to 1951 census there were 13,540,000 people in the non-agricultural sectors in India and more than 4,600,000 worked in the large and small scale industry. Their employment in big industry was favourable to trade unions. The capitalists also had their own organisations at the time of independence. The non-rural petty bourgeoisie, as different from the middle class, was conservative and aligned with the rural rich. Each of these classes was able to engage in class and nationalist agitations during the twentieth century.

It would be Stalinist to call this nascent national effort as running dog of imperialism. At the time when India looked for autonomy in foreign affairs the Western powers led by the USA, expressed their hostility to its path of capitalist industrial development as well as its attempt to charter a different course in international politics of cold war. Birla's Bombay plan was not welcomed by the West. This contradiction cannot be explained by the theorists of One World System who regard the independence of the Third World States like India only as that of sub imperialism. One does not gain from this insight as far as this analysis' application to India is concerned. We do not concern ourselves with any grandoise goals that the State here in this country may have entertained. We do not look for any conspiratorial designs of the bourgeoisie to establish class rule or of the workers to establish a real people's republic through the Telangana type insurrection. We look at the functional flexibility of the Indian State for accrual of power and empowerment of different sections of the people internally by extending the benefits of infrastructural developments for balanced regional development of the classes of the country. In that context it developed its maneuverability in the foreign affairs as well.

Its sense of extending protection is signified by the following: (a) Absence of agricultural tax, provision for subsidized infrastructural inputs into agriculture from the community development projects through the Green Revolution to sectoral protection schemes for different segments of the rural population. (b) Changing of the procurement prices in the wake of the peasant agitations, particularly after it declared that there was no land that was surplus and could be distributed to the people. (c) It provides for free and compulsory education and cheap health services to the masses. These are unbelieveably cheap, particularly the higher education facilities, especially in the non-technical stream. (d) Restrictions imposed on the industrial houses with regard to the labour relations, e. g ., in relation to lock - outs, retrenchment, minimum and living wage. Minimum wage has been introduced in the urban sectors and in some States it has been introduced in the agrarian sector. (e) The State in India since the days of the Bombay plan that had asked for protection of the Indian industry continues to perform that role. During this decade the demands of the Indian business, in relation to the policies of liberalisation, for protection are heard by the State that manage recurring social contradictions.

II

Given this functional flexibility, of protecting different strata and classes of society, how does one understand the essence of the State. The literature on the issue has grown in volume in the last decade. With finesse and insights it has brought out the 'decreasing' capacity of the State to manage societal turmoil, overload of violence and deformities in the democratic process and constitutional values primarily owing to its shrinking class or social essence. The characterisation of soft (Gunnar Myrdal's expression)[36] and strong State continue to inform the literature. Myron Weiner does it in the context of the fate of the minorities.[37] Akbar and Sengupta[38] for siege in Punjab in the 1980s and violence. At the same time dominant streak of authoritarian responses of the State have been underlined by others in the wake of the Emergency.[39] This phase of the State is compared to the populist phase of Bhutto's authoritarian Pakistan.

Approaches

In 1990 Yogendra Yadav reviewed the theories of the Indian State. He looked at both its ontos and telos. He looked,

'... at the phenomenon from within and from without, placing its present in the past, and anticipated future, judging its significance, and choosing the worthy course of action.'[40]

Unpacking the writings, he classifies them as Liberal, Marxist and Culturalist. He suggests the titles as politico-institutional for the liberal, politico - economic for the Marxist and State and Society themes for the cultural classification. The problems with this trifurcating are quite a few. First, the politico - economic approaches need not exclude the politico - institutional. He does not mention this dimension. Second, in the politico - economic there are liberal, Marxist and agnostic approaches which again he ignores. Third, in the category of politico - economic he includes Gramscians like Sudipto Kaviraj. And Gramscian analysis is regarded as detonation of Marxism from within.[41] Fourth, the cultural perspective has since been enriched. Apart from the State versus Society approach of Rajni Kothari others like Partha Chatterjee have made substantial contributions.[42] More significantly, gender and ecological approaches have developed analyses of the Indian State as patriarchal and harmful.[43] The newer perspectives focus on differance, meaning to differ, or rather to defer, used to open spaces within institutions to dislocate the ties of an institution to any stable present [44], i.e., if there is a stable present. The basic criticism from these perspectives is of the Nation State and narratives supporting it are in need of deconstruction. It would be one thing to use the cultural difference for constructing the modernist secular evolving national identity through integration and not assimilation. It is quite another thing to use the cultural - gender and ecological-perspectives and other cultural axes of analysis like ethnicity, language and the rest for communalist integration/secessionism and terrorist politics. The Marxists need to work out their analyses with reference to these newer perspectives in order to pursue their own version of the modernist agenda in late capitalist societies pursuing liberalisation.

The survey is a useful key to understand the literature on the subject a decade ago. We propose to detail these for we discover that the issues of the functional flexibility, role of the middle class therein as the State's ontos is implicit but not explicit in only some of the writings. Not in Gramscian concept of relative autonomy. They focus on the role of the bureaucracy. They relate the crisis of the State to the structure. Classical Marxists use the concept of One Class to understand the character of the Indian State. Some other Marxists use the concept of multi- class character of the

State to understand its nature. We prefer functional flexibility to relative autonomy, which is more didactic and available in the Gramscian critiques predominantly. The word functional is used not to denote the State's function of system perpetuation but to denote a process in which the State itself is a significant part of the process of achieving the secular, modernist and capitalist agenda incrementally without any blueprints of social engineering. In this functionality we notice a continuum in external and internal terms. In the external terms it implies strengthening of the State and internally to lead industrial development and preserving a secularist ideology. The position of the historians is closer to ours here. As we noted earlier the position of the capitalist class at the time of independence played a crucial factor in favour of the people and the State.[45] (a) In the struggle between local and foreign capital, owing to the backing of the Indian State the Indian capital became less xenophobic.[45(a)] (b) The process of consolidation and social change through the mechanism of democracy made a qualitative difference to ordinary life, life styles and perceptions of the people. This meant a growth of democratic institutions, development of infrastructure, small scale, public sector and big private sector industries, the Green Revolution and generally further growth on capitalist lines with the State being a significant actor and not the market. It intervened in the market on prices, labour legislation. In the 1980s, e.g., it intervened in the wake of the peasant agitation for increased procurement prices. Not only the rich farmers but the entire peasantry benefited from this. Our concept of functional flexibility is rooted in the specific Indian reality and not in the south Italian transition from feudalism in which is rooted the concept of relative autonomy.

Unlike Yadav we do not look for a telos of the Indian State. He favours reintegration of culture and power. He says 'the recent inclination among social scientists to take up the question of culture, power and interests together is a welcome sign in this direction.[46] He suggests a need to shift from a European to the Indian agenda for understanding the Indian State. One does not know if there is an or the Indian agenda. Historians are divided between two viewpoints about India and the role of the State. They are not agreed on the issue of the place of change in India and the role of the State therein. Some believe that India did not witness change, while others underline the fact of change. Yadav is not concerned about this. He is concerned about some ethical mystical order. What is so typically Indian about this is also not clear though. The worst critiques of the western political order do not deny the original ethical dimension of the Western Liberal State in terms of freedom.

In the classification of political economy he looks at the writings of the Communists, and academics like A.R. Desai, Ajit Roy, C. P. Bhambri, Pranab Bardhan and Sudipto Kaviraj. Two ideas emerge from these which have relevance for us. The idea that the State is part of the material base in India (Bardhan) and that the essence of the State is reflected in the intra-class conflict (Bhambri). Bardhan's analyses are more erudite and combine the role of the State both as part of the material base and as an agency of development after noting Bhambri's intra-class essence of the State. Implicit in Bardhan's analyses is the idea of functional flexibility that one needs to focus on after the fundamentalist point of class essence of the State is made. The third significant idea comes from a more eclectic source : Rudolph's focus on democracy as developed by the Congress by the middle of the 19th century. Of Nehru's strategy he says 'the Nehru strategy was based on a coalition of urban and rural interests united behind an ... urban oriented industrial strategy. Its senior partners were India's small ... but politically powerful administrative, managerial and professional urban middle classes and private sector industrialists... the junior partners ... were rural notables, mostly large land owners who survived intermediary abolition and blocked the ... implementation of land ceiling legislation'[47]

Their earlier article's[48] argument of the command polity (1956-57 to 65-66) which later developed authoritarian traits (1975-77) and demand polity (1977-80) with shocks (1967, 1974-75, and the deaths of Nehru and Shastri) led them to theorise on *Stateness* in their later work. Their idea of Stateness reflects the flexibility of the State when they say,

'... paradox of a State that has, over the four decades, since independence, alternated between autonomous and reflexive relation with society in which it is embedded'[49]

This flexibility is expressed in terms of autonomy and constraints on it. This flexibility is not related by them to the role of the middle class or to class structure.

The writings subsequent to the review with regard to the ontos of the State are of Budhadev Bhattacharya and Dipankar Gupta.[50] Bhattacharya's view of the State, like Desai's, is that in the socio-economic formation the State is an agency of the bourgeoisie is the continuation of the classical view that the communists held.[51] Gupta's view that nationhood should be recognised since the developmental role of the State can be understood in pursuit of national interests and not just class, multi class or regime specific interests. Gupta's emphasis on the non-economic factors is helpful in our focus on the State-Society simultaneity. In looking at practice against the theory of one class character of the Indian State, Gupta points to the growth of the petty commodity producer in the *lal dora* belt of Delhi.[52] We noticed above the policies of the State help small sector to grow all over the country. This is possible if the nation operates as a reality in the policy goals of the State. Class analysis cannot deny this. Marx notes that this happens when the class represents the nation as a whole. In his own words,

'The class making a revolution comes forward from the very start, if only because it is opposed to a class, not as a class but as the representative of the whole society as the whole mass of society confronting the one ruling class.' It can do this because initially its interests really is as yet mostly connected with the 'common interests of all other non-ruling classes.... Its victory therefore, benefits many individuals of other classes which are not winning a dominant position, but only in so far as it now enables these individuals to raise themselves into the ruling class.'[53]

As for the Indian State representing the Indian society as a whole and its reflection in development policy the following may be noted during the period of Indira Gandhi whose rule is diagnosed by many as bringing on the political crisis of *over-centralisation* and the *powerlessness* of the Indian State. During her period the protection to the poor is seen in the granting of pattas to the rural poor for their plots of land, the various poverty removal schemes that she had initiated apart from the Green Revolution, the labour legislation preventing retrenchment of the workers, taking over of the whole sale trade in food grains. The nationalisation of Banks and the abolition of Privy Purses was a help to small taxi drivers and rickshaw pullers in towns through bank loans in and around Delhi. These very people had rallied for her during her fight against big capital. It is during her regime that Karnataka witnessed a radical implementation of land reforms under Devraj Urs. As a general point, not related to the rule of Mrs. Gandhi, it must be said that in terms of social mobility it would be an interesting exercise to see the professional profile of the sons of workers and poor peasants in the last fifty years. The point is that the State manages the social contradictions not just in the interest of the propertied class that rule. Apart from that it looks at social contradictions from the perspective of the interests of the nation, even while its policy pivot is pursuit of power. That was in case of Mrs. Gandhi's domestic and foreign policies. It is also during her regime that the spread of molecular capital in the Hindi belt increased cutting across caste and communal lines. The State has to currently integrate this capital.

The issue of ontos with relation to the non-ruling classes becomes more significant in the condition of absence of a vibrant workers' or a peasants' movement in the organised sector of the economy or polity. In that context the need to look at repression of the mass becomes timely since the cause of that repression may not have much to do with absolute poverty. It may have to do with relative poverty. It is not being anti-Marxist to look to relative deprivation as a causal explanation for revolt in the society. This revolt then is of the haves rather than of the have-nots. For a person like A. R. Desai the alleged repression against the poor is a product of the class nature of the State. The other side of the dialectics is that the State also uses instruments of coercion to protect the deprived from the aggressions of feudal remnants and from the emerging sections of society like the middle castes' violence against the scheduled castes and the communalist attacks on the minorities.

In the context of the anti-feudal role of the Indian State we notice Sudipta Kaviraj's view of structural crisis of the Indian State with reference to the feudal order a little out of place. He suggests that the Indian State is passing through a structural crisis. It cannot deal with crises. It fails to carry forward the tasks of capitalist development owing to the over-centralisation during 1971-87. This led to the growth of incompatible regional demands because the compact between the rich farmers and the bourgeoisie broke down as in Punjab. He has written the obituary of the

Indian State. He regards the responses of the Indian State as pre-capitalist and,

'...is proving incapable of providing the most vital preconditions for bourgeois development, preconditions of political stability.'[54]

The problem in case of Sudipto's writings is that one cannot engage in factual data to refute him or corroborate him since he believes in the fetish of theory and theory's logic. If you assume that the structural crisis is linked with the Indian State becoming more and more feudal than formal logic can only take you in that direction. One can only pose some issues. What are the feudal practices that the Indian State is engaging in. If this is with reference to use of the coercive State machinery then why regard it as a feudal practice and why not the practice of all democratic States. Second, is the making of political turmoil of the capitalist class' or the feudal classes ? We know nothing. Is the turmoil of the rich peasantry aimed at weakening the Indian capitalist development? Is it against the State engaging in the process of primitive accumulation? Did Indian capitalism require agricultural surpluses for capitalist development? Did the Indian State perform the role of the agency for that primitive accumulation even though from the beginning it never imposed an agricultural tax? Is it not an investor?

But perhaps Sudipto Kaviraj can turn around chameleon like and say that he talked about over - centralisation and not feudalism as the incapacitating factor of the Indian State. For a minute even if we grant that the period of over centralisation that he mentions as the cause of Indian state's powerlessness could be characterised as such does the subsequent picture of coalitions and lack of assertion on the part of the State since atleast 1992 in regard to the demolition of the Babri Masjid the State in India is now capable of getting on with political certainty and helpful for capitalist development? If capitalist development is related to expansion and the renewal of capitalist economy then how would he regard the period of liberalisation which began in 1980 and not after 1987. Since the coalitions were marked by support of the CPI(M) surely Kaviraj will not be saying that the State was moving towards Peoples Democracy and therefore it was not interested in having capitalist development.

At a more substantial level the issue can be related to the role of the middle classes in instigating and handling political conflicts in the Indian society. One section of the middle class could be interested in injecting revolt by using cultural symbols for capturing political power, as at the other end, the party of monopoly bourgeoisie, the BJP, would be interested in using the communal card to come to power. How does the section of the middle class that mans the State and is engaged in managing violence respond to the insurgencies and revolts of the different sections of the society and not just the rich peasantry? A close look at the Government's policy since the time of the formation of the seven sisters in the North-east shows that the State has used both its coercive and accommodating strategies for solving the problem. In fact negotiating with the insurgents/terrorists was started during the regime of Mrs. Gandhi and not by Pandit Nehru. In 2002 National Democratic Alliance (NDA) Government has negotiated with the BODOS and the NSCN (I-M). The formation of the States in the North-east was also undertaken during her regime and not under a left wing, right wing or any other dispensation. Again one notes here that the State shows its capacity for functional flexibility. These cannot be dubbed as feudal. The reference to middle class utilising agitations is not our invention. The middle class did this in combination of the caste factor with regard to the linguistic agitations during the 1950s.[55] Prafulla Mahanta leadership in the Assam Movement in the 1980s very much did the same. The social mobility of the middle peasant and its alliances during agitations in the 1980s show this as well in party mobilisations in the 1990s, e.g., in UP, Bihar and lately Gujarat (2002).

Kaviraj's diagnosis is closer to the Huntington thesis of non-governability of Third World democracies that he developed in the 1970s for the Trilateral Commission and that was developed much later by Atul Kohli with reference to India. In the context of social mobility and the breakdown of the earlier compact Francine Frankel also looks at the incapacity's of the Indian State. The advantage of a strong empirical base is with Kohli and Frankel and not Kaviraj. The latter consciously rejects an empirical approach. Instead of making a positivist argument against Kaviraj we quote from Marx on method of studying each of the forms empirically. He says,

"... by studying each of ... forms of evolution separately and then comparing them one can find a clue to the phenomenon, but one will never arrive there by the universal passport of a general historical - philosophical theory, the supreme virtue of which consists in being pure historical."[56]

The super theory of Gramsci and the lack of empirical data are some of the strengths of Kaviraj, he will think. Insights of Marx are not relevant for Kaviraj. Kohli has now defended Indian democracy.

Kalpana Wilson adopts, like Kaviraj, the Gramscian view of Passive Revolution and provides a different explanation of the failure of the Indian State. She regards the State as an arena of class struggle and posits the function of the State and of the dominant classes that disorganise the subordinate classes in order to achieve hegemony. The State in India has failed to achieve this hegemony. The reason in her case is the existence of the multiplicity of the modes of production in the Indian social formation. Some of these modes are of pre-capitalist nature and they articulate themselves in the political arena of the State as communal and caste ideology. Finally she relates the failure of the State in the ideological sphere to the crisis of accumulation owing to the class alliance that forms the Indian State.

In case of Wilson what is new here is her view about the ideological disarray of the Indian State owing to communal and caste ideological orientations which are the articulations of the pre-capitalist modes of production. We suggest that both caste and communal assertions are related not to pre-capitalist modes of production. Rather they are related to different sometimes over lapping bourgeois interests. We do not want to repeat ourselves on the issue of accumulation. However the running of parallel economy and the refusal of the professional classes, which are part of the middle classes, to file their tax returns could cause such a crisis rather than a breakdown of the alliance between the rich peasantry and the bourgeoisie. We also notice that in the latter part of the 1990s the private investment in industry has not picked up since the State investment has not increased. This is a circular logic in which only certain sections of the bourgeoisie are involved and not the rural classes.

With regard to the communal and caste ideological articulations we believe that these also do not have to do with the pre-capitalist modes of production. The literature on caste and class coincidence or lack of it is known. The related literature on the modernising role of the caste voting blocs is also known. The struggle of the OBCs and V. P. Singh's opening up the caste gadfly is also known. That move was to casteise the recruitment to the State since the State was being viewed as a milch cow. As for the communal mobilisations and their use by the BJP the analyses by Ashgar Ali Engineer[57] shows this to be a petty bourgeois phenomena and the writings of N.L. Gupta[58] show these to be related to pro-monopolist BJS (whose new incarnation is the BJP. Aijaz Ahmed's analysis of the State in the Middle East and South Asia, barring India, shows that the petty bourgeoisie may be in need of such mobilisations. The intermediate and auxiliary classes, he says

"...occupy a strategic field in the economy and politics of their countries, thus obtaining powers and initiatives which make it possible for them to struggle for political dominance over other classes, including the bourgeoisie. Thus elements drawn from these classes play a role in the construction of political reaction as well as in the process of radicalisation and even revolution.'[59]

In India some sections of these classes have awakened to the value of capturing political power. The political parties, in the wake of the decline of the Congress, are utilising this reaction for their own right—wing purposes. Some sections of this class while not being in power could also disarticulate the poorer classes on slogans that are beneficial to the bourgeoisie. For example the struggles for civil and human rights and not on issues of poverty, hunger and development could be such a dis-articulation. In this once again it is the middle class intellectual with the left liberal image and orientation who would be involved and he may have nothing to do with the feudal mode of production.

Finally related to the functional flexibility is the issue of the role of the middle class with regard to the system of distribution. It is skewed distribution that could lead to a crisis of revolt. This is not taken up by Wilson. It is relative deprivation that may cause dis-articulation and not the atavistic argument of pre-capitalist ideology. The issue of development and distribution is taken up by Terence J. Byres.[60] Supporting Gramscian analyses of Kaviraj, the author weaves the politico-economic with the chronologic-politico -economic dimensions of the Indian State. He links State

Planning to class structure to unravel the process and draws support from Partha Chatterjee. For him the State is an institutional ensemble involving bureaucracy, corporations, banks, sub central organs of power, representative assemblies, the police, the army, the law courts and the judiciary. The civil society is the site of primitive accumulation, habitat of classes and locale of class struggle. As an arena it is marked by class cohesion against subordinate classes for accumulation and of important class fractions leading to class frictions since they are enmeshed in the exploitative relationships.

In this the paradox of State power which is interested in capitalist development but has to accommodate non-capitalist or pro-capitalist classes that may develop powerful ideologies, in opposition to capitalism: ideologies of populism and neo-populism is unenviable. His analysis shows that there is a relative weakness of the urban bourgeoisie in all this.[61] From our perspective the ideology of populism is as much bourgeois as any other aspect of bourgeois life, and the relative weakness could be in relation to certain conjunctures associated with the dynamics of struggle for power in the political arena. As for the State this is related to the incapacity of the personnel to anticipate, respond in time and think out strategy for responses at a given time momentarily. To that extent that this is related to the dialectics of the politics that seizes the middle class. That the bourgeoisie shows its incapacity cannot be deduced from this dialectic.

Byres moves closer to the culturalist perspective of State and Civil Society. Chatterjee and Kothari elaborate on this. Chatterjee relates his analysis to hegemony. In functional terms Chatterjee describes the paradox of the interventionist State as being a manager and mobiliser of investible national resources for industrialisation and expansion of capital and the problems linked to the political process related to the federal structure and the problems generated by deprivation that in turn get related to ethnicity, language and other cultural issues.[62]

Both Byres and Chatterjee underline the issue of distribution of resources after they critique the developmental strategy. This is crucial to the functional flexibility of the Indian State. On the issue of distribution they however do not refer to relative deprivation. The discussion on distribution must also take into account the question of the nation and the principles underlining the system of distribution. The Classical and the Marxist political economy talks about distribution in great details. The issue in the national context is also significant. In case of the two analysts we do not know if they believe, like some classical Marxists, that class societies lead to the contradiction of absolutisation of riches and poverty. Further that there is no possibility of the poor and other sections of society on the margins of the rich from developing and prospering. In case they do then what is expected is only a breakdown of the capitalist system. If they do not then the nature of tensions in the political process that cause the paradox need to be analysed and so also their leaderships. The response of the State as well needs to be analysed in terms of its capacity to accommodate the aspirations of the people making newer demands. From a Marxist perspective it would be difficult to sustain the position of break down of capitalism. What is the Gramscian position we do not know from the authors. If they also believe in such a break down then there appears to be a resonance of the non-governability thesis.

To Kaviraj and Kohli we can add the names of Byres, Chatterjee, Frankel and Rudolphs. Rudolphs view that the Indian State's interests in themselves come in conflict with consumer and voter sovereignty, i.e., with democratic governance. For Francine Frankel India witnessed by the end of the 1980s conflicts that '...are all aspects of the social turmoil accompanying the collapse of the Brahminical order' and the emergence of other social and caste groups. The mobilisation of the backward classes was on caste lines. She says, '... among cognate groups that cut across class differences to maintain the segmentation of the poor around distinctive social, ethnic and religious categories, except in Uttar Pradesh and Bihar where the struggles were waged cutting across *varna* lines but significantly for the purposes of... replacing upper castes as political leaders.'[63]

In this paradox class politics has been marginalised for both Rudolphs and Frankel.

Kohli and Shue use the Weberian categories in their comparative perspective, to describe the paradox as that of over-centralisation and powerlessness of the State. The State as a result is unable to handle social fragmentation and political violence. The State gets attention at the political level because it is interventionist and mobilises the free floating economic resources. It is the source of social and political fragmentation. He says '...spread of egalitarian values, and of competing politics within the context of India's low income democracy and interventionist State have greatly politicised social conflict in a manner that has greatly contributed to fragmentation of India's political society.'[64]

This attitude towards the State being the cause of social and political conflict is further developed by Rajni Kothari during the decade under discussion. Both in his earlier book and a recent article[65] his position is that the State in history and during contemporary times is against Society, especially its petty bourgeoisie in history and human rights activists and the Dalits in the contemporary period.[66] The reason for its hostility is its essence, which is that it has lost its autonomy since it pursues narrow interests of the neo-rich and its allies in its internal functioning and dealing with the people. He says that the Indian State with its fast disappearing Brahminical order '... has become at once more centralized and more oppressive, especially vis-a-vis the deprived, the weak the marginalised (both traditionally marginalised and more recently marginalised) and the victimised sections of society by the 1990s.'[67]

He considers that traditionally the State and Society relationship was one where the society was democratic. In contemporary period the State has long ceased to be democratic, particularly with the arrival of Mrs. Gandhi on the scene , and the perpetuation of terror by the State against the Naxalites, the 'terrorists' , and the so called dacoits, i.e., any one who is found unwanted. For him human rights assertion in India is her democratic tradition.

This Bharat versus India view leads to the following prediction. He says, ' ...a precipice of a gathering decline, at any rate for the larger masses of the people afflicted by the failure of the social order to save them from destitution, disease and disorder', or '... opening of new creative spaces in which the people are found to manage things differently, away from the statist and globalist perceptions, with a new outburst of local democratic initiatives, emergence of new regional coalitions providing scope for new ways of organising both the human economy and the human polity' quite different from the Leviathan perspective.[68]

There are empirical, historical and theoretical problems in Kothari's position. At the empirical level let us take the case of criminalisation of politics. This criminalisation got reflected in a big way in the Indian Parliament during the regime of V.P. Singh. This was five years after Mrs. Gandhi's assassination. It is of course just a coincidence that during Singh's ministry Kothari was nominated to the Planning Commission. The process of criminalisation accelerated with the coming into power of the non-Congress governments.

Historically it is a myth that the society in India was progressive and the State an obstacle. We believe that at different points of time the State and society simultaneously progressed, depending on one another. At the initial stage if the State depended on Society, as in case of Chola history initially, the society also depended on the State for the expansion of the nuclear region into the periphery. Historians have looked at the Indian State from the liberal, Marxist and eclectic perspectives. R.S. Sharma suggests that State arose as a result of social differentiation and caste hierarchy.[69] Marx showed that class does not show any democratic urges in society. The State was there in the village community for the collection of revenue by Irfan Habib and Satish Chandra and for hydraulic functions.[70] The revenue functions were performed with fairness and not in a predatory manner. At the conceptual level the State in India has been characterised as *segmentary, feudal* and *patrimonial*. This is true of the State at different points of time. These concepts assume or show different patterns of the State and society relationship. The eclectic perspective of Chattopadhyaya is significant. He talks of the reciprocity of the State and society even when he recognises the role of the 'danda' (State coercion). The period of the peak of Indian State's power is marked by the rule of Ashok and Akbar. Both States were marked as Patrimonial. The concept of the Patrimonial State is borrowed from Weber's analysis of Sultanism. Athar Ali describes the features of the Mughal State: a *jagir* system, revenue system, absoluteness of sovereignty, religious and ideological traditions, blending with Akbar's rationality. It created an absolute sovereignty and a composite nobility rather than repressive or segmentary. Unlike in the Segmentary State, sovereignty continued to be in the State in absolute and ritualistic manner. This sovereignty was used to extend the reach of the patrimonial State to peripheral regions. The manner of this extension even while the danda was used was through a process of integration rather than assimilation. This process in any case neither shows the State to be repressive nor the society to be democratic.

The recent researches of historians with regard to the *portfolio capitalists* in which they show the State to be bad light are too preliminary to be based upon. In any case some of these writings find the autonomy of the petty merchant- trader wanting to be industrialist as the native or indigeneous roots of colonial rule. We consider this as one of fluidity. Sometimes the State was leading the society on the path of development and democratic urges and at other times it was the society. There was no democratic Bharat that Kothari pits against India as far as Indian State in history is considered. From our perspective of the middle class, we can say that even in the late Mughal period the intermediary classes had powerful and strong elements that depended on the State for their survival and expansion —as does the bourgeoisie today. The portfolio capitalists as much depended on the State as do the present day capitalists even if one keeps the differences of scale and nature of their enterprises.

Theoretically, how far is it correct to accept one sided version of analysis that attempts to integrate colonialism to the indegenous lineages by suggesting that the local mercantile activity suffered at the hands of the State and that it was the Colonial State that was later welcomed by them. In the Indian case the danda and the dharma (path of righteousness to be followed by the king) of the State brought order to the society and helped to integrate it.

The contemporary State in India is a case of more egalitarian use of power. Power here does not imply extraction of surplus alone. It implies rendering of service and curtailment of extraction for social goals. The developmental strategy of growth with justice suggests a rejection of the philosophy behind the colonial as well as predatory liberal State. The concept of power did not belong to the 19th century England. It had its Indian roots in its rejection by both Nehru and Gandhi. Along with the 'danda' there is also the goal of poverty alleviation and eradication of inequitious social evils. The middle class, described by Kothari at one place as lumpen, has to use or wield that power. To call the whole of the lass as lumpen is rather an unacceptable proposition. The middle class in India has used State power in different phases with different models of development. In the Nehru phase it used it for development - a phase described by Kothari as pursuit of happiness. It used it against right wing and in foreign policy the USA in pursuit of power during Mrs. Gandhi's time. Kothari's critique of this stance of the State is the most trenchant and perhaps is an indication of his ideological and political biases. Today since the second prime ministership of Mrs. Gandhi the same middle class has moved in the direction of liberalisation of the economy. Yes, it is true that the middle class may be having its own self interest in increasing power through selective globalisation. It may retain the idea of redistribution.

Let us look at the untenability of the charge of lumpenism from another perspective that is upheld by Kothari. Elements of the same middle class lead non-government grass-roots movements as well. He had hope from these. Further we noted that the political movements, like that of linguistic Reorganisation of States had middle class leaderships. The current Human Rights activists come from the same class. So do the leaders of the Dalit movements. The responses of the State to these movements do not show the other section of the middle class in lumpen light. Again on both sides of the divide there may be self seeking motives of certain elements. These motives cannot be the only criterion to judge an entire class. If that is done then it is to beat the State with any stick available. The approach then is used to beat the State. The point is made by Dipankar Gupta who says, 'The concept of civil society in India draws its intellectual charge as a cultural critique of the Indian State.... In critiques of this kind the take off point usually is a consideration of India's history, and her peculiar cultural genius. Lest it be misunderstood, the claim no where is that Indian culture is superior (or, for that matter inferior) to other cultures, but that tradition are always closer to the people, and represent their aspirations more authentically.'[71]

The tradition of Indian society had very little of democracy to it and that initiative for change came from both sources: State and Society at different points of time. It is therefore better to modify the State versus Society approach and to lean away from its British and the French tradition.

To summarize, the review suggests the following:

(a) Indian State should be seen as part of the productive process and not just as a derivative of the material base. (Bardhan)

(b) Indian State and society have a certain simultaneity and not a deterministic priority of one over the other. (Chattopadhyaya).

(c) The ontos of the State reflects inter-class and intra-class alliances and schisms and can not be regarded as an instrument of the single class. (Bardhan, Bhambri)

(d) The State and the nation need to be seen beyond a mechanical application of classical class conflict. (Marx)

(e) The inter and intra class - schisms and alliances are functionally handled by the middle class whether occupying a position in or out of the State power. It engages in functional flexibility for the benefit of different sections, segments and classes of society. It handles conflict with a certain fluidity at different points of social conflict to extend the unity and sovereignty of India. This impinges on distribution and its nature. In managing social conflict the State in India shows a felicity at some times, a moribund strategy at other times in matters of extending avenues of participation. In this context the idea of Stateness (Rudolphs) and of State helplessness in face of revolt (Kohli, Frankel) have to be viewed as an empirical analysis of certain moments in the Indian State. That holds true also for those who regard history of the Indian State as being increasingly authoritarian (Kaviraj, Byeres, Wilson). Authoritarianism is not the medium of existence of the Indian State. Democracy functions here as much or as less as anywhere else with Indian characteristics.

(f) The middle class itself is heterogeneous. It shows the signs of the dialectic of the community and individual oriented episteme. It could be secular and modern and communal, casteist and traditional.

(g) The middle class could also adopt different strategies of development from within the historical experiences of the liberal State and combine them with certain features of socialism and / or equitous basis of justice.

(h) Being heterogeneous class the middle class leads the State through soft and hard options. It could well traverse the path of liberal Predatory State or welfareist path as much as combine this with a communalist or secular ideology. It has kept open the option of the State led development as well as the market oriented liberalisation.

(i) We regard the State-coil society approach of Kothari as empirically, historically and theoretically untenable.

We examine in the next section in detail the role of the middle class in the 1990s and the next section looks at the function of distribution of the Indian State.

(j) Relative Autonomy argument is to be replaced by one of functional flexibility.

III

External and Internal Intersection

Theda Skolpol's[72] designation of the State as crystallisation at the intersection of external and national conditions can be miniaturised with reference to the middle class in the internal dynamics. Her treatment of the autonomy of the State with regard to the Great Depression suggests that the autonomy is linked to the Weberian concept of bureaucracy, legislators and the role that the lobbyists played, including some trade union leaders. At the external level by the beginning of the 1990s as a fall out of the end of the cold war and the self- destruction of the USSR, the uni-polar moment with, the USA as the hegemon, arrived. It meant new pressures on the States since the process of globalisation involved the sameness effect on other States. Globalisation, with its structural adjustment programme and marketisation with flush-finance prescription meant a new hegemony for the Third World States. States like India, that were not viewed favourably in the Cold War period by the USA, now came under new pressures for loss of manoeuvreability with the collapse of the Soviet Union. Among the developing world it was a unique case of independent country unlike States of Brazil, South Africa[73] and the peripheral States of the South Asian region. The Indian position on the continuation of NAM, pressures on international arms control agenda in favour of nuclear monopoly of the five nuclear powers, the positions at the Earth Summit and in the World Trade Organisation came in for pressures that the State had to handle which it did in keeping with maintaining as much sovereignty as possible. These pressures were posed to it with the dialectic of growing closer to the USA and having differences with the USA.

In the 1990s it tenaciously struggled to retain real sovereignty on issues of Pokharan - II and the arms control diplomacy though it made compromises on the issues related to the Earth Summit and not WTO in 2003. Again it is the 1990s that it had to fight a *war like* situation in Kargil with the backing of the West on the issue though it is not clear if there is a quid pro quo on it. Those who have managed the foreign policy issues have adjusted to the situation keeping in mind India's vital interests on global issues they claim. At the regional level tensions continue despite the new possibilities elsewhere after the end of the cold war. The globalisation of the new uni-polar moment has not only meant the greater U.S. role in the region. It has also meant that the earlier phenomenon of small weapons being used in transnational terror continues. However owing to the unstable coalitions that came into existence in India, after P .V . Narasimha's government, were not able to respond to the new challenges. This was also the case with the V.P. Singh's Government as well since he himself hardly had any vision on foreign policy. The new decade has seen a pro-US shift in foreign policy under the NDA Government with all its dilemmas in the context of the Afghan and Iraq war. In both cases a new US ordered order is the reality to be contended. Bandwagoning and balancing are the two nodal points of the possibilities in which autonomy of the Indian State will operate in the future.

Middle Class Schism: Composition, Role

The middle class composition of the State stands at the point of crystallisation of caste, communal, class and cultural conflicts that bedevil the Indian polity. It stands at the changing cross section of the class alliances with caste and communal coincidence or lack of it. It stands at the bifurcation of the process of the nation - in itself becoming a nation - for - itself with all its pros and cons. The elements of this class whether out of, or, in the government are supporters of this or that regime. There are hardly any that are against the system. Those that emerge in that category from time to time get either marginalised or absorbed in the democratic system. That is how terrorism's trajectory seems to be working. Their critique is grounded in relative deprivation that its sections outside of power feel across the length and breadth of the country on issues of standard of living, way of life, or sheer desires of capturing State power. The entire array of the leaderships of dissent are beneficiaries of the system's development booms from the basic food items, toilet paper, computer facilities, rail, air and road travel, and, other benefits in an atmosphere of luxury, composite culture and alleviation of poverty and a reasonable sense of self-reliance and security. Aijaz Ahmed says of compositeness, 'In a nation so very heterogeneous, negotiations between universality and particularity, between migrancy and a sense of place, is a daily experience ; even the Constitution of India has to recognise twenty languages....One has a profound sense of belonging to it all of it and yet the knowledge that one would not understand even a fraction of it.'

The alternative elites are supporters of this or that regime and not critics of the Indian State per se. In terms of intra class conflicts the middle class stands at the point of optimum of change from episode to episode suggesting pragmatic compromises that are the truths of the State. So is the story about interclass conflicts. Thus does the middle class help the process of integration and development while some elements of it tie themselves in right wing or extreme wing radicalism to upturn the original vision of the Constitution.

The middle class is distinct from and apart from the intermediary classes in India. Its socio-economic base is the rich, middle and to a lesser degree the poor peasant with a sprinkling of the Dalit and tribal elements from the countryside. Its roots in the small towns are in the petty bourgeoisie, trading and commercial interests. In the metropolitan centres its lineages can be traced to the first and second generation of skilled workers, white collar workers in the private and public enterprise, among the professional families. This new petty bourgeoisie therefore is composed of the soldier, policeman, bureaucrat, judge, advocate, technocrat, journalist, doctor, school, college and university teachers, aesthete, playwright, actor, local and regional level leaders of party organisations, social activists in the Gandhian mould, leaders of RSS organisations—especially pracharaks, non-government organisations, sportsmen, leaders of trade unions, revolutionary violent organisations, insurgency, terrorist movements and members of elites of police and para-military organisations. As a group it is a mixed caste and community unit. Its reach is all

India. Its consciousness is all India in terms of what India has to offer and what it needs to be.

In terms of political traditions it has had a varied background. It has been part of the nationalist movement as well as spear head of the communalist politics. In 1935 Pandit Nehru said, "Most of those who have shaped the Congress policy during the last seventeen years have come from the middle classes. Liberal or Congressmen, they have come from the same class and have grown up in the same environment. Their social life and contacts and friendships have been similar, and there was little difference to begin with between the two varieties of bourgeois ideals that they professed."[74]

Nehru also notes the propensity of some elements of this class to move in the direction of the communalist politics.[75] This duality is witnessed in the intermediary classes of the Peripheral States that Aijaz Ahmed analyses with reference to South and Eastern Asia. That duality was expressed in terms of reactionary and revolutionary politics. During the freedom struggle we notice the emergence of the revolutionary and the terrorist struggle along with the socialist and communist politics apart from the communalist and the Congress movement. The middle class dynamics of the party politics in the provinces was predominant before the advent of the Gandhian phenomenal expansion of the Congress into the peasantry which meant the alliance of the middle class with the peasant masses. The jelling of the two sections, the emergence of the Congress as an umbrella organisation of the freedom struggle, the emergence of the mass Kisan fronts in the Congress ruled States, the peasant agitations under the joint leaderships of the democrat Congressman, Congress Socialist and the Communists and the struggles for the partial demands of the peasantry in the late 1930s and 1940s were events that did not leave a possibility of a subaltern consciousness being suppressed or alienated. Very few Gramscian Organic intellectuals emerged.

This middle class was charged with a vision of service and social distribution in governance as was the case represented by the split in case of Orissa's middle classes. The post Independence developmental strategy had its own hiccups in the Nehru-Rajagopalachari, Nehru - S.P. Mukherjee and Nehru-Purshottam Das Tandon controversies or the differences that Nehru had with

Patel, or, the Nehru-Prasad controversy over the Hindu Code Bill. One fact was clear that the Nehru strategy of development accepted by the Constitution had its critics from the right wing leaders and sectarian Communists. This could not be compared to the differences that the Indian businessman had with Nehru during the Freedom Struggle when Nehru announced his ideas of socialism as President of the Congress. But it did show that the right wing was hostile to the Nehru model of development, foreign policy, composite culture and scientific temper that the project of enlightenment would approve of. The incipient splits turned out as monsters, as it were, for the State in India during and after the lifetime of Nehru. As for the Communists they left the path of insurgency, accepted the constitutional democracy as an arena of struggle apart from conducting trade union and political campaign within the system. In 1950 Nehru had told the Chief Ministers in one of his letters about the right wing threat that India faced. In 1998 the right wing negation came to rule the roost and is threatening to control India for more time and more drastically and perhaps more violently with truth being a dispensable commodity. In 1992 the moral authority of the office of the Prime Minister declined owing to inaction of the then Prime Minister P. V. Narasimha Rao, who failed to use power to prevent the destruction of the Babri Masjid by the BJP, RSS and its other organisations. This episode reflects the insensitivity of the middle class Hindu man. Of that insensitivity Verma says '... the average Hindu middle class person had a very undeveloped sense of social sensitivity to the over all good of his community. He attached little priority to the need for an altruistic interface with society. His motivation to contribute to its betterment, without the notion of personal gain, was weak. He saw no great reason why he should identify his personal welfare with the well being even of his immediate environment. His concerns were restricted to himself, his family, and, at lower scale, his clan or caste.'[76]

The view of the self seeking, money making middle class *bania,* untouched by enlightenment, is referred to by Thornburn with regard to *banias* of the undivided Punjab before the partition. Verma's characterisation may be valid for some sections of it. Not for the whole class. He himself praises the developmentalist and social service perspective of the same class during Nehru period. He comes heavily against the newer elements of this class in the phase of liberalisation. He says, 'Together, the old and the new members of the expanded middle class inhabited a landscape singularly denuded of any feature of principle or morality. The real defeat was that of ideology, for two reasons: one, the very valid goal of social justice was overwhelmed by the cynicism of those who were its most eloquent votaries; and, two, the wave of caste consciousness that Mandal unleashed put on the back burner the real issues that needed to be confronted : poverty, illiteracy, disease and exploitation.'[77]

We agree with Verma's Hindu consciousness of sections of the petty bourgeoisie. This may be true in Punjab,[78] families in Uttar Pradesh, Madhya Pradesh, Maharashtra and Gujarat. All these are places where the BJP has come to acquire a base. They combine the knowledge of importance of money with the view that they can use the communal card to come to power and turn it away from the egalitarian and composite character that it has so far had. It is yet to be seen if their scholars are influenced by the enlightenment philosophy in analysing the troubles here. One wonders if they ever use the Bhakti or the Sufi traditions for their analysis of the ills of the Indian society, or even the Buddhist ones. The entire ideology of the Hindutva is expansionist in geographical reach, it is patriarchal in its view of empowerment of women and has nothing to offer to the ecological movements. For tribal identities they offer only assimilation in the name of mythology of the Ram.

This may not be true of the social activist, the revolutionary leader or even the liberalisers in the State administration. Verma has no space for the first two kinds except in so far as he recognises the role of non-government organisations like Self Employed Women's Association, Deccan Development Society, The Social Work and Research Association in Tilonia or social agencies like CASPLAN, DEEPALAYA and other NGOs like Shramik Vidhyapeeth and the Community Education and Development Foundation, Comprehensive Rural Health Project, Gita Propagation Societies, Common Cause and Satya Sheel. He upholds them for their commitment to service and anti-statist orientation. He, of course, owing to the nature of the book, has not included those innumerable individuals who consciously reject the consumerist life styles in their personal life, who are not media savvy, who keep groping for avenues to do service to the people, those who are still engaged in the day to day struggle of the trade unions, who fight battles with terrorist organisations at the political level as well as with the communalist but who are not necessarily anti-State. The lull in the political arena of the working class and the trade union movement, like those of the Bank Employees and the Central Government Employees, are not a reflection of the demise of the ideology of the left wing politics. Some of these organisations have been middle class and their ageing leaderships have to pass on the baton to the new generation. Second, the Communist parties who have controlled these organisations have a political agenda of defending simple liberal values, processes and structures of governance from the communalist take over.

Since we notice that the middle class is heterogeneous in origin, episteme and political roles let us look at its contribution in the direction of liberalisation which is part of the enlightenment project, though not necessarily its social distributive one. We look at a narrow circle of the sections in the bureaucracy that has helped adoption of the policy of liberalisation. The role of the current bureaucracy has not been favourably looked at, particularly in case of the contrast it has with its role in the Nehru period. But those who were not in favour of the 'licence raj' of the Nehru strategy will find the current one as better in contrast to the developmentalist vision. The bureaucracy was made more professional during Rajiv Gandhi's phase. Gazetted officers, Non gazetted officers and the commissioned officers form the cultural capital, exploit the resources under them in their favour, and are prepared to get politicized (if it helps in pursuing self interest). Caste heterogeneity exists in it. Political lineage's and linkages with the corporate world and international finance of its members are known. Caste coalition and caste heterogeneity within the political executive re-enforce each other.[79] The negative dimension of it is reflected in the politician -bureaucrat-police-smuggler nexus that has emerged in the recent decades reflecting in bomb blasts, communal riots and terrorist politics. Scams, scandals and Jain diaries on Hawala symbolise the corruption, and terrorist dimensions in the 1990s. Professionalisation also continues.

Liberalisation

Within this large segment emerged an 'episteme community'. It has been exposed to the Western economic experience and rationality, shares a similar intellectual landscape, is split between fast and slow changers within liberalisation and its irreversibility; and this community is involved in the three moments of the liberalisation during the Prime Ministerships of Mrs. Gandhi, Rajiv Gandhi and P.V. Narasimha Rao.[80] The first reform era began with 1990-91. The second reform era with Yashwant Sinha in the 2000 period. Removal of fiscal deficits meant its decline from 2.3 per cent of the GDP in 1990 to 0.7 per cent of the GDP in 1993. Yet a sustainable budget situation could not be achieved by 2000. Trade and payments regime and domestic financial condition underwent a change. Described as most autarchic in 1991 the trade and payments regime witnessed a change. In the first two years the measures in this area were (a) the removal of import licencing requirements for most imports although prohibitions on the import of consumer goods remained; (b) the beginning of a programme of tarrif reductions; (c) restrictions on inflows of foreign direct and portfolio investment were significantly increased; (d) a number of export restrictions were removed or relaxed (although some remained). Between 1991-95 the trade and payments regime was highly liberalised. The financial sector was similarly liberalised. Financial reforms were based on the Narasimhan Committee. The RBI carried out the necessary changes in the banking system. Bank restructuring was also taking place. Interest rate ceilings were being removed, and interest rates were being freed to a considerable extent. Efforts were made to tackle the telecom industry. Monopoly of Indian Airlines was broken. Entry was permitted into the airline and other industry. Power sector was reformed. Economic growth accelerated during the 1990s though it declined in 1998-99.The growth rates reached 7&8 per cent in the late 1990s. By 2003 the projected growth rate is 6 per cent.

Impact

The impact of the liberalisation process is being continuously analysed.[81] The policies have benefitted different segments of the middle class with the urban and rural spread. A classification of the middle class is now available on the basis of this newer analysis. The reports classify the middle class households into five categories on the basis of income after making a margin for inflation and unaccountable money. The categorisation for 1985-

86, 1989-90, 1992-93 and 1995-96 is as follows: Lower Income Group income less than 25,000; lower middle had between 25001-50,000; middle income group had between 50,000 - 77, 000 and upper middle between 77,000 - 106, 000. This categorisation was available for both urban and rural families. Distribution pattern shows (a) proportion of low income group declined from 65.24 to 58.84 in four years and sharper decline in subsequent three years. (b) The proportion of high income group went up from 1.07 to 1.44 in the pre-reform period, while in the pro-reform period there was an increase from 2.33 per cent to 3.56 per cent. The number of low income group households remained the same in both 1985-86 and 1989-90, whereas between 1992-93 and 1995-96 their size declined by ten million households. It is pointed out that the number of low income group households was higher (90 million) in 1992-93 compared to 1989-90 (83 million). This was owing to bad years of 3 per cent growth of the GDP in contrast to 5 per cent growth. In these bad years the poorer households were badly affected in contrast to the affluent ones.

Stratification

Income growth rates also showed that the upper sections of the middle class benefited during 1989-90 to 1995-96. For example in the 1989-90 years middle, upper middle and higher were 20 million households that swelled to 34 million by 1995-96. Between 1986-90, about 14 million households were added. Also during this period there was inter class movements of households between different income groups. The resultant change of distribution showed that in the low income group , the number of new entrants almost equalled the number of households moved up the income ladder and as a result their size remained more or less at the same level as in 1986. All other groups had net additions ranging from 70,000 to 5.5 million. The lower middle group had maximum increase. In contrast, in 1995-96 the number of low income groups shrank from their level in 1992-93 at about 9.7 million, which in fact is slightly more than the total number of households added during this period The net addition to other groups was also positive ranging from 2.2 million in the high income group to 11 million in the lower income group. This trend was noted for both urban and rural centres.

Consumer Pattern

In terms of consumer durables, one notices the increasing change in pattern of possessions within the five income groups. In 1993-94 mechanical wrist watches increased from about 6.3 million in 1985-86 to 10 million, of which 75 per cent were the rural buyers. On an average each household owned 4.7 durable goods (a list of 31 was made). The increase from 1993 - 94 quantity of 586 million was marked by 705 million in 1995-96, a rise of around 20.3 per cent in two years. Even allowing for increase for population , the average ownership per house hold went up from 3.72 in 1993 to 4.27 in 1995-96. The number of durable goods owned by each household seemed to have grown at annual rate of 9.6 per cent between 1993-94 and 1995-96.The goods that showed impressive growth were Black and White T.V. sets (16.1 per cent), colour T.V. sets (14.80 per cent), Refrigerators (13.1 per cent), Washing Machines (25.5 per cent) and Quartz watches (15.8 per cent). More than 80 per cent of the house holds owned mechanical wrist watches in 1995-96. Every second household owned a radio and a transistor.

Rural Household

These goods have penetrated in the rural areas indicating the reach and the richness of the middle class. Rural house holds, which account for 71.2 per cent of the households in the country, account for 52.2 per cent of ownership of durable goods. The average ownership of the rural household was only 3 compared to 7 in urban areas. Among the durable goods mechanical wrist watches and bicycles penetrated to more than 50 per cent. Radio and transistor penetration rate was 42 per cent. Generally, for most of the goods (other than bicycles) penetration in the rural areas was lesser than in the urban areas. The reasons for low level of this penetration are threefold, viz., different life styles, low income and the lack of infrastructure, e.g., electricity. And yet the survey notes '... life in Indian villages has been undergoing drastic changes in the 1990s. Increased migration to cities and industrial township has led villagers to get acquainted with what the urban markets have to offer. Villagers who work in urban areas become trend setters and invariably guide the tastes and requirements of compatriots in rural areas. This has slowly led to the breakdown of the urban rural divide.'[82]

It must also be noted that the market expanded at the annual average rate of 4 per cent before the reforms and after the reforms it doubled.

The maximum benefits came to the urban and rural income groups in the highest income slot. The number in the over Rs. 5,00,000 at 1995-96 prices went up from 200,000 in 1993-94 to over 350,000 in 1995-96, an increase of 33.8 per cent per annum. The growth was faster in the higher ranges of income, e.g., the number of households with income over Rs. one million nearly doubled over the two years while households with income of Rs. 5 million per year shot up by two and a half times. In all cases, rural growth rates were higher. This is attributed to smaller base of rural segment, where there are few households at these levels of income. The urban sector witnessed greater number of households proliferating.

The survey does indicate *social mobility* from the lower to the middle class. Other points to be noted are the middle class stratification, its penetration into the countryside, spread of the market and the durable items into the villages, and the change in the life style in the countryside. The distribution during the liberalisation decade has helped (a) middle class, (b) allowed for inter and intra class mobility (c) has helped to bridge the rural-urban gap and (d) led to a pyramid like structure of the middle class with the apex showing off its two to three cars households and the possession of almost all the 31 durable items mentioned in the survey. So, this expresses the heightened consumerism at the top.[83] The dialectic of unending quest for consumer items to ape the upper sections of the society and the bare minimum of mechanical wrist watches and bicycles show also the difference between different segments of the middle class as well as its distinct character from the other sections of the society. In political terms functional flexibility of this class is evident from the fact that within the liberal developmental projects it adopted one model in the pre-1984 era and quite another in the decade under study. Within this change the State has still not given up the protectionist perspective for the Western interpretation of market economy, human rights and poverty alleviation. What is disturbing is in the realm of ideology and limits of change.

That segment which is attached to the BJP and the RSS aims at reinterpreting India within what they call 'creative nationaliasm' 'cultural nationalism' or Hindutva and speaks untruth, half truths and outright falsehoods about the last fifty years of the State. It may choose the repressive way out. Desai says the following "Hindutva's task is different on two main counts: first in contrast to agglomeration of localised identities which made up the Indian nation must now construct a more unified bourgeois class whose commercial and (familial) proprietary links stretch from the villages to the Western metropolis, and second, that the circumstances of effective abandonment of redistributive and marginally welfarist development...."[83] This cannot be a teleological outcome, though.

It is possible to imagine that the high- income group families may be interested in identifying themselves with the higher sections of big bourgeoisie. There is however no empirical basis for this to prove. At the theoretical level one imagines that the top managerial class through various avenues identifies itself with the processes of globalisation, if they support the option that the big business in India wants to opt for it. It is also possible that independent of this the middle class' creamy layer, owing to its own linkages with the international funding agencies and/ or the NRIs, may wish such an option to be exercised. However, as far as the big bourgeoisie is concerned it is demanding of the Indian State a certain protection from international competition. Therefore, the big bourgeoisie, while still wanting a larger share from the national cake may not clamour for jettisoning the distributive aspect of the State. If it did, apart from the possibility of social contradictions becoming acute, the middle class itself may join a more radical option than the one on ecology and/or human rights. If it goes radical definitely large sections of it will not like to go communal or acquisitive.

There is therefore the possibility of the radicalisation of politics which the State with democracy may find it difficult to ignore. The other option is that the middle class forgets its own interests, joins the band wagon, if one exists, for globalisation with full blown market model of growth. In that case it would be ironic, though not beyond the realm of a theoretical possibility, that it may play the communal card for a modern liberal predatory policy of the market model of growth. The heterogenous character of the middle class would prevent it from playing such a monolithic role. Only some segments of it, in *moffusil* towns may opt for it under conditions of political frenzy and social terror that might accompany the communalisation of the political process. The middle class has used the caste mobilisations for various demands since the 1950s.[84] Communalism has fed on capitalist and middle class interests during the freedom struggle. In more recent times the communal card has been used by the non-Congress parties to come to power.[85] There are allegations of the Congress communalising the situation in Punjab, or, offering soft Hindutva in Gujarat in 2002 and making compromises with it. That historiography has anti-Congress pathology at its heart. Congress was always pitted against the BJP-Akali link up in Punjab. Communists joined up with the BJP in 1967. In Gujarat the Congress has been able to retain its vote base in 2002 among the Muslims. In fact it is turning the corner from the post-Babri hostility of Muslims towards it. Communal riots have also reflected the conflict in the petty bourgeoisie. It has very heavily been used by the RSS since Independence. The RSS helped in communalising the Assam environment at the time of the elections to the Assembly in the 1980s.[86] So did it in Kashmir during the Governorship of Jagmohan. In all these segments of the middle class have contributed by participating in these or providing leadership to them. Such a role for coming to power has been played by middle classes.[87]

This however cannot be taken to mean that the entire middle class has become communal. Firstly, the individuals who have been involved in opening up the economy are modern and secular ones and are not in the communal parties. Second, democratic and secular parties still enjoy a preponderant position in the political and electoral scene despite their faultlines among individual elements. Third, the traditional left parties, though not at the centre of the political stage in terms of electoral votes do exercise considerable clout in terms of articulation of political agenda of secularism and distribution. Fourth, is there a crisis of accumulation which dictates the State to go communal? Will communalisation help? Has it exhausted its potential for development? These questions require an economists eye and there are quite some who do believe that the potential of 19th century predatory State does not exist. Further, the demands of protection that are being made by the Bombay club, and, not just by them are ones that need not have any communal colouring to it. The Bombay Plan during Nehru's time did not need any communal colouring to it. The need of State intervention continues, even if one were to comply with the demand that the second stage reforms towards liberalisation continue. Gradual reforms are taking place in the education, improvement of the labour force, in the financial sector, for example, in the insurance industry. Restructuring of State owned enterprises is on under Arun Shourie though questioned by the Supreme Court. The labour reform and removal of restrictions on small scale industry are on the demand board.

Disinvestment

The disinvestment of the industries has gone beyond the strategy of Opposition even from within the BJP and the NDA Government. In January 2000, Modern Bakeries was the first undertaking to be disinvested and the Hindustan Lever bought it. This is a subsidiary of Dutch multinational, Unilever. Another seventy firms were listed for this process, including Maruti Udyog, where Suzuki is the major partner, Air India and some companies in the petroleum sector. Some PSUs have started down-sizing themselves like the Steel Authority of India. It has proposals to reduce its work force by atleast one third, has even created a board level position and engaged international consulting firms to consider shedding non-core activities and divest non-performing assets. The only major means of dealing with labour redundancy is to operate voluntary retirements that give four times the normal retrenchment compensation and promise of employee stock options in disinvested firms. Recent trends in stock market have dampened the euphoria about employee stock even in information, communication and entertainment-industries.

The communalisation of the polity may be the need of the BJP. Let us take its efforts to communalise the security agenda. It sought to communalise the Pokharan - II tests and called them Shakti tests. This failed miserably. N. Ram, who condemns the tests themselves as anti-human, makes a point that shows that the BJP could not communalise this in electoral terms. He says, or ...Congress (I) President Sonia Gandhi is reported to have attacked Vajpayee government's nuclear policy on several counts. "…. The saffron debacle in Rajasthan, Delhi and Madhya Pradesh proved beyond any doubt that the masses of the people… were not willing to buy the pseudo - nationalist and chauvinist agenda based on nuclear hawkishness ...."[88]

In an interview Natwar Singh had claimed the Pokharan - II to be the part of the Congress programme. But nowhere ever did the Congress communalise it.

One agrees with Desai's warning about a worst case scenario. As far as communalism is concerned there is disagreement. To regard it as a structural need of the State for purposes of accumulation is not borne out either by the needs of the big bourgeoisie or the constraints of politics that Hindutva has to face. Even in terms of the current elections of September 1999 the BJP with all its bandwagon of parties has not been able to put up candidates for all the Lok Sabha constituencies. The election on Gujarat riots shows that this is not true. Desai touches on the theme of distribution that we need to look at next in the new section. Empirically Desai has to prove that capitalism needs petty-bourgeous reaction.

IV

The State in India, as enjoined by the Constitution, has to bring about justice. It is a concept that in class societies has an underpinning of inequality from Bentham to Rawls. All theorists have suggested a re-organisation of society for bringing about justice which would be facilitated by the removal of social, institutional and economic hindrances. In the last analysis they have suggested re-distribution atleast since the time of the Great Depression in the 20th century. Within the Marxist framework the element of inequality remains but not to the detriment of the dispossessed in social terms. In it the State retains its bourgeois birth-marks for it is the agency of determining the theory of reward. What role does the State perform in a State which is also a nation State in the making? It has to cater to the callings of different segments of society who may be at different stages of historical development in an unevenly developed economy, polity and consciousness. In its pursuit of good society, in the context of the hitherto colonised one as India was, the State would mean prosperity, participation and peace. For this the principle of justice was economic growth with justice and not just the strategy of economic growth. It did not have the luxury to pursue the strategy of predatory processes of primitive accumulation first and then bring a protracted introduction of democratic methods of governance. It needed a strategy that would spread liberal economy, secular consciousness and social justice through a democratic polity in a society that Nehru said was still religious. The State and the market exist and have to function for the benefit for all. Property had to be controlled and not eliminated. In that sense it was no socialism. In that sense also no Communist party was putting socialism on the agenda. They were asking for the benefits to the deprived in the urban and the rural sector through structural reforms.

Development Strategy

In contrast to their demands of structural change in the countryside the Congress adopted the strategy of abolition of intermediaries, development of infrastructure, community development projects, industrial policy resolution, introduction of democratic decentralisation through the three-tier system of Panchayats, White and Green Revolution, nationalisation of Banks, abolition of Privy Purses and allowance for the growth of the small sector in the industry that is now represented in the Confederation of Indian Industries, apart from the chambers that represent big business like the FICCI and the CII. At the social level it followed the policies of protective discriminations, protection of labour from layoffs, retrenchment, lockouts, stoppage of *begari,* forced labour and untouchability. The extension of franchise, the gradual change in the Centre - State relations, the Panchayats acquiring new status of the third tier of the Centre - State relations and the strategy of accommodating, coopting and fighting the most violent wing of the insurgent and terrorist outfits has extended the possibilities of democratic participation to those sections of the society that have benefitted from the State developmental strategy even in terms of education. The protection schemes have targeted the most deprived through the development corporations that are now sought to be liberalised.

The management of the scientific and technological revolution on the principles of self reliance,[89] and, now on the principle of selective liberalisation has not led to an adverse defense and development[90] relationship that could pose the security dilemma. It has also not impacted adversely on the security of the country[91] vis-a-vis external environment. The Science and Technology Plan relevant for the end of the century portrayed the following picture: in terms of individual security science and technology has meant increase of life expectancy from 27 years in the 1940s to 56 years by 1990. It recognised shortcomings: mortality is 95 per one thousand live births, 10 million active cases of tuberculosis, one third of leprosy patients of the world live in India, and disease caused by modernisation like cancer, heart diseases, accidents and diseases due to environmental and occupational pollutants. In food the target is 225 million tons by 2000 A.D. for the population at the present rate of population growth. By the end of the 1980s India was producing 154.2 million tons. Therefore the new issues of politics where the Indian State has to face the challenges are in area of health, food and ecology. Much more needs to be done.

From the perspective of liberalisation India stands out in four major areas according to an international survey that is market friendly. These are stock market, strong science and engineering capabilities, with a large pool of competent scientists and engineers, and strong education in basic science and mathematics, strong business schools and its strong labour force and judicial independence.[92] In the field of agricultural sector poverty alleviation shows both progress and paradox. The 1980s saw the growth in food production to 18 million tons. The spread of Green Revolution to Western and Central India accounted for this. Poverty is high here. Rice and wheat output increased. Today greater investment is needed in the agricultural research and optimal distribution is needed. Basing himself on the data of 1993-94 C. H. Hanumantha Rao says '... the proportion of people below the poverty line was lower than in 1987-88. However, the rate of decline over this period was lower than in the preceding decade, despite a series of good monsoons and the spread of green revolution to the poorer States in the eastern India.' He suggested that India needs 7 to 8 per cent growth rate combined with 4-5 per cent of agricultural growth rate for a decade to generate employment in urban and rural sector to empower the poor.[93] The strategy adopted for the rural poor in the changed circumstances of the mobility of the rural poor at the intermediate and lower levels is to have increased investments to the rural areas, higher priority to the rural areas, higher priority to the rural infrastructure and social sectors and substantial development roles being assigned to Panchayati Raj institutions. This priority is irreversible though some question it.[94]

Distribution

The principles of distribution along class lines suggest Liberal and Marxist paradigms.[95] Principles of distribution change from time to time and place to place. These are related to production. For Marx at the centre of production is exploitation, or, the relation between profit and wages. This involves a fight between the two. Surplus is appropriated through rent for which relations of landed property are crucial and interest for which banking is crucial. Further competition in the market mediates the distributional parameters. The market may itself allow for increase in wages and thus the profit is partly siphoned off. It is possible that the market for labour in comparison to profit may be advantageous.

In this economic process the State cannot be wished away both historically and theoretically. Even for the creation of the market, saving it from failure or saving the people from its failure and modifying the market mechanism the State intervenes. This is all too well known. The interventionist State as in India creates conditions for the operation of the market by removing the vestiges of feudal property and labour relations. Not just the introduction of the wage system but also the protection of the wage earner from the ravages of the market find the State engaging in having public distribution system in essential commodities and passing of labour legislations to protect them. Again to help the farmer it decides on the procurement prices of agricultural commodities and not just the food commodities. It has no land tax. It subsidizes agriculture even now during the period of the State agreeing to the WTO conditionalities. At the other end it exposes the industrial sector to international competition and/or protects it from it and the working class actions. Distribution leads to relative distribution and that in turn leads to social turmoil to be dealt with by the State.

This functional flexibility is possible since the State has a multi-class ontos and a middle class personnel. Both help in the extension of the societal processes and that in turn help the State to extend integration. The middle class in and out of power deal with much of this dialectic and the ordinary people are mobilized on class and cultural ground in this struggle of consolidating or acquiring power. Through cooperative and conflictual strategies the State meets these confabulations. In the process it may strike new alliances by making them more broad based or contracting them as the personnel deems it fit. But one thing is very clear : there are no grand rational choice designs and coalitions that are available with the State. It could down the social ladder and /or extend democracy. All this may not and perhaps will not lead to either the liberal or the Marxist utopia. The situation promises the continuation of the State, its multi class ontos, its functional flexibility, its middle class composition and the dialectic of middle class conflict. The situation may change if there is the unbridled liberalisation and the consequent social situation worsens.

Let us not forget that the peculiar features of the liberalisation policies have their own social paradoxes. There is an uneven economic impact in different States of India. Industrially more advanced States of Gujarat, Maharashtra and Tamil Nadu have prospered. Bihar and Uttar Pradesh have been on the slide in terms of economic growth rate. These two latter States combined with Orissa, Rajasthan and Madhya Pradesh have shown poor performance in the reform period. The per capita income has declined here, according to the NSS survey. The Union budget reduced subsidies on the social sector. The country's poor are at the constant figure of 34.4 per cent.

Opposition

The protest against the liberalisation regimes is existent though is not strident. In such a situation it is possible for the present Government to enlarge the consensus on the reform agenda. However despite this enabling situation the Government is not going ahead with quick pace of the second phase of reforms nor in the direction in which it is being suggested by those who are not satisfied by the Indian reforms. Krueger and Chenoy say "...achieving further reforms will increase the pay offs from those reforms already undertaken, but simultaneously will increase the pay offs to be achieved by still further liberalisation."[96]

The trade unions, though weak, currently do not agree with the privatization drive. Some unions made proposals to take over enterprises to prevent privatization of IPCL. BHEL officers association made a similar proposal few years ago. In the mid-90s, workers unions and officers associations in a PSU made a proposal for acquiring the ailing Iron and Steel Company Limited at Burnpur. Government had reservations about them and so did not receive them enthusiastically.[97] This resistance to privatization under globalisation is muted but not absent. If this is combined by the resistance of the business groups seeking protection then this may become more strident. The business groups have sought protection from the Government against the impact of liberalisation especially in the soft drinks industry to mention one.[98] The social sector has witnessed negative developments. In contrast to the pre-reform era in the post reform era there is a declining trend in the budgetary allocations of both the Central and State governments for various sub-sectors of the social sector, namely health and education. The plan expenditure between 1985-90 at the rate of 33.5 per cent of the total expenditure was reduced to 28.3 per cent between 1997-98. The development expenditure , v e notice also registered a slide. It came down from 56.4 per cent to 49 per cent in the same period.[99] Liberalisation growth led to jobless development. In the first half of 1990s, employment had increased by 1.2 million people but in the same period 35 million people were added to the labour market. The income disparities between the poorest rural man and the corporate employee have widened.[100] Discontent will be articulated by old and new social movements. The old social movements have not yet exhausted their potential even though the left is existing in pockets. So was the BJP till 1997. The new social movements on the gender, ecology and sub-regionalism need to go beyond issue based movements and make the project of modernity stronger albeit with alternative policies by joining with the All India perspective, as they do in the context of their State Governments' foes. The structure of representation is claimed to be shifting in favour of the Dalits.[101] The Dalit representatives in various elected bodies are not seeking structural change. They are seeking developmental funds. The Mayawati politics in UP similarly represented that and did not engaging in structural reform to help the Dalit masses. It was with the BJP and not with those who would seek alternative politics. There is a need to do so. The change in power structure in the villages has not changed in social terms.[102] The NDA Government means that the upper castes, the petty bourgeoisie and the middle castes (through regional parties) support the BJP but not necessarily its programme. In any case the Dalit, middle caste and tribal mobilisations of the BJP in Gujarat have not been for structural change but against even reservations. More than that the mobilisation is for mythological characters. The alternative will rest on the dominant sections of the middle class, the dalits, the Muslims and the poor if they join up with the Congress, and so join up with its base of different segments of the population. Congress has adopted the strategy for the poor and it needs to combine its orientation for the poor with the policy of liberalisation. There is yet time to prevent the possibility of authoritarian polity to emerge under the BJP umbrella or under the direct RSS command ultimately.

References

1. Nicolas Poulantzas, *Political Power and Social Classes,* London, New Left Books, 1973.
2. Ved Marwah, *Uncivil Wars,* New Delhi, Harper Collins, 1995.
3. N. L. Gupta, edited, *Communal Riots,* Gyan Publishing House, 2000.
4. Yogendra Yadav, 'Theories of the Indian State' New Delhi, Seminar 1990.
5. Fareed Kazmi, *The Politics Of India's Conventional Cinema,* New Delhi, Thousand Oaks, London, Sage,1998.
6. Pranjali Bandhu, *Cinema In Focus, Black And White of Cinema in India,* Trivandrum, Obyssey, 1992. p.16.
7. Sumita S. Chakravarty, *National Identity in Indian Popular Cinema,* Delhi, Bombay, Madras, Calcutta, Oxford University Press, 1993.
8. Lalit Vachani, 'Bachchan- Alias: The Many Faces Of film Icon', Christiane Brosius and Melissa Butcher, edited by, *Image Journeys, Audio Visual Media and Cultural Change in India.* New Delhi, Thousands Oaks, London, Sage,1999. p. 220
9. Nikhat Kazmi, *Ire In The Soul, Bollywood's Angry Years,* New Delhi, Harper Collins, 1996. p. 50.
10. Christiane Brosius, ' Is This The Real Thing? Packaging Cultural Nationalism', In Christiane Brosius and Melissa Butcher, *op. cit.,* pp. 99-136.

11. Jean Louis Commoli and Jean Narboni, ' Cinema/ Ideology/ Criticism', in Bill Nichols, *Movies and Methods,* Vol.1, Calcutta, Seagull Books, 1993. p. 24.
12. Amiya Kumar Bagchi, 'Markets, Market Failures, And The Transformation of Authority, Property and Bondage In Colonial India', in Burton Stein and Sanjay Subramaniam, edited, *Institutions and Economic Change in South Asia,* Delhi, Bombay, Calcutta, Madras, Oxford University Press, 1996. p. 60.
13. Karl Marx, *Theories of Surplus Value,* Vol. 2, London, 1969 quoted in Anthony Giddens, The Class Structure of Advanced Societies, London, 1973. p.77
14. Pavan K. Verma, *The Great Indian Middle Class,* New Delhi, Penguin,1998.
15. C. B. Macpherson, *Life and Times of Liberal Democracy,* Oxford, OOP, 1977.
16. David Held, ' Beyond Liberalism and Marxism?', in George Mclennan, David Held, Stuart Hall, edited, *The Idea Of The Modern State,* Philadelphia, Open University Press, Milton Keynes, 1984.pp. 80-109
17. Brajadulal Chattopadhyaya, ' Political Process and Structure of Polity in Early Medieval India' in Herman Kulke, edited, The State In Modern India, 1000-1700, Delhi, Calcutta, Chennai and Mumbai, Oxford University Press, 1997. pp. 195-222.
18. Herman Kulke, 'Introduction', *ibid.*
19. Burton Stein, 'The Segmentary State: Interim Reflections', in *ibid.,* pp.137- 161.
20. ibid., p. 145.
21. Pranab Bardhan, *Political Economy of Development in India,* Delhi, Bombay, Calcutta, Madas, Oxford University Press, esp. pp. 36-37.
22. ——, ' The State against society: The Great Divide in Indian Social Science Discourse' in Sugata Bose and Ayesha Jalal, edited, *Nationalism, Democracy, Development: State and politics in India,* Delhi, Calcutta, Madras, Mumbai, Oxford Paperbacks, 1998. pp.191-195.
23. C.B. Macpherson, *op. cit.*
24. Brajadulal Chattopadhyaya, *op. cit.,* pp.214-215.
25. R. S. Sharma, *The State And The Varna formation in The Mid-Ganga,* New Delhi, Manohar, 1996. p. 86.
26. Nordlinger, 'The Return To The States: Critiques', *American Political Science Review,* Vol. 82, No.3 September 1988.
27. Abu L - Fazl Allami, *The Ain-i-Akbari,* translated by Blochmann, M. A.,Third edition, New Delhi, Oriental Book

Reprint Corporation, 1977. Part 1, p. 174.

28. *Ibid.*, p. 232.
29. *Ibid.*, p. 279.
30. Burton Stein and Sanjay Subramaniam, *op. cit.*
31. Francine R. Frankel, *India's Political Economy, 1947-77, The Gradual Revolution,* Princeton, Princeton University Press, 1978.
32. Francis L. Carsten, 'Interpretations Of Fascism', Walter Laquer, edited, *Fascism, A Reader's Guide,* Penguin, 1979. P. 479.
33. Bipan Chandra, *Communalism in Modern India,* New Delhi, Vikas Publishing House Pvt. Ltd. 1984. p. 36.
34. B. B. Mishra, *The Indian Middle Classes, Their Growth in Modern Times,* Delhi, Oxford University Press, 1978. pp. 367-368.
35. Aijaz Ahmed, ' Class, Nation and State', *Lineages of the Present,* New Delhi, Tulika,1996.p. 46.
36. Gunnar Myrdal, *Asian Drama*, New York, Pantheox, 1968.
37. Myron Weiner, ' Minority identities', in Sudipto Kaviraj, edited, *Politics in India,* Delhi, Calcutta, Chennai, Mumbai, Oxford University Press, 1997. He says ' what seems most likely to intensify ethnic conflict is the deterioration of the political institutions.' Pp.241-242.
38. M.J.Akbar, *The Siege Within,* Middlesex, 1985;
    ——*Riot After Riot, Report on Caste and Communal Violence,* New Delhi, Penguin 1988;
    Bhabani Sen Gupta, *India; Problems of Governance,* New Delhi, Konark Publishers Pvt. Ltd., In face of what he calls overload of violence the ' State appears powerless to end…inter peoples' wars, and is often found enmeshed with it in a partisan way.' p. 272.
39. L. I. Rudolph, and S. H. Rudolph, *In Pursuit Of Lakshmi,* 1987. They point out the articulation of cultural dissent and regional nationalisms and the increasing incapacity of the State to handle these. p. 396; Paul Brass, The New Cambridge History of India, *The Politics of India since Independence,* New York, Port Chester, Melbourne and Sydney, Cambridge, 1995, p. 335.
40. f. n. 5, p. 17.
41. David Held, 'Central Perspectives on Modern State' in *op. cit.,* pp.29-75
42. Partha Chatterjee, *The Nation and Its fragments,* OUP. 1997. He notes that cultural difference has challenged the post colonial State as it did the colonial State.
43. *A Derrida Reader, Between The Blinds,* Introduction and Notes

by Peggy Kamuf, NY, Columbia University Press, p. xvii.

44. Criticising the developmental model so far followed in India, Gadgill and Guha say, 'The relentless transformation of the natural world into the world of artefacts, brought out so vividly for us by the satellite, has most asymmetric implications for... different constituents of Indian society...' and '... one sixth of India's population are the real beneficiaries of economic development....' Madhav Gadgil and Ram Chandra Guha, *Ecology and Equity,* penguin, 1995. pp. 3-4.

45. Aditya Mukherjee, 'Indian Capitalist Class and Foreign Capital', *Studies in History,* No. 1, January - June, 1979. p. 144.

45 (a). Aditya Mukherjee and Mridula Mukherjee, 'Imperialism and the Growth of Indian Capitalism in the Twentieth Century', *Economic and Political Weekly*, 4684, Vol. xxiii, No. 11,1988.

46. Yogendra Yadav, *op. cit.,* p. 20.

47. L.Rudolph and S. Rudolph, *op. cit.,* p. 50.

48. ——, 'Regime Types and economic Performance' in Sudipto Kaviraj, *op. cit.*

49. f.n.47.

50. Budhadev Bhattacharya, ' Dominant Mode of Production and The Character of the State in India' in Ghanshyam Shah, edited, *Capitalist Development, Critical Essays,* Felicitation Volume in Honour of A. R. Desai, Bombay, Popular Prakashan, 1990; Dipankar Gupta, ' Theory Against Practice; A Critique of the theories of the Capitalist State with special reference to India' in Ghanshyam Shah.

51. Budhdev Bhattacharya, *ibid.,* p. 146.

52. Dipankar Gupta, *ibid.*

53. Marx and Engels, *The German Ideology,* Collected Works, 1845-47, Vol. 5, Moscow, Progress Publishers, 1976., p.60.

54. Sudipto Kaviraj, 'A Critique of Passive Revolution' in Partha Chatterjee, edited, *State and Politics in India,* Delhi, Calcutta, Chennai and Bombay, Oxford,1988., p.86.

55. Robert D. King, *Nehru and the Language Politics of India,* Delhi, Calcutta, Chennai and Mumbai, Oxford University Press, 1998.

56. Marx, Letter to the editor of Otyecestvenniye Zapisky (Notes on Fatherland) end of 1877. *Selected Correspondence.* p. 71.

57. Ashgar Ali Engineer, edited, *Communal Riots in Post Independence India,* New Delhi, Sangam Books, 1984.

58. N. L. Gupta, 'The Reactionary Role of the Jan Sangh', New Delhi, *Secular Democracy,* April, 1968.

59. Aijaz Ahmed, *op. cit.*

60. Terence J. Byres, 'State, Class and Development' in Terence J. Byres, *The State, Class Development Planning and*

Liberalisation in India, Delhi, Chennai, Calcutta, Mumbai, 1997.

61. *Ibid.,* p.72.
62. Partha Chatterjee, *op. cit.,* pp. 211-212.
63. Francine R. Frankel and M. S. A. Rao, editors, *Dominance and State power in Modern India,* Delhi, Oxford University Press, 1990, pp. 509-516.
64. Joel S. Migdal, Atul kohli and Vivienne Shue, *Domination and Transformation in The Third World,* NY, Melbourne, Cambridge University Press, 1994.
65. Rajni Kothari, *State Against Democracy, In search Of Humane Governance,* Delhi, Ajanta Publications, 1989. Rajni Kothari, ' Rise of the Dalits and the Renewed debate on Caste', in Partha Chatterjee edited, *op. cit.*
66. Yogendra Yadav, *op. cit.,* p.18
67. Rajni Kothari, 'Rise of Dalits and the renewed Debate on Caste', *op. cit.,* p.442.
68. Rajni Kothari, *State Against Democracy, op. cit.,* p. 95.
69. R. S. Sharma, *op. cit.*
70. Quoted in Sumit Guha, ' Potentates, Traders and Peasants: Western India, c. 1700-1870', in Burton Stein and Sanjay Subramaniam, *op.cit.,* p.71.
71. Dipankar Gupta, *Rivalry and Brotherhood, A Study of the BKU,* Delhi, Oxford University Press, 1997, p. 125
72. Theda Skolpol, *States and Social Revolutions: A Comparative Analysis of France, Russia and China,* Cambridge, Cambridge University Press, 1979.
73. Rajen Harshe, *Imperialism in the Twentieth Century,* New Delhi, Sage, 1998.
74. Quoted in Pavan K. Verma, *op. cit.,* p. 15.
75. *Ibid.,* p.17.
76. *Ibid.,* p. 128.
77. *Ibid.,* p.122.
78. S. S. Thornburn, *Mussalmans and Moneylenders of Punjab,* New Delhi, Mittal Publications, 1983.
79. B. P. R. Vithal, 'Evolving Trends in The Bureaucracy', in Partha Chatterjee, *op. cit.,* p. 228.
80. Vanita Shastry, *The Puzzle of India's Industrial Policy,* University of Boston.
81. I.Natarajan, *Mimeographe,* 1998, New Delhi; CAER,1998.
82. *Ibid.,* p. 20.
83. *Ibid.,* p.60.
84. Radhika Desai, ' Culturalism and Contemporary right, Indian Bourgeoisie and Political Right', *Economic and Political Weekly,* March 20,1999. 705-707. Looking at the logic of

liberalisation, Jayati Ghosh points to the danger of authoritarianism. She says 'Government and bureaucracy are still critical in economic functioning, whether explicitly or implicitly, and this is in a context in which economic and financial powers are being further centralised, both vis-a-vis the State governments and within the various agencies of the central government'. Jayati Ghosh, 'Development Strategy in India: A Political Economy Perspective', Sugata Bose and Ayesha Jayal, *op. cit.,* p. 180.

85. Robert D. King, *op. cit.,* p. 73.
86. Government of India, *White Paper on Punjab,* GOI Publications.
87. Monirul Hussain, *Assam Movement,* Class, Ideology and Identity, Delhi, Manak Publications Pvt. Ltd. in association with Har-Anand Publications, 1993.
88. Ted Robert Gurr and Barbara Harff, *Ethno- Political Conflicts in World Politics,* Westview Press, Westview, 1994.
89. N. Ram, *Riding The Tiger,* New Delhi, Leftword Books, 1990, p. 12.
90. Baldev Raj Nayyar, *India's Quest for Technological Independence, Policy Foundation and Policy Change,* Vol. 1, New Delhi, Lancer,1988; N. Vittal, ' Information Technology for Defence and Development', Talk delivered at the National Defence College on March 20, 1993, *National Defence College Papers,* New Delhi, 1994.
91. Emile Benoit, *Defence and Economic Growth in Developing Countries,* London, Lexington, 1974.
92. David J. Louscher and Michael D. Salome, *Technology Transfers and U.S. Security Assistance: The impact of licensed Production,* Westview, Boulder and London. 1987.
93. 1998 Global Competitiveness Report of World Economic Forum Quoted in Nirupam Bajpai and Jeffrey D. Sachs, 'Strengthening India's Strategy for Economic Growth', *Economic and Political Weekly*, July, 18-24/25-31, 1998, p.1935-42.
94. C. H. Hanumantha Rao, Agricultural Growth, Sustainability and poverty alleviation' *ibid.,* pp. 1943-47.
95. V. N. Rao, ' Economic Reforms and Poor: Emerging Scenario', *ibid.,* p.1950.
96. Anne O Krueger and Sajjid Chinoy, 'The Indian Economy in the Global Context', Anne O. Krueger, *Economic Policy Reform,* edited, The University of Chicago, Chicago and London, 2002, p. 43.
97. C.S. Venkata Ratnam, D.P.A. Naidu, *Privatization and Labour,* SAAT and ILO, New Delhi, 2002, pp. 129-30.

98. Baldev Raj Nayyar, Business and India's Economic Policy, Economic and Political Weekly, September 19, 1998, ff. 2453-2468.
99. P. R. Panchmukhi, Social Impact of Economic Reforms in India, A Critical Appraisal', *Economic and Political Weekly,* dated March 4, 2002, pp. 836-45.
100. Smitu Kothari, 'Whose Independence, The Social Impact of *Economic Reforms in India, Journal of International Affairs,* Vol. 15, No.1 pp.85-116.
101. Sudha Pai, 'New social and political movements of dalit: a study of Meerut district', *Contributions to Indian Sociology,* 34, 2, 2000.
102. Roger Jeffery, Craig J. Jeffrey, and Patricia M. Jeffrey, 'Social and Political Dominance in Western UP: A response to Sudha Pai', Contributions to Indian Sociology, 35, 2, 2001.

2

State in Pakistan

The State in Pakistan stands at the intersection of national, regional and global cross currents of competing interests. Externally it is caught in the cross-currents of its search of leadership of West Asian Muslim States (strategic location being the largest Muslim populated State) in the Western side of its geographical reach. Its strategic location is on the route to push for warm waters from the North, especially from Afghanistan and Central Asia makes it a sought after entity for strategic games in the region. Its desire to score over the Indian preponderance and policy towards J&K makes it search for security push into Afghanistan to seek tactical depth and J&K to get water works. The core of this concentric relevance is its reliance on the US, the NATO countries and China.

The internal dimension has no fewer complexities for it to negotiate. It stands at the cross roads of creation of internal wealth, legitimation process among peoples at different stages of - nationalisms of five regions (one seceded from it in 1971) since the time of the creation of Pakistan as an artificial union without nationalism. Given the centrifugal forces in these different regions, as a State Pakistan has to balance between the contradiction between the creation of wealth and legitimacy. As a desirous 'nation' it has to balance between the centralising tendencies germinated by the logic of its external strategic location and the central position that a modern institution like a professional Army has teleologically occupied, internally.

The two cross currents of the internal and the external ultimately have to revolve around the issue of the people and the standard of living. If it produces wealth, the issue of satisfying demands is raised. If it succeeds in its external policy with an economic spin off its impact on the society's well being will determine its legitimacy and through it its security. In its search for legitimacy it can opt for democratic, authoritarian, totalitarian or theocratic processes. The legitimation process is related to the political structures and that to the democratic transition, if at all. Depending on its success in meeting the demands for well being, the democratic option may be available. In built in the slip between expectation and its satisfaction, the proclaimed promise and increasing denial will show up its eroding base in the form of political revolt independently of the regime types. The revolt here has axis both of the absolute and the relatively deprived, apart from the issue of nationalism.

In Pakistan, the received wisdom from the West is that since it is not a totalitarian government its authoritarian government is acceptable to the West. Second, as a corollary it can get away with murder if it serves various extra-regional purposes. This not only impinges on its regime types but also makes the issue a little more complex. There are the 'civilian' and the militarist regimes. Further the argument is that the former are the more democratic, or were atleast expected to be and the latter are authoritarian or atleast assumed to be. The difference may not be much since a Bonapartist regime was the nomenclature given to the most popularly elected one, i.e. of Zulfiqar Ali Bhutto. In any case whatever the difference there is no denying the fact that they would be creating conditions of some version of capitalist economy under authoritarianism. This is also true of the parliamentary and the presidential types building capitalist mode of production.[1] The second be neo-liberal, welfarist or even socialist, as per the position of Immanuel Wallerstein.[2] Within the capitalist argument there are different versions of the [3] economy's nature and thus also of its State. Does it follow a dependent mode and therefore become a Peripheral State or does it follow a self-reliant mould and become a Semi-Periphery or independent? That precisely is the case of Pakistan and India from the perspective of the New Left intellectuals like Wallerstein, Hamza Alavi, and Aijaz Ahmed writing on Pakistan and India, respectively. The latter two regard Pakistan to be a Peripheral State. At another level the difference is that one is pursuing State capitalism and the other pursuing private capitalist road, as do India and Pakistan, respectively.

The issue of the nature of the economy is tied to the nature of the Pakistani State's ontos and that in turn to two dimensions of it. One, what is its relationship to the economic power structure and the other to its capacity to transit to a modern democratic polity in the context of the forces that shape and get shaped by it. The issue involves the relationship of the military and society and the professionalism of the military. In this dialectic of its development lie the roots to its militarism and its supposed democratic options. Since the issues of both democracy and militarism are currently the two defining features of the debate in Pakistani civil society it is necessary to go into the dynamics of its militarism in the Pakistani polity. Further why is it that it fails to deliver goods despite its enumerated successes in the economy and pervading hold over State administration? That raises certain sociological issues not just of the military profession, or the profession's linkages with the society, but also its external linkages and the process of transition from within military industrial complex that a polity witnesses.[4]

The State in Pakistan has its own theatre like its colonial predecessor. The State in all its Hobbesian majesty is standing alone to intervene in the processes of war sometimes as a *trip wire* or at other times as a *frontline* one closer to foreign interests but oblivious of its negative spin off internally. It deals with 44 foreign States apart from the European ones[5], unlike India, say some of its commentators, but quite unable to raise its permanent place either in the Muslim World or the comity of nations without the US-Chinese support. In fact, if a foreign commentator is to be believed, its experiment as a State is in danger if the US abandons it.[6] A more dispassionate view makes the same point.[7] Both want Pakistan to survive in the interest of the US and not for the sake of Pakistan. This is sheer tragedy of this theatre in which the importance of the people is that of mere onlookers.

Internally the theatre is made more splendid and therefore more tragic by the talk of democracy by those who especially Leviathanised the State, namely the Army. Ayub's Basic Democracy was claimed to have civilianised the polity. Yahya's holding of fair elections and LFO resulted in secession. Zulfiqar Ali Bhutto's talk of Islamic socialism slumped into Islamisation and authoritarianism. The Islam of pirs and sufis opposed Zia's attempts at Islamisation fad. The theatre of Benazir and Nawaz

Sharif's interlude of corruption and nepotism, debt traps were Army's mascots in the name of civilian regimes. In this distance of tragedy and farces one notices the sombre reality. A recent report in the *Dawn* suggested that a brother killed his sister for having converted to Islam.[8] Talk of Islam is the most farcical apart from Bhutto's talk of Islamic socialism. The society and its people are not moved by it. Duncan says of the Zia regime, 'While Zia's parliament existed, between 1983-88, the Islamisation programme slipped. It was alien to the people who made up the Parliament: their sort of Islam was the traditional, rural Islam, of pirs and shrines and poems."[9]

Zia had also banned eating of meat on a particular day. The Pakistanis were spending the rest of the six days collecting meat for that day only.[10] Fighting for *jehad* led to inter ethnic fallout in Sindh.[11] The shadow of Islam turned Islamabad, in the words of an American ambassador, as

'Rather like a New York cemetry; half the size: but twice the dead.' [12] A Baloch Khan commented about Pakistan's links with the US and *jihad* thus, 'First the British, then the Pakistanis, now the Americans' and went on to say ' we are allergic to the United States. We are against you. You always try to be nanny, or come marching in with a big stick.'[13]

In Kashmir this Afghan *jihad* meant that by June 2002, 180,000 Pakistani troops and 250,000 Indians faced each other along the banks of Jhelum.[14] When asked about Talibanisation about Afghanistan, Musharraf said slightly irritably 'I have never been to a madarsa, but I do know that all this talk about their teaching militancy is just hearsay.'[15]

At the time when NWFP Government adopted legislation on Sharia in June 2003 the same Musharraf said that he is not for Talibanisation.[16] The irony is that the same leader has to speak different languages on the subject of Islam. If one relegates it to tradition he still continues to visit mosques, as did Ayub. The fate of Bhutto's socialism was that his realpolitik ironically linked him to Islamisation to seek legitimation in 1977. The case of Zia is that he could do little about the segmented and sectarian ethos of the Pakistani society despite his Islamic orientation in his personal and public life and Army organisation. Yahya Khan stands out to be the only one who did not pander to Islam and is also the one whose regime witnessed the idea of Islam becoming the broken thread for West and East Pakistan. The point is whether it is a militarist or a civilian regime type it resorts to Islamisation but fails to unite the country into nationhood. Still the tragedy is that no one yet has looked at the liberationist potential[17] of Islam in Pakistan. Malik had pointed to its nationalist and social aspects. Islam could provide for both a nationalist and revolutionary possibilities. These are not worked out by any scholar or political leader in Pakistan. Faiz Ahmed Faiz's is one of the few lonely voice that one heard.

This chapter examines the State of Pakistan from the perspective of regime types to lay bare the distorted dynamics of 'democracy'. It further looks at its ontos to see its class essence and developmental strategy to suggest that it has pursued dependent capitalist economy in a way that has preserved the narrow base of the Pakistani State in terms of classes despite its transition from colonial to peripheral imperative. Further its militarism is examined to suggest that this is a structural and policy option that it's strategic location and historical antecedents offer to Pakistan. It has its internal and external linkages. It is part of the distorted process of social change without political revolution that effectively fights feudal interest conclusively. Finally it looks at the nature of political revolt that Pakistan has faced in the process of its 55 years' history, taking in view its unevenly developed proto-nationalisms, sectarian conflicts and other social issues like gender in different parts that composed it and add to its existential blues.

First part of the chapter looks at the approaches to the State. The second section looks at the ontos of Pakistan. Here we focus on the regime types and foreign connections. Section three looks at its militarism in terms of its praetorianism/corporate interests and the role of ISI.[18] The last section looks at the nature of political revolt of the peoples of Pakistan. *Dependent State of Pakistan in the throes of transition from precapitalist stage to peripheral imperative belies any theory of militarism, democracy and nation formation. Its militarism and failure to form the nation State are the products of its being caught up in the logic of its historical underdeveloped antecedents and existential structural economic linkages with U.S. military industrial complex and strategic interests. Its core of militarism can be explained only in terms of external and internal linkages and historical lineages that add to it that sombre blend of having stagnated at the cross road of the broken old world and aborted new world. That appears to be the existential condition of this fragile, if not failed, State. Its nascent Civil Society making no differece. Its liberalised economy and participation in the War on terror after September11, 2001 generates hopes of its transition to democracy,*[19] *which was never on the agenda. Authoritarianism will be its qualifying mark.*

Approaches to the State

The State of Pakistan has been a focus of study by innumerable indigenous and foreign scholars. Their approaches can be divided into three, *viz.* structural-functional or liberal, political economic and cultural. In the latter there are two strands, viz the State and Civil Society approach and the Islamisation approach. The first approach examines Pakistan's early failure as a democratic polity and hopes that its fragile present strengthens democracy in the future. The second one looks at Pakistan as a dependency and ascribes to it its dependent economy and authoritarian nature. The last approach of State and Civil Society hopes that the future emerges as the new organisations of civil society, especially the women organisations raise their banner. The Islamist approach is linked especially to the Zia phase and not just to that to suggest that the issue of nationhood is addressed by it so is probity in national life. We do not however notice any analysis that takes stock of the Pakistani State from the perspective of ecology or class formation and dissent within the Marxist framework. Practically every approach does talk about the autonomy of the State of Pakistan in its functional aspects. We do not have any work that uses the concept of relative autonomy as propounded by Gramsci. Pakistani scholars notice the decreasing Stateness in volatile situations like the one in East Pakistan and Sindh despite the increasing significance of the Army in the governing structures and political process as one having corporate interests. In contrast, theories about India are richer.

Liberal Approach

Idea of Pakistan. A sympathetic observer of Pakistan, William Rushbrook looked at the original rationale of Pakistan as it was in the minds of the elites and the masses that supported the idea of Pakistan. He says about the elites "Elite-landowners, public servants, men of business, politicians, and religious leaders—each with particular interest of his own ...sought no radical changes in the political and social organisation to which they had become accustomed under British rule."[20]

Unlike this desire to be ensconced in the continuity of patronage and pampering of the martial races by the British Colonial State the masses had a different vision of the idea of Pakistan. They wanted radical change. To quote from Rushbrook "Masses had rallied to Mr. Jinnah because they were hoping for the creation of an Islamic state. What exactly this would imply in the shape of formal institutions, the masses did not know, and perhaps did not greatly care; they look for a polity in which the Islamic ideals of social justice, of benevolent rule, of responsiveness to popular needs, and of the protection of the poor from exploitation would provide the governing principles of political life and economic progress."[21]

This reading of the peoples' mood seems to be fairly accurate for the people of India had been used to benevolent or patrimonial State, as defined by Weber, atleast in the north of the Vindyas. Despite the fact that the Mughal State was feudal and extracted revenue ruthlessly it also provided for benevolence and protection to people against corruption and excesses of the administration. Further it also helped within its framework the entrepreneurial activity though not of the Tudor magnitude in England. Briefly the people who settled for the idea of Pakistan had no inkling of the future polity. The movement for Pakistan was based only on elite politics of a constitutional variety in which apart from the idea of the Muslim homeland and the desire to be free from the Hindu 'domination' there was little that was offered. Jinnah's charisma and realpolitik till 1946 did not produce anything for Pakistan in the future heartland of Pakistan—the Punjab, which was under the secular control of the Unionist Party. Sikandar Hayat Khan and Chottu Ram were the secular leaders of the undivided Punjab. Khizr Hayat Khan's leadership also did not allow the Muslim League to form the government till 1946. Ian Talbot says "The Punjab had always been a key province for Jinnah's aims to represent Indian Muslim opinion. The raising of the Pakistan resolution in 1940 increased the region'a importance still further. At the time Muslim League could claim some influence with Sikandar's ministry through the Sikandar-

-Jinnah Pact, but it was at best a very tenous hold on power. More over Sikandar increasingly distanced himself from the Pakistan's scheme because of its unacceptability to its Hindu and Sikh allies."[22]

Talbot observes that the lack of support to the Muslim League remained, till owing to the war conditions, and, the British rural policies eroded the support base of the Unionist Party and that led to the support to the Muslim League. In other provinces this remained the scene too. Even this idea was not widely shared by all the Muslims of undivided India. Not even in the provinces that became Pakistan. The struggle that the charismatic leader and his outfit conducted was around constitutional reforms. He had a single minded desire for a Muslim homeland.[23] There was therefore no way in which the common man (in the provinces that became a part of Pakistan) and the immigrants, could have any idea of the future vision of Pakistani State.

Structural Approach: *Polity and Process*

In the absence of a strategy of social change liberals focused on the structural functional aspects of the polity. Pakistan did inherit institutions of governance that the British had created in the provinces. Mohammed Waseem writes of it and examines politics around those authority structures. He says "...the authority structures of the state, as inherited from British India, provide a focal point for the country's politics."

And further ascribes to them unprecedented position thus "it is essentially to the structural dynamics of the state that we must ascribe the primary responsibility for shaping the political events throughout the post-independence period."[24]

He discusses the processes and the structure of the Pakistan movement and notes the kind of alliances that the movement had to make in the making of Pakistan. He suggests

"The All India Muslim League leadership entered the Muslim majority areas in two phases: first it sought an understanding with the local political forces, especially the Unionist Party in Punjab, Krishak Praja Party in Bengal and unexpectedly, Congress in Sindh. Secondly, it launched a movement of mass mobilization, undercutting the respective political parties in the provinces."[25]

He notes that in the framework of the Pakistan's State system, elections were considered dysfunctional in as much as the political elite lacked a well-established constituency in the country. This led to the continuance of the bureaucratic polity as a military regime of Ayub.[26] Its interventionist role and its regime types following economic goals have created the conditions where informally the State only created "clientilistic relationship between the bureaucracy on the one hand and the tribal and landed elite on the other."[27]

Waseem's hopes of the system's capacity to absorb dissent are brighter than his diagnosis for he attributes to the State an increasing capacity to absorb dissent through elections of 1953, 1968-69, 1977 and 1983. The post 1988 elections and the coming into power of a conglomerate of parties under the JUI and BNA are evidence of his democratic desires. He expresses them thus:

"Their presence in the government at various levels reflected the principle of constitutional legitimacy in the sense of rule by public representatives."[28]

His caveat to this desire is that the elections are beholden to the hold of the military and bureaucracy over the polity. Eight years later, writing in the context of the changes that Musharraf had brought about in the polity Waseem expresses the pathos of democracy seekers thus:

"The latest constitutional reforms proposed by the Musharraf government not only avoid addressing the problems facing democracy in Pakistan but may also destabilise the federalist framework of the State still further."[29] L.F.O. is a proof.

We do not have an explanation to this pathos here. It does not just reside in the structural formation of the State of Pakistan but in the correlation of classes that determine the character of the civilian and military governments. It is suggested here that a better way of looking at the regime types is to look at them as a continuum on the same scale of class structure and political institutions. They are Janus faced-half military and half civilian. To prove the point following may be noted. First, Governor General Muhammad Ali aligned with Ayub when the Constitution making was taking place. Second, Ayub attempted to civilianise his martial law administration by giving it the name of Basic Democracy and devolving power to civilian bureaucrats. Martial Law Administrator, Yahya Khan is praised for allowing the first and the last ever free and fair elections to be held in East and West Pakistan with his L.F.O. (Legal Framework Order). This brought the Awami Party to majority in Pakistan before Pakistan's break up. Zulfiqar Ali Bhutto, the popularly elected leader of the civilian government, had his autocratic lineages and orientations. He was a martial law administrator. He was a *wadera,* a minister in Ayub's government; he was aligned to Yahya Khan in preventing Sheikh Mujibur Rehman to become the Prime Minister of Pakistan and in the conduct of the ill-fated military operation in East Pakistan. His own prime-ministership is described as Bonapartist. We are currently not interested in raising the issue of any one's psyche. We are interested in looking at the double face of the Pakistani State and therefore point to the inability of Waseem to explain this regime type. If he does that then there is no possible scope for the optimism that he posits in the Pakistani elections. They are not separated from the power structure that the state structure represents.

Failure of Democracy: *Muhammad and Munir Conspiracy*

The subversion of the democratic structure was achieved very early for no fault of the civilian elites. Mcgrath shows this. He calls the experiment with democracy in Pakistan a failure. He had examined the period of Constitution making and found that the Constituent Assembly had made tremendous progress but Munir and Ghulam Muhammad were in league with Ayub to subvert the democratic experiment. He does not blame the civilian leaders since they had done an excellent work of giving the new nation a constitution. He blames the Pakistani leadership as well as the foreign Press for this failure. To quote him,

"But it was the success, not the failure, of the assembly which brought about its demise. It had succeeded in producing a Constitution which was democratic and therefore unacceptable to Ghulam Mohammad."[30]

On the culpability of the then leaders of Pakistan he says "When those who destroyed Pakistan's democracy wrote their histories they placed a large part of the blame for the destruction on the victims. Supposedly it was the people, because they were not 'ready' for democracy, who were charged with being the underlying cause of failure."[31] This was the position taken by Munir who, as Chief Justice, had justified the take over by Ayub. Mcgrath points to the immense job put on the shoulders of the leaders of the Constituent Assembly and the post-Jinnah leadership, especially in the context of having to provide for a constitution in which East and West Pakistan were to be put in the same constitution. At another level then one could point to the difficulty in terms of the uneven articulation of the proto-nationalisms and maturation of class structures as the cause of this stifled growth. We must also note the reasons forwarded by the early civilian Pakistani leaders against democracy were those that had been forwarded by Simon, Stratchey and Sealey who declined to give either freedom or democracy because they thought Indian people were not fit for self-governance.

Post-1988 Democracy: *Lack of Institution Building and Personality Clashes*

William L. Richter points to the difficulties of the Benazir Bhutto government that came to power after the 1990 elections. He summed up the strains on the polity thus "the fabric of Pakistan's democracy was stretched and stressed, if not actually torn."[32]

Richter points to the conspiracy that was indulged in by President Ishaq Khan who was once upon a time a Zia loyalist. This had paved the way for the 1990 elections. Post-communist blues in foreign policy marred subsequent government of Nawaz Sharief, problems of globalisation's impact on economy and law and order situation. The issue that rocked the government was the rape case of Veena Hayat. This put Ishaq Khan for the first time in the tight spot.[33] The critical issues that the Nawaz Sharief government could not handle were the orientation of the State towards student unrest,[34] 125 million unemployed, scandals involving BCCI and the Pakistan Industrial Development Corporation.

Richter views these elections as a hope for a party system to emerge in Pakistan and this he thought augured well for Pakistan's democracy.[35] This optimism gets jolted by developments during 1993-98. Pakistan is confronted with the problems of splintering of parties. Parties not being entrenched. Family feuds of the Bhutto family emerged. Confrontation between Benazir and Nawaz Sharif intensified. Accusations against the Army of plotting against Benazir were made. Political assassinations, sectarian violence, scandals, scams and corruption, and failure of the Benazir and Leghari relationship.[36] The grounds on which Benazir Bhutto was dismissed were not of her making alone. They were reflective of a perennial situation of distorted development. These grounds were: (a) political violence, (b) manipulation of the judiciary; (c) political interference with administrative postings; (d) use of draconian measures against political opposition; (e) tempering and corrupting national institutions, (f) rampant nepotism and disasterous state of the economy.[37] All these are related to the constitutional amendment that was introduced by Zia. This amendment gave discretionary and overriding powers to the President by amending Article 53(b). The then Supreme Court on the grounds of historical necessity approved the amendment. Second, most of the economic problems and political violence are related to the state of the polity since its inceptions when the violence against the adians or Ahmedias started. What was new was violence related to Murtaza Bhutto's assassination and alienation between daughter and mother, Benazir and Nusrat Bhutto. The problems of corruption related also to Mr. 10 per cent that Mr. Zardari, husband of Benazir Bhutto, was called. Third set of grounds that related to the economy was connected with the processes of globalisation.

The last civilian government of Nawaz Sharif came into conflict with the Army on both foreign and domestic policy and lost out despite the fact that Benazir, as an opposition leader was a changed person. On the basis of his survey of Pakistani politics Ziring concludes that Pakistan as an idea and Pakistan as a reality are quite different. Commenting on the reality he says, "Pakistan would be sustained in the condition of the classic administrative state."

He further suggests that the political process as a political phenomenon have nothing in common with the democratic experience for he says, "The vast majority of Pakistanis are a gullible congeries of factions, clans and tribes and their manipulation by traditional, as well as contemporary power brokers remains the central focus of political experience."[38]

To conclude this part we notice that commentaries on Pakistan's liberal route of democracy range from optimistic (Waseem), realistic (Ziring) to pessimistic (Mcgrath). An Indian commentator of the Pakistan scene reflects the last mood, as well.

Contemporary Pakistan shows up a picture of rootlessness of the democratic institutions and political system. Venna Kukreja says of this " Even after five decades of its creation, Pakistan is struggling to establish a viable political system. Democracy and democratic institutions have yet to take roots. Long spells of military rule and even longer periods of religious, ethnic and economic turmoil have battered its polity. And since the 1990s, relentless Islamisation has made things more difficult and has done enough damage to Pakistan itself."[39]

Development in Pakistan has not led to democracy she notes and wishes it does by allowing political participation. The issue is not of just why development has not taken a democratic root. Obviously we are talking about the liberal democracy in this section. We need to note that democracy is not the logical outcome of liberalism. Constitutional oligarchy is its twin in Lockean argument. The growth of oligarchic institutions called parties and the transformation of class and other conflicts into plural conflicts only takes a State to the liberal democratic direction. Both these conditions were and are not available to Pakistan. Its creation was an artificial construct. It has not been able to cohere as nationhood, a pre-condition for a modern European nationhood as in England. It did not boast of a middle class and a petty bourgeoisie that could replace the proto- nationalist aspirations of its peoples at a micro level. All that it had by way of modernity at a macro level is its elements in bureaucracy, military and support from the Western powers. It would therefore have been a matter of surprise if it had led to the fulfilment of the liberal agenda that the scholars are talking about. It does not even have a liberal community, let alone a liberal democratic one. This is not to say that there are no liberal elements. They are very much there. There are as much Marxists though negligible. But there are no determining liberals and marxists. That they pose a danger to the state is well brought out by the fate of Faiz Ahmed Faiz who had prescience when he talked about the blowing away in the air of the powers that be. Iqbal Bano had sung that so beautifully to rising crescendo of the clapping of Pakistani audiences in the 1980s. This not only coincided with Zia's death but also a presaging of the brush with near death that Musharraf had in the air before he even staged his coup. At the time when the drama was coming to an end in the air this remark is relevantly made about

Musharraf. "Needless to say, Musharraf was one of the last men who wanted the plane to crash; he was, after all, on board.... Musharraf conduct, at best, fully justified his reputation as a risk taker and, at worst, was reckless."[40]

The democratic shoots in terms of popular elections and partyization that were becoming the basis of hope were grounded and dashed by his coup and subsequent authoritarian elections as noted by Waseem above.

State and Civil Society Approach: *Neo-patrimonial Civil Society*

Ziring, Iftikhar H. Malik and Anita Weis subscribe to this European approach to democracy in Pakistan. Once the liberal approach concludes that the institutionalisation of democracy has failed in Pakistan, scholars have taken to the other Western approach that is useful to discuss the project of democracy from Western perspective. The European experience of the transition from feudalism to capitalism via the creation of civil society in place of feudal solidarities is being used to look at the possibility of good governance of Third World developing States. We notice that this is happening in case of post-communist East European societies, post-Mao Chinese State and current Central Asian States. The theorists of subaltern history usually reject this clamping of categories over societies with their specifically different political processes and local polities. Let us however turn to the argument for Pakistan.

Iftikhar H. Malik adopts the approach to debunk the Pakistani State as it has evolved and focuses on the Civil Society owing to the emergence of a new intermediate class that is leading it and imposing on the political agenda of Pakistan a new agenda. He thus articulates the gulf between the Pakistani State and the Civil Society.

'Civil Society is rooted in democracy, constitution, and issues pertaining to the national economy and security. It entails establishing public confidence in domestic and foreign policies through a corresponding system of accountability to discourage corruption and contain militarism. Such a society is an essential pre-requisite for political culture, based on an independent press, and judiciary, an efficient educational system and thoughtful planning in which the state encourages voluntary participation rather than operating as a coercive institution and embodies the broad principles of mutual acceptance and tolerance."[41]

His view of civil society is not like the one in the German tradition where it is an ally of the State but in the British tradition where it is supposed to be watching and checking the state on behalf of the individual. He has further Pakistanised his Civil Society to include in it drives of primordialism and fight against authoritarianism. He says of it,

"The civil society in the perspective of the developing world is an interface between primordial social groups and political authority and is a continuum of changing processes and scenarios, with internal and global features, exerting an unbridled influence, in most cases contradicting the civic dictum of a given society."[42]

He pins his faith in a new relationship between the State and Civil Society of Pakistan since he posits a political change in the nature of the state in post-colonial society after the 1980s. On the political agenda is the transition of the State from authoritarianism to democratic participatory State with a new political culture and wider economic opportunities. The core of this new political culture is the growth of a new intermediate class. He says it is a cross regional class providing youthful leadership to the masses. We notice that the notion of this class is rather hazy in his work. He does give us a clue about it. He says of it "a comparatively youthful society, most of whose members have been brought up as Pakistanis, are not only demanding an efficient and congenial government but also raising voices against a continued monopoly of feudal interests over policies. They are not comfortable with the existing oligarchic tripolar relationship between the bureaucracy, the military and politicians which smacks of age-old dynastic elitism and so demands accountability are becoming louder."[43]

His faith in the civil society is linked to the dismal performance of the Pakistani State in the realms of social sector and in matters of poverty alleviation. It must be pointed out that he is not looking for mass politics as an alternative to the present elite politics. Rather it is a plea for an alternative elite politics within the given structures. He puts his faith in the judiciary, press, active campuses that would promote healthy counter culture. In all this he suggests that the gender issue is a new and significant addition on the agenda of the Civil Society. What is remarkable about this author's faith in the Civil Society is that he thinks that it will help in generating Pakistani nationalism by making ethnicity an integrationist force as opposed to its regionalist divisive orientation. To quote him,

"A democratic state, helped by responsive and representative institutions, is geared towards the political consensus and is strengthened by a strong and vocal civil society. Ethnicity in such cases, emerges as the integral part of civil society, rather than being simply an anathema to centrist, monopolistic and particularistic tendencies."[44] He hopes for a new covenant.

The problem with the view is that we do not know either the structure of the new intermediate class or its roots. We further also do not know about its orientation except that it is not committed to traditional paternalistic political culture. But no evidence. Further how different his middle class is going to be from the earlier middle class that has been absorbed so far in the system. One of the institutions that he pins his hope on is the judiciary. Let us look at the judiciary. Mushahid Hussian and Akram Hussain said of the judiciary that it is a strong pillar of the Pakistani Civil Society. They said of the judiciary,

"The judiciary has upheld the rule of law, defended civil liberties and contributed to breaking political deadlocks, thereby serving to push the political process forward."[45]

The experience is different. It was Justice Munir who fumed against the civilian political leaders to justify the introduction of martial law by Ayub Khan. Hussians themselves agree to this. Further we also know that during the Zia period the judiciary gave the doctrine of 'historical necessity' when he amended the Constitution to accrue to himself extra constitutional powers as President. Again we notice that in the wake of the current demand of the Opposition that President Musharraf give up one of the two offices, viz of the President or that of the Army Chief, he has done none of this and the court has decided in his favour.[46] Hussians are right in saying that the judiciary has grown but not at the expense of the Army's rule or authoritarian governance. In that sense the judiciary does push the political process as an actor in it and as a part of the authoritarian legitimation process.

Another issue that is new and this has not been raised so far is the one about gender. The women's movement grew up in the atmosphere of the 1980s. This is a significant one that even the post-modernists also raise and so go more in the direction of tradition. But this is not the position of Iftikhar H. Malik. Another scholar looks at this issue within the democratic framework. This is a significant issue and has received public attention during the regime of Nawaz Sharief involving a relative of Ghulam Ishtaq Khan in a rape case. We also noticed that after Musharraf went back to Pakistan from Agra he agreed with a journalist's view, in a Press conference that was televised live, that the role of lady activist in India during the Agra summit was against the traditional culture of Pakistan. She is a human rights activist of Pakistan. Anita M. Weiss focuses on the growth of the women's movement especially against the wrong interpretation of women's role in Islam and their open opposition about girl rights in the atmosphere of the 1980s. On the civil society, and on the role of women in preparing for the International Conference on Women, she says

"A civil society is emerging in Pakistan, one engineered neither by state nor the elite groups, but emanating from enthusiasm, commitment, perseverance of individuals agreeing to work together to achieve envisioned goals."[47]

The problem with this approach is that there are no abiding processes that would strengthen the Civil Society. These relate to a resurgent secular educational system, middle class formation, the general improvement of the dependent nature of the civilian bureaucracy on the Army, or even the improvement in independent vernacular or English media that can strengthen the enthusiasm of Malik and Weis about the Civil Society in Pakistan.

Secondly, it may also be pointed out that the political culture in Pakistan is neo-patrimonial, as well as opportunist, and not like the one that emerged in the West. Given its IMF led and State led private sector economy it has not produced competing economic organisations that would man the Civil Society and partake in the political process against the State. Its economy has been described as rentier, peripheral and State led by economists like Haq, Javed Burki, Omar Noman and Hamza Alavi. Jinnah had to ask private business from Calcutta and Bombay to come to Pakistan to give Pakistan credibility. For private capital to develop Martial Law Administrator, Ayub Khan founded Pakistan Industrial Development Corporation (PDIC). Zia-ul Haq had to call out private capital. Bhutto had to rely on the leevers of the State to attempt to deliver on the social sector. The immigrants (Mohajirs) brought skills from the North of India but not much of capital or organisations. The point being made is that the Pakistani Civil Society does not seem to be matured either to be composed of economic individuals or organisations to be effective opponents of the State. Much more needs to happen. It is in the genesis stage. In that sense Lawrence Ziring's observation is more in tune with the ground reality. He says,

"Before Pakistan can achieve coherence, before it can assume the role of a nation-state, it will have to construct a civil society."[48]

In other words the intermediaries that Malik notes and women activists that Weis observes are too few and far between. The intermediaries may as well be getting coopted as has been happening, says Kukreja.[49] There is in any case no sign of any significant legislation being made on the basis of demands made by the liberal intelligentsia that one can expect to man the civil society. S. Akbar Zaidi says of its recent role in the context of Musharraf's coup and politics,

"Decaying, corrupted and dependent on donor funded projects, the NGO led 'civil society', thinking that General Musharraf was some sort of a liberal, secular, military leader, threw in the lot with the military government as soon as it took over power in October, 1999 and suffered from 'praetorean liberalism' and this is closely aligned to the US and the Western capitals."[50]

The relevance of the approach lies in the fact that it raises relevant political questions with regard to the future of democracy, construction of nationalism and the liberation of women in the State of Pakistan. In the absence of a radical class movement this is the other alternative to enrich the authoritarian experiment or the Administrative State as Ziring calls it. Nothing happens in the political domain without the propulsion of the economic. Further it may be pointed out that some radical theorists, like Gramsci theorised upon the Civil Society to conduct a political struggle against Capitalism and its State. Here the Pakistani scholars are trying to use it for the defence of the capitalist state. In other words subvert its original intent by emptying its revolutionary kernel.

Bureaucratic: *Administrative State*

The skills that the Punjabis and the North Indian Muslims brought to Pakistan helped to form its elites, administrative, military and political. The three got into a symbiotic relationship with the military dominating the scene though originally it is the civilian bureaucracy that had dominated the Pakistani polity. The three-fold division of the elites and the initial significance of the bureaucrats are noted by Hashim thus " Since its birth Pakistan has been governed by its elites, mainly bureaucratic, military and political. The bureaucratic elite who had formed an important element in the power structure since the very creation of Pakistan gradually became more assertive, frequently gaining their steadily increasing power at the expense of the political elite. An important contributory factor in this development was the fact that at an early stage in Pakistan's history some erstwhile bureaucrats occupied the political positions of Governor General and Prime Minister. They brought with them the traditions, outlook, and attitudes typical of the bureaucrats. Their sympathies were slanted more towards the bureaucracy than towards the political institutions. The military coups of 1958,1969 and 1977 further strengthened the power and prestige of civil bureaucracy."[51]

The Pakistani bureaucracy continued very much in the British tradition, in that its system of relationship between the Secretary and the Minister, the recruitment of the generalists, and the cadre system helped it to perpetuate its hold. There are specificities of Pakistan's problems of bureaucracy as well. We noticed above that the people who came from North India brought with them their skills. These were the bureaucrats and the Punjabis combined the illustrious group. The two groups that dominated the bureaucracy and through it Pakistan are the Punjabis and the North Indian immigrant. This was felicitated by making Urdu to be the national language. This language policy worked against the other Muslim majority areas, like the Bengal, Sindh, Baluchistan and the NWFP. Linguistic policy has a great link with power. In Pakistan English is followed by Urdu and then by Punjabi, Sindi, Siraki, Bengali, Pashtun and Baloch languages. The Administrative elite was dominated by the English and Urdu-speaking groups. English and Urdu formed the language of power. Below these came the mother tongues.[52]

The imbalance was sought to be corrected by introducing the quota system for the adequate representation of the provinces in the bureaucracy in order to remove the disproportion of provincial representation. By 1970s the system increased the provincial representation. Upper Sindh, and to a lesser extent the Punjab are over-represented in the rural bureaucracy while rural Sindh, Baluchistan, the Northern Areas, and Federally Administered Tribal Areas, and Azad Kashmir are under represented; that such inequalities are positively correlated with rank but such inequalities are reduced says Kennedy.[53]

Bureaucray is conservative said Karl Manheimm in his study of the German bureaucray in Ideology and Utopia.[54] Weberian bureaucracy is not known to be radical either. Macaulay's bureaucray in India was no exception. Trained to be the British steel framework, the ICS did not have the commitment of the kind that Gunnar Myrdal[55] talked about in Asian Drama with regard to India. In India Nehru expressed the need of making the services commit to be the servants of the people and engage in community development and decentralised democracy. The bureaucratic reform of the CSP in the Ayub period only strengthened the bureaucracy's commitment to the dependent economy, provincial prejudices and the Army rule. Bhutto discovered that his effort at improving the social sector and nationalisation was being thwarted by the bureaucracy, whom he unsuccessfully tried to tame. He introduced reforms to overcome this and also made out of turn promotions and transfers. He introduced several policies for administrative reforms. These were abolition of the CSP Academy and adoption of the uniform pay scale. This reduced the comparative advantage in salary structure of the CSP officers. And the introduction of the lateral entry.[56] Zia-ul Haq reverted to the pre-Bhutto phase and restored the significance of the bureaucracy. This got disrupted during the Benazir Bhutto period that carried the practice of lateral entry of the bureaucrats and change them at will.

The institution of the bureaucracy declined with passage of time. It became a junior partner of the military bureaucracy. The significance of the bureaucracy reduced owing to the following factors. The intellectual calibre of the bureaucracy declined since their training suffered. In other words their intellectual and institutional decay took place. The reasons of the decay are varied. First, the strategy of frequent transfers caused demoralisation. Second, the decline of educational standards in academic institutions. Best brains of the bad educational system did not join the civil services. Third, the courses of the training institutes are superficial and that evaluation of the participants is soft leading to further decline. Fourth, arbitrary mechanisms of decision making further eroded their self-confidence. Their reliance increased on the political boss.[57] The ideology of Pakistan Studies and Islamisation of education did not produce good social science.[58] On Pakistan Studies Rehman says that these contain all the three elements of political, historical and sociological studies and is meant to disseminate State-supported ideologies. In Pakistan it refers to politics or religion and use of emotive symbols like *jihad* and martyrdom. The military bureaucracy has gained at the cost of the civilian bureaucracy.[59] At the time of independence the three sections of the elites shared equal power. But now it is the military bureaucracy that has gained in prestige, power and a corporate position.[60] Generally speaking it is through the bureaucracy that the landowning classes were well entrenched in the State and through the lever of the State the bureaucracy controlled nascent business class.

Liberal Political Economy Approach: *Mehbub-ul Haq and Papanek Model*

To begin with, the economic strategy developed till the beginning of the Ayub period was on the basis of an alliance between the bureaucracy and the merchants. No structural reforms had been introduced. This led to political dissensions since it had benefitted the merchants and the bureaucrats and both from the same ethnic background, namely Punjabi and immigrant. The strategy had also led to regional imbalance since it drained wealth out of Bengal.[61] During the Ayub period the model of growth was the one that young Mahbub-ul Haq preached, after being freshly trained in the US institutions. The western model of modernisation was the framework and private capital for economic growth was the strategy for economic development. It had no dimension of social welfare.

This laissez faire economic strategy had produced the following results. First, it produced regional disparities. Second, aggregate performance in industry and agriculture led to the rise of per capita income. Third, during the second and third five-year plans GNP grew at 5.5 per cent annual growth rate. Fourth, GNP per capita growth was 3.3 per cent throughout the sixties. Fifth, during 1960-65 there was rapid industrial growth. Seventh, large-scale manufacturing sector in the first half of the sixties developed. Eight, there were substantial inflows of foreign capital. Ninth, Green Revolution and liberalisation in industrialisation allowed for growth since the bureaucratic controls had been removed.

The success story had its obverse. First, protected industrialisation produced its uncompetitive industries. Second, Green Revolution was confined only to the Punjab. Third, the land reforms denied individual large holding by providing for ceilings but did not lay down ceilings for family holdings. Fourth, generous productivity exemptions were made. Fifth, landed elite was largely unaffected by the strategy of economic change,[62] beneficiaries were the urban classes, merchants and landed classes. Sixth, regional imbalance and social inequity rose by the end of the Ayub period and this led to social tensions and revolt.

Bhutto's populism brought about an initial change in the economic strategy. Free enterprise of Ayub was described by such rhetorical phrases as 'loot and plunder' by Bhutto. His strategy of nationalisation was welcomed but soon turned to be a source of corruption. During 1972-74, 41 units of small and medium size were nationalised. Consumer goods sector was untouched. Credit policies benefitted rich peasants, small landlords and smaller industrialist capitalist. With the takeover of the rice husking business the private sector lost its confidence in the Bhutto reforms and the unity of the private and public sector broke down. The confidence of the private sector was shaken when in the context of scarcity as a result of floods ghee (processed fat) was nationalised. Flour mills and cotton ginning were also nationalised. As a result the petty bourgeoisie was alienated. Steel production had its internal contradictions since it could not be fully consumed by the internal market. The nuclear industrial sector helped the Army. Like in the Ayub period the Bhutto economic strategy also relied on foreign aid.

The Zia period from 1977-79 was marked by a renewed emphasis on the private sector as the fifth five year plan indicated, denationalisation of the rice husking units and flour mills. Under

Islamisation project he opposed usurious capital against all economic rationale. The basic change and turn around in the economy came from the external push from two different directions. These were the money that came from Pakistani labour working abroad especially in the West Asian countries, especially from the Saudis. Second, the US renewed interests in Afghanistan after the Soviet intervention there in 1979 was a boon for Zia. Before this President Zia described Carter's economic aid as 'peanuts.' It is during the Reagan Presidency that economic aid started pouring in, in the name of aiding the Afghan Mujahiddeen. The ISI also increased its economic importance as well as internal surveillance role. Zia's rule is not known to have made any economic difference to Pakistan. Zia avoided any revolutionary changes and moved within safe grooves. He is known to have provided economic stability, claim the best of his friends.[63]

Till the Zia period the evolution of economic policy in Pakistan indicated following stages. (a) 1948-59: focus on private sector and market, period of Mehbubul Haq; (b) 1958-72: Private sector, economic management and market identified by Mehbub-ul Haq; (c) 1972-77: State sector and State management added with focus on the social sector. This was again identified with Mahbub-ul Haq; (d) 1977-92; Laissez faire-private sector called out along with focus on marketisation, denationalisation and growth of clientalist economy; (e) 1992: Liberalisation-aim of becoming a middle level country.[64] (f) In 1999, Musharraf launched a strategy of economic reform. By the time he had taken over, the economy was heavily dependent on foreign loans, with 56 per cent of the budget going for debt servicing. Foreign reserves were a mere $1.45 billion. Tax collection had plumeted since, as Burki had noted, the tax evasion was massive and all the sources of revenue collection had not been tapped. He suggested the imposition of tax on five exceptionally dynamic sectors, viz, agriculture, commerce, small-scale business, transport and real estate, which were undertaxed. Both Norman and Burki pleaded for attracting foreign capital and internal resource mobilisation. They also suggested a legal framework for economic transactions to stop corruption. Burki pleaded for the possibility of Pakistan transiting to a middle income country.

By 2001 agriculture had recorded a negative growth of 2.5 per cent. Rice crop showed a decline of 21.2 per cent, unprecedented since 1974. The growth of bollworm in Punjab reduced the total cotton crop by 1.6 per cent. Large scale manufacturing sector increased marginally in Fy 2001. Trimmed growth indicated a slow down from 6.6 per cent in Fy 2001 to only 15 in the same period in 2002. Similarly growth excluding sugar decelarated from 6.7 per cent to 3.8 per cent in respective periods. The social sector, even according to a changed Mahbub-ul Haq, is appalling. All economists have pointed to its total neglect in terms of education, health, poverty alleviation, and prcvision for women and provision for schoolgirl.

Musharraf reforms to reduce poverty, focus on debt reduction and on other social indicators has received praise from the IMF in 2001 thus,

"Over the last two years, Pakistan has established a record of sound macro-economic management and timely implementation of structural reforms."[65]

Once Pakistan became a frontline state in the War on Terror Musharraf's fortunes became brighter as had been the case of Zia-ul Haq in the wake of the Afghanistan factor after 1979. The West and the US removed sanctions that had been imposed in 1998 owing to its nuclear explosions. Pakistan's external sector became a success story. The investment scene, which had touched an all time low since 1966, improved. Growth rate remained sluggish at 3 per cent since the 1990s.[66]

Briefly the review suggests that the Pakistan's economy is primarily private sector oriented. Its domination is by foreign capital, without which it cannot be bailed out. It has focused on economic growth. This strategy led to crisis in the social sector as much as to the crisis of survival of the Pakistani State by the end of the 1990s. Despite the claims of Burki that it may be poised for a breakthrough into a middle income country it is clear so far that that dream is nowhere to be realised. Secondly, it is noticed that the military regimes have done better in terms of economic performance than the civilian governments have done. Thirdly, the civilian governments have served the economic interests of the military regime, whether out or in formal power structure. Fourthly, all the economists agree that the Pakistani State is peripheral, rentier or clientist both in economic and strategic terms. The clientist nature of the State is commented upon in the context of the US interests in South Asia. Tariq Ali says that by 1980 the developments in India, Iran and Afghanistan and the coming into power of President Ronald Reagan required that Pakistan become an agent of serving US interests.

"Not surprisingly, India has perceived Pakistan as, in effect, a large US Base, designed to pressure it into itself becoming a pliable, pliant republic, safeguarding western interests."[67]

In that context he predicted grim future of Pakistan and gave an alternative vision of it either as a confederation or as a renewed polity by restructuring the polity from top to bottom by listening to its dissenting voices. This has not happened in the subsequent developments. Pakistan has once again become a frontline state and has once again come away from the brink of a 'failed' state owing to its regaining the status of the US client under Musharraf. Pakistan is the structural imperative of the US geo-strategy or to put it otherwise it is embedded in the global reach of the US capital.

New Left Approach: *Dependent State*

Hamza Alavi propounds the dependency thesis and Aijaz Ahmed provides the insight into the narrow ruling caste of Pakistan's State. Alavi unfathoms the structural imperative in the economic aspects and politics of Pakistan. The structural imperative is that of peripheral capitalism. It means that the Pakistan economy and its class structure are not feudal or capitalist but linked to foreign, especially to the US finance capital. Alavi says of this "...that landowning classes in Pakistan are not located in a feudal mode of production and therefore, are not locked in a structural and antagonistic contradiction with the bourgeoisie and the forces of capitalism. On the contrary, being located within the the structure of peripheral capitalism along with the indigenous bourgeoisie, it too, progresses in keeping with the logic of capitalist development."[68]

The economic strategy of metropolitan capital for Pakistan was to give tied-credits, apart from funding pharmaceuticals. As a result the local purchaser had to buy from the predetermined seller at hiked prices and had no option but to buy in this fashion. The local purchaser had to compensate for this high price by over invoicing and selling the machinery in black market. At the end of the logic it is the consumer who finally paid for this tied scheme. Apart from such dealings with private capital the foreign funds have come in the State sector, where again the tied credits have played a part in overpricing of goods.

Along with this the new dimension was that Pakistan soon became a strategic partner of the US. Both factors have only established an unequal relationship to the disadvantage of Pakistan. As a result of this the US-Pakistan relationship has had its own ups and down and Pakistan was left to fend for itself in 1965 when it talked of a rejection alliance with China and thought about Non-Alignment. The situation changed once again in the late 1970s, when once again, the owing to its strategic interests, US was able to make Pakistan its Frontline State and again in 2001 this repeated itself. In each regime the precise nature of the relationship has varied.[69] The State of Pakistan has regenerated the social order as well as this dependency. Says Alavi "It serves the necessary conditions for the reproduction of the social order in which our three economically dominating classes are ensconced. That role of the State in civil society is secured by the 'structural imperative' of peripheral capitalism, a concept that we put forward as a key concept for understanding the inter-relationship of the state and civil society and the mode of operation of the state in class based societies."[70]

The features of this dependency are that Pakistan is part of the One World System in terms of trade. It does not develop an indigenous bourgeoisie in terms of State capitalism that may develop the capacity to face State monopoly capitalism that the US represented, as per some Marxist economists. Second that the dependent status of the state in peripheral capitalism allows for autonomy of the State[71] in dealing with the internal crises. The concept of relative autonomy is subscribed to by Weberians[72], Marxists[73] and Gramscians.[74] The Weberian concept focuses on the role of a technical intelligence that a State has and is in need of a legitimacy. This concept was developed by Theda Scokpol to include not only the bureaucracy but also the legislators and lobbies of economic interest in the context of the Great Depression in USA. Further the issue of legitimation is carried forward in the framework of Habermas.[75] The Marxian version relates it to Bonapartism.[76] Gramscian concept is related to the nature of peaceful change in the Third World countries and how these are the continuation of the colonial legacy. The analysis of Alavi takes on the flavour of class but not of Marxian analysis since he ultimately has to come to terms with the oligarchy of the military and bureaucracy in Pakistan.[77] Bureaucracy provided the continuing link from pre- to post-independence. It was initially preponderant while the Army was in disarray. Later it became the junior partner with its decline and the increasing penetration of the Army in the economy and polity of Pakistan.

The oligarchy becomes a ruling caste in the analysis of Aijaz Ahmed. He refers to intermediate classes with reference to those sections of society that come between workers and capitalism in Peripheral States. From the segment of these intermediate classes emerges a governing caste after the dissolution of the feudal State.[78] On the relationship between metropolitan centre, State and governing caste in the regions of peripheral states he says, "What defines the main experience of these is the externally inserted presence of the metropolitan bourgeoisie, the growing generalisation of capitalist relations and commodity production at home, and the emergence of the peripheral capitalist state as the articulating principle for the external and internal dynamics."[79]

There is no class leadership here; it is the leadership of a governing caste.

A significant dimension of this is the external dimension that constructs the military apparatus under the needs of the US. The post-colonial States are highly interventionists and owing to the fetishization of the State "the struggle to find a niche within the State apparatus"[80] takes place.

Such is a transitional state to industrial and capitalist relations and is led by merchant-criminal-politician-bureaucrat network. The emergence of a governing caste takes place owing to the fact that the polar classes are weak.

Both authors, Alavi and Ahmed, underline the role of the following elements in the State of Pakistan. (a) Its peripheral character, (Alavi) (b) its transitory role in formation of capitalist mode of production, (Ahmed), (c) US penetration to enlarge and modernize the military apparatus, (Ahmed), (d) fetishization of the State (Ahmed) or State autonomy, (Alavi), (e) the emergence of a governing caste from within intermediate classes owing to the weakness of the polar classes, and the former provide for right wing and left wing radicalism. The relationship between the external and the internal is suggested by Gardezi thus,

"Pakistan's neo-colonial alliances facilitated the development of an oversized military and bureaucratic state apparatus, which has used direct physical coercion to reserve the relations of production which allow the domestic bourgeoisie and feudal classes to appropriate surplus value."[81]

The discussion on peripheral state leads inexorably to the idea of militarist dimensions of the State of Pakistan. There is however no discussion on militarism in general or in relation to South Asia, despite the fact that there are references to the Bismarkian State, Bonapartist State and other authoritarian experiences in Europe. The militarist dimensions of the South Asian scene need to be analysed. A beginning in this direction will surely lead to a study of Pakistan and then to Bangladesh since it is in these two countries that military coups have taken place. In contrast it would also be necessary to delineate the contours of civilian- military relationship in India and the role of military in internal security aspects. A history of militarism raises the issue with regard to the profession of the armed forces, their relationship with the government, their relationship with the internal and external aspects of the polity, their relationship with peripheral capitalism, the linkages of classes with the Armed Forces. Western literature on militarism has attempted to understand these various aspects through various concepts dealing especially with the civilian-military relationship, armed forces and society relationship, internal and external relationship, and, development of political culture and militarism.[82] We will look at the dimension of militarism in the section on Pakistan's militarism. Pakistan's State has been described from this perspective as praetorian /corporatist. They are used in the same breath, though they mean different things in the European context.

The State of Pakistan has been described as a failed State. This is rather a harsh assessment, at the first sighting. The break up of its territory, chaos of its dependent economy, the anarchy in polity marked by Kalashnikov-drug culture, the political mobilisation of its segmented society and the failure of its formal electoral machinery to provide for regime change conjour up images of it being a failed state. The other side of the story testifies to the Stateness of this State. That Stateness is symbolised by its coercive State apparatus and its capacity to handle crises, the autonomy of its Army to intervene and the position of the ISI to be a State within a State. We notice that the symbols of its power-Army, Police and paramilitary units are financed liberally and have intervened in the crisis situations successfully with the exception of Bangladesh and to a lesser extent in Sindh. The Baluch situation is under control after the flash in the 1970s. Sindh has burnt in the 1970s and 80s but is relatively quiet since the 1990s. Afghanistan has remained turbulent but since the Taliban regime and the post 'War against Terror' has given the Pakistani State leverage to intervene in Afghanistan currently. In terms of internal turmoil Pakistan is in a period of relative calm and so less stressful is the Army.

Another reason for believing in the strength of Pakistan's Stateness is the penetration of the military in the economy and the polity of Pakistan. Under Musharraf for the first time now the National Security Council will have a role in formal decision making structure. Till Musharraf had taken over the triumvirate of the President, Prime Minister and Army Chief were the key figures of the State. Now that situation has changed and the formal Army presence exists as a constitutional body. The transition from Jinnah charisma to Liaquat Ali to Ghulam Muhammad-Munir duo to Ayub and through Bhuttos, Sharief and Zia to Musharraf has meant a concentration of power, and not fragmentation of power, in a narrow circle of decision-makers. The governing caste was narrower than oligopoly under early rule of classes, i.e., landowners, bureaucrats and business. The first reflected a Lockean attempt at constitutionalism. The second beginning with Ayub marked the beginning of the Bonapartist authoritarianism. The subsequent experiments have meant further narrowing the base to include in decision making only the expert of violence and that too in the military sector and ISI. From such a reading of the historical development of regimes in Pakistan we notice that democracy was never on cards nor was it ever a reality in Pakistan. Finally, Pakistan will survive till it serves the US strategic interests.

If by liberal democracy we mean constitutional oligopoly then it was nearly there. That was a Lockean project that did not object to electioneering or even a monarchy. In fact till the 18th century the critics of Locke did not concede to Locke the significance of elections.[83] The Bonapartist regime believed in constitutionalism but not democracy. Even if we recognise the Bhutto regime as Bonapartist we notice the duality of the significance of elections. He came to power through free elections. He is charged to have rigged them in 1977, atleast on the reading of Zia's evaluation of them.[84] There is no commentator of the Pakistani State who has not said that the military regime undermined democratic regime. This is a faulty evaluation. There never was a democratic government in Pakistan. Bhutto's was the elected Bonapartist government. There were Lockean regimes in the initial and subsequent periods. The difference being in institutional terms. In purely historical terms we notice that democracy was ushered in the British Isles in the latter half of the 19th century. The growth of parties as modern bureaucracies or ones based on iron law of oligarchs led to democratic government on the basis of adult sufferage after 1928. Marx had said in the middle of the 19th century that the introduction of the adult sufferage would bring the working class to power. The fear of the working class did lead J.S. Mill to balance his adult manhood suffrage by plurality of votes. That fear was removed by the coming into existence of the political parties.

Further it is only in the twentieth century that pluralism took root in the Western societies and that became an argument for polyarchy and not democracy, as understood in classical Greek sense. Participation, in both cases, was considered finally of a periodic relevance.[85] In the post-cold war era democracy was equated with only a technique to elect governments. It had no moral dimension.[86] For a brief period was democracy identified with social development to be overturned by the neo-liberal agendas of the late 70s and 80s in England and USA. Now there is a talk about the collapse of Liberalism.[87] By another reading there are atleast five versions of liberal democracy.[88] These five versions are thus described by him: One Class model, Protective model, Developmental model-I&II, Pluralist, elitist and equilibrium model and Participatory model. Pakistan perhaps proximates to the first and which is more in the nature of the immediate products of the middle class revolutions in England, France and US War of Independence. At that stage there was only talk of constitutionalism and not democracy. Locke, Rousseau and

Jefferson were the theorisers of democracy and money, property or the farmer was considered the backbone of democracy. We need to look at Pakistan in that context. The singular significant feature of this context was the emerging rule of the middle class through Parliaments and Parliament in England legislated money to be the highest value.

Jinnah's Charisma: *as a Muslim and not a 'democratic' Leader*

In Pakistan we notice that the initial years of its existence were very complicated but some similar to the ones which were prior to the late 19th century democracy in England. It had charismatic leader but no political parties to follow him or take over from him. It had economic interests to defend but no middle class worth the name. It had only naked bureaucracy not as a representative of a new middle class but as an extension of the ruling landed class. In subsequent years its penetration into the business class made the latter a junior partner. It had unprecedented problems. The administrative problem of finding a solution to the refugee settlement—a task undertaken by Jinnah himself was Herculean. Jinnah wanted to kill two birds with one stone. He wanted to transfer power to the Centre as well as also solve the problem with the help of an efficient administrator. Thus the Mamdoot and Murdie fights in the Punjab remained to vex Jinnah and Liaquat Ali. The centralisation of power began then only and not after Jinnah who is generally portrayed as one with liberal democratic vision for Pakistan. Let us be fair to Jinnah. Any number of books try to counter pose him to what came to be known as Pakistan. He was a liberal in the 1920s is well known. His break with the Congress at that time is a liberal one in the context of Mahatma Gandhi's mass politics. This was more in the nature of the break that C.Y. Chintamani or Lala Lajpat Rai would have had with Gandhi. Jinnah's ferocious break with Gandhi and the Congress is not on liberalism but on Muslim communalism and the demand for a State on the basis of religion. He emerges as a leader of the Muslims not as a liberal but as a Muslim communal leader, and only then a liberal Muslim leader. The constitutional history linked with Jinnah is history of Muslim communalism trying to jockey for space through argument, if possible, or through mass mobilisation if necessary. That is how Pakistan resolution culminated in the birth of Pakistan.

Jinnah had to give way to juniors under his wings as much as Gandhi or Washington did. In the latter two cases there were theorists and institutionalisation. In the case of Pakistan there were provincial leaders who had become national leaders with the emergence of Pakistan and who had no first hand experience in party making or operating a party and bureaucrats. Their parochial thinking made it difficult for them to meet the challenges that confronted them. The provincial nature of the new reality in the context of Partition and the manner in which the Radcliffe Report was implemented along with bringing East Bengal and Punjab together would make any leadership run for the available resources to unite. That alternative was possible only with the bureaucracy. Hence the three sections of the elites, namely bureaucratic, political and military came together in an equal relationship to unite Pakistan on the principle of centralisation. The mistake lay in not recognising the need of federalist structure. In the absence of a dominant party there was also the possibility of only the Army emerging as an institution playing that role. The problem then was not in the civilian leaders but in their stars.

Authoritarian Governments: *Jinnah Approach and Civilian Governments*

Jinnah as Governor General concentrated power in his hands and opted for an Islamic State, despite his famous speech to the Constituent Assembly before the announcement of the Radcliffe Report. As Governor General he chose the cabinet of Liaquat Ali. It was composed of I.I. Chundrigarh, Ghulam Muhammad, Sardar Abdur Rab Nishtar, and Fazlur Rehman. A little later he appointed Zafarullah Khan. Second, the problems of provinces of Pakistan were handled by him in peculiar authoritarian manner. He dismissed the Khan Saheb ministry in NWFP since it was a Congress Ministry and then went on to dismiss the M. A. Khuhro Ministry in Sindh because it had opposed the making of Karachi as the federal territory for making it the capital of Pakistan. He also interferred in the affairs of the Punjab Province and on the opinion of Governor, Sir Francis Murdie, wanted to dismiss Mamdoot ministry and install Daultana in the post. In Bengal he stood for Urdu despite the local demand for Bengali. This however he could not do. In January

1947 he exorted his audience to "sacrifice and die in order to make Pakistan a truly great Islamic State."[89]

The political practice followed by Jinnah in the early years of Pakistan does not indicate that he was laying down healthy democratic principles. This was unlike Mahatma Gandhi, who had laid down his life for healthy principles of secularism and giving material aid to Pakistan that led Godse to commit the assassination. In matters of Parliamentary Government and provincial administration Jinnah had shown by practice the centralising tendencies.

Liaquat Ali: *Centralising Interlude*

The story of democracy is not very different under Liaquat Ali Khan. On his limitation, Macgrath says "Liaquat continued Jinnah's policy of attempting to increase the power of the centre at the expense of provincial government. In the provinces however, Liaquat did not enjoy the same strength as he did at the national level. Some in the local political leadership considered him a refugee and therefore an outsider. His administration was hampered by the fact that he and the Muslim League lacked social and economic policies which might have helped him to build a political base in dealing with local leaders."[90]

Liaquat relied on Nazimmuddin as the Prime Minister. He used emergency powers under Section 92(A) in the provinces to establish his control over them. He dismissed the Mamdoot Ministry of Punjab. Subsequently formed a council of advisors for Mudie, the Governor of Punjab. He set aside a bye - election in Mymensinh. He gagged the press after Suhrawardy filed a case against it and had previously called him an agent of the military. He was distrustful of any opposition and the parties that were formed during his time were small and liquidated soon. Under pressure from Maulana Maududi he introduced the idea of Islam in the Objectives Resolution that was to become the basis of subsequent Constitution making. The term remained vague so that it was interpreted by some leaders, like Zafarulla Khan and Ishtiaq Hussein Qureshi, as to mean that it was to be the unethical foundation of the Constitution. For Ulema it meant that the Constitution would abide by the Shariat and therefore superior to the Constitution.[91] it would in any case have been difficult for any one to define democracy in terms of Islam.

Consequent upon this the Assembly appointed a Basic Principles Committee, which further set up subcommittees, to go into drafting a constitution under the chairmanship of Maulvi Tamizuddin Khan. Liaquat Ali further submitted an Interim Report and since it was not popular for it retained only Urdu as a national language, it was withdrawn by November 1950. Further the Liaquat Government attempted to Islamize the polity. In February1951 he set up a Committee to bring Government laws in accordance with the Objectives Resolution. In March the Constituent Assembly instructed the Federal and provincial governments to take steps to institute Koranic instructions in schools and universities. It passed a resolution that the purpose of research was to make the Muslim population of the country truly Muslim. The major problem that confronted Liaquat was provincialism and he was engrossed in it till he was assassinated in Rawalpindi on 16th October in 1951.

Ghulam Mohammad: *Centralisation and Concentration of Power*

The process of centralisation and concentration of power continued during the period of Governor-Generalship of Ghulam Mohammad. During this period the Constituent Assembly was able to frame a constitution under the leadership of Prime Minister Bogra, the new Prime Minister, who was after Jinnah the Governor General. How did this change come about is not clear? After the death of Liaquat Ali a meeting at Rawalpindi, which was shrouded in mistry, decided on the new alignment of offices. The country was presented a *fait accompli* by a cabal.[92] The new Constitution was marked by provisions for a parliamentary system, judicial review, federal government, fundamental rights, democratic Pakistan based on Islam and nominal position of the President. After the success of Bogra in getting the Assembly to frame a Constitution Bogra, went to the US, with Ayub Khan and in his absence Ghulam Mohammad staged a coup against him. Bogra, trusted by the US, negotiated an economic and military package. During his absence Ghulam Muhammad staged a destabilisation once again throwing democratic principles to the wind and in this he used Punjab leaders, Mamdoot and Daultana. It was easier for him to do so since he was able to establish his relationship both with the military and bureaucracy which had grown in self-confidence. While Bogra was en route to Pakistan, the US discovered of the intentions of Ghulam Muhammad. It announced increased military package. Bogra was removed and asked to form the Government again with Ayub in the position of the Defence Minister. Soon it was further made clear to Bogra that he would not preside over the meetings but Ghulam Muhammad would instead. This is for the first time that the Army Chief became a Defence Minister. Power was therefore further being concentrated and the Army being integrated in the decision making while the US played its cards of developing friendly and strategic relations with the new Muslim State. The coup meant a reversion to the old style of politics and subversion of the newly framed Constitution. It meant in practical terms that the attempt to have a democratic structure of governance of the Parliamentary kind was not acceptable. Further it also meant that Pakistan as a Federal State was also not acceptable and West Pakistan was to be made into One Unit.

There was no discussion on this coup since the press had been gagged. Behind the scenes the Army was also growing in strength with its Kashmir policy, economic resources being augmented by the US for the military and the US making the polity a part of its military alliances in the context of the Cold War. In the US-Pakistan relationship the civilian government had hardly any role to play. It was Ayub and his military that was responsible for it.[93] Two events that had bolsterd the Army was the anti-Ahmadi riots in the Punjab and the friendship that Ayub enjoyed with the US. Suhrawardy's reaction to this change of the new government was that Pakistan was on the verge of dictatorship once there was the propaganda that the civilian leadership was found incapable of giving to Pakistan a Constitution. The inexperience was proved by the quick succession of civilian ministries that led to political instability.

The reality as it emerged by 1954 showed that the bureaucracy was in command and the Army happily on the ascendance though not equal to the bureaucracy. Waseem Mohammad says of this "When Ghulam Mohammad abrogated the Constituent Assembly in 1954, and the bureaucratic supremacy over political institutions was publicly demonstrated, the military's complete loyalty to the new civilian order was also symbolised by General Ayub's presence in the so-called 'cabinet of talents' under Mohammad Ali Bogra."[94]

Subsequent civilian leaders acted irresponsibly not because of any thing but the stripping of the Constituent Assembly of any powers after Ghulam Mohammad's coup and the justification provided to it by Justice Munir. The Munir-Mohammad duo had laid the foundations of an autocratic government.[95] Ghulam Ali and Iskandar Mirza dominated the scene upto the time of the Martial Law. During 1949-58 a dozen ministries had been dismissed.

It needs to be underlined here that the period witnessed the assertion of authoritarian government, peripheral economy, Islamic orientation of ideology, non-federal Pakistan and cold war alliance with the US that showered on it economic and military aid and support in the UN and outside in the Cold War context. Initially the Kashmir question and the Indo-Pakistan hostility is related to the Pakistani desire to incorporate J&K as its homeland. Sumit Ganguly says of this "The second factor underlying the origins of Indo-Pakistan conflict is Pakistan's irredentist claim to Kashmir. As the putative homeland for the Muslims of the subcontinent, Pakistan sought to incorporate the Muslim majority state of Jammu and Kashmir into its domain."[96] The British and the US representatives were involved in delaying the solution to the Indo- Pakistan conflict in these early years since the British representative wanted the US to get involved in the conflict on the side of Pakistan. This he finally did, after initially dragging his feet.[97]

We notice then that the development of events in Pakistan towards a denial of democracy and establishment of authoritarian government were part of the transition of Pakistan from the colonial to peripheral imperative. In this both the external and the internal factors played their role. Internally it is the alliance of Ghulam Mohammad, Justice Munir and Ayub Khan and externally it was the role of the US plus Bogra added to this internal triumvirate. In all these the dramitis personae had little democratic experience and behaved exactly as they could have given their own training and Pakistan's challenges and strengths. Pakistan was not on the verge of a democratic revolution. It was not even in a stage where even a conservative Edmund Burke could plead for its cause. He had done this in support of the

American case for war of independence. Pakistan had not launched any liberation movement, it had no mercantilist class to support it, it had no middle class to support an ideology of liberalism and its politics under the colonial rule had been pro-feudal. Its experience of working with institutions was with regard to emasculated undemocratic institutions. It had no mass party to build consensus among competing societal interests.

It therefore reneged from the case of constitutional oligarchy that John Locke pleaded for. It could only be considered a State that was at the boundary of semi-feudal-semi-colonial stage during the period of 1947-58 and one where it had promoted authoritarian governments under the control of a civilian bureaucracy. In this the military was an equal if not a junior partner. Structurally this was the context of its further militarisation. We shall come to this in the next section. Let us continue to further probe the exact nature of the civilian regimes in its history. Pakistan's civilian governments should be seen as a variant of authoritarian rule helping Pakistan economy to transit from the colonial to the peripheral imperative. This is true of the rule of the next popularly elected civilian leader in the 1970s-Zulfiquar Ali Bhutto, or for that matter the regimes of Benazir Bhutto and Nawaz Sharief during the 1990s. The story of the two civilian Prime Ministers, namely Junejo, under Zia during 1983-88 and Jamaly, under Musharraf, from 2003 onwards will be discussed in the section on militarism.

Zulfiquar Ali Bhutto, a *wadera,* i.e., belonged to landed class (not to the middle or business class). He was a minister in Ayub's Government. He was an anti-India baiter in the context of Tashkent Agreement in 1965. He incessantly played on the anti-India sentiment in his propoganda against Ayub's alleged surrender in the Tashkent Agreement. He had a dubious role in the arrest of Mujib-ur Rehman of East Pakistan and the Army debacle under Yahya Khan in Bangladesh. He was elected by popularly held elections. He was the leader of a new Pakistan Peoples Party, architect of Shimla Agreement with India. He is regarded as a developer of the State sector in Pakistan. He introduced land reforms like Ayub Khan. Known for espousal of development of the social sector in Pakistan, he turned out to be one who only helped the growth of the military influence and landed estates. Further he prepared the ground for the military take over. He is described as a Bonapartist by some left wing analysts. Aijaz Ahmed says of him "The political party he then created, namely the Pakistan's Peoples Party (PPP) was a classic formation of radical elements, on the one hand, drawn from the petty bourgeois of Punjab and Sindh, and on the other hand, substantial elements of the landlord class -the latter, however, consisted typically of those who (a) were hostile to the biggest landlords of Punjab (the top stratum of semi-feudal power in Pakistan and (b) were committed to capitalisation of agriculture, which involved restrictions on the extent of semi-feudal ownership (hence the land reforms..)"[98] He was Martial Law administrator.

This Janus faced power block cracked in favour of Pakistani conservatism. The radical elements of his party had diverse social background, greased his propaganda machine, made him take populist measures like take over of trade and granting to the Soviets certain contracts and generally radicalising the atmosphere captured by the slogan of *roti, kapra aur makan* (food, clothing and housing). However we notice that the radical wing was purged. The business was alienated. The landed classes deserted him. The bureaucracy got demoralised owing to transfers and the practice of lateral entry and personalisation of the State apparatus.[99] Briefly his transition is summed up thus "Mr Bhutto switched from a populist to an authoritarian mould."[100]

He is described as a power broker by some and Bonapartist by others. Waseem calls him a representative of an intermediary regime that Kalecki had mentioned in the context of Third World regimes especially with reference to India. And it is the steps of this regime that led to the coming back of the Army. The demand for denationalisation began during his tenure. The business classes refused to invest in industry since the nationalised ghee (processed fat), rice husking and cotton business. He tardily implemented the land reforms. Further he used the Army to quell revolt in Balochistan and he instituted a conspiracy case against the Baloch and Pashtun leaders. He created nuclear infrastructure that made the Army happy. The growth of corruption and the mishandling of the opposition brought the conservative PNA alliance (supported by the US)[101] to oppose his politics and in this context the murder of Kasuri's father cost him his life under Zia. People of his on PPP got alienated. But Waseem describes the conservative backlash. In response to this conservative backlash Bhutto had gone over to the strategy of Islamisation but that did not help him. Of course Waseem does not call it conservative. He calls it political mass activity. He says "Steps such as nationalisation of industry, compulsory wage increases and what is considered unguided public activity led to rampant disinvestment, flight of capital and finally military come back in order to stem the tide of political participation by the masses."[102]

This is a rather facile way of looking at both the military and the mass movement that occurred during the last days of Bhutto's regime. Bhutto's method of dealing with the PNA Opposition does not show him to be a leader who was interested in bringing about either a renewed structure of democratic governance or develop a party system that could sustain civilian governments by having a smooth transfer of power. Further the manner of his dealing with the Opposition left much scope for the Army to intervene.

A Zia friend, K. M. Arif informs us about a mini martial law that Bhutto had planned. Further the way he handled the Opposition by being revengeful. Kasuri's father's murder sealed his fate. People became restive owing to Bhutto's authoritarian ways. It is alleged that law and order worsened and three divisions were placed in Sindh, Lahore and Hyderabad under the martial law. Disaffection in the Army spread. Bhutto had started meeting the corps commanders himself. He had appointed the Mamoodur Rehman Commission on the misdeeds of Ayub regime but had not published them. This happened in order to put a veil over his questionable role in the East Pakistan conflict. He reneged on his promise of holding elections by going on a foreign trip to Islamic countries. This put pressure on the Army. The political crisis was between the PNA and Bhutto. Once the PNA leadership was arrested, says Arif " ...the people became restive and resentful under the authoritarian rule of Mr. Bhutto's revengeful government, joined the movement which took a decisive turn to the right."[103] Less said about personal traits, better it is.

The subsequent elections marred Bhutto's reputation and thus began his downslide. In a country where not the civilian leadership but the military interpret national interest not just differently, the possibilities of the coup were bound to be high. Zia took the position that Bhutto's ego rigged elections and party interests rather than national interests were behind Bhutto's policies and therefore this warranted the military coup. The White Paper on elections highlighted the nature of rigging of the elections and his alleged offer to give Makran to the Soviet Union. In that context he told the PNA leaders that he would not hesitate to call upon the Army. Even if one gives concessions to the pro-Zia nature of Arif's narration of events one thing is clear that the opposition to Bhutto's regime was conservative and relied upon the support of the Army, the US landed classes and radical petty bourgeoise and democratic elements in Sindh and Balochistan. In terms of ideology and social development Bhutto was himself now a new embodiment of conservatism since he identified with Islamisation of the polity by taking the following measures. He promised enforcement of Shariat laws within six months. Alcohol was prohibited. All forms of gambling were banned. Nightclubs and bars were closed. A promise to prepare a legislation to deal with corruption was made. Friday was to be observed as a weekly holiday. And finally he said "Then make me the Amir (ruler) and not the parliamentary system.'[104]

Waseem's intermediary regime had fallen apart with radical students deserting the Party and the petty bourgeoisie giving up. It is not clear here whether the stratum of farmers was part of his regime or feudal landed estates were. Burki is of the view that as a result of the Green Revolution that Ayub had achieved a new class of farmers came into existence. Hamza Alavi was of the opinion that such a class never came into existence and that the land reforms that were attempted by the Ayub regime allowed the large landlords to retain family estates since there was no ceiling over them. The ceilings were only on the individual holdings. Business became antagonistic and landlords also going away from his new compact. The egalitarian politics was a non-starter. The steel sector also had internal problems since it had no foreign market and the local market did not have a sufficient absorption capacity. The land reforms were also turned around and the *wadera* part of the lineage made its appearance in them as much as it did in his Islamisation sans socialism.

Bhutto Jettisoning the Possibility of Liberal Islam

What is the most tragic part of his rule, though lesser than the circumstances in which he was assassinated, is the killing of the possibility of a resurgent Islam taking roots in Pakistan. There were signs of this possibility. Let us have a peep backwards. In his speech before the Partition riots, Jinnah wanted the Pakistanis to live as citizens and the State was to treat them as equals. Second, the Constituent Assembly gave a vague place to Islam in the Objectives Resolution. The Constitution framed by the Assembly that was subverted by Ghulam Mohammad was of a liberal nature in terms of Islam. The Ayub leadership was that of a devout Muslim in private matters but a modernist in public affairs. Yahya was a thorough bred Western secularist. Bhutto was given to Islamic Socialism. There was no talk of the 'ghazi' and 'jihad' yet taking shape even though Jinnah had said that Pakistan should be an Islamist state. Even Jamiat's Madudi was arrested.

Yet the compulsions of the Muslim League to assert Muslim identity, the intervention of the Jamiat-I-Islami, despite the arrest of Maulana Madudi, the riots against the Ahmadiyas and the Qadians, the assertion of the provinces, the reaction to the Bengalis' and Sindhis' opposition to Urdu and the compulsions of office during Bhutto's time, and, eagerness to stay put there with the help of conservative Islam led to the increasing assertion of the conservative streak of Islam. Zia-ul Haq symbolised it during his tenure. Processes of weakening contemplation of democratic structure, accompanying disrepute of the civilian leadership at the hands of the bureaucracy, assertion of the authoritarian methods of governance with increasing reliance on the Army, peripheralisation of the economy and the resurgence of Islamic process of legitimation marked the civilian leaderships. How were these to be differentiated from the military regimes is a moot point. To begin with let us note that the original Pakistan's leadership's attachment with democracy is questionable. Whether this was a matter of conviction or convenience is not sure. Macgrath says "The leaders of Pakistan's movement had a general idea that the new state would be a democracy of the Western type, but it is uncertain whether their allegiance to parliamentary democracy was based on conviction or convenience."[105]

Second, the bureaucracy was Macaulay's to maintain the steel frame of imperialism. The early leaders acted in defence of making the political structure of Pakistan authoritarian and first step in that direction was centralisation. It is possible to give credence to a view that Pakistan should be a union, like it was done in India in the context of the seccessionist tendencies and demands. But to have subversion of any political autonomy and democracy only shows the intent of the leaders to impose authoritarian governance. Third, the Constitution making was also marred by the demands being made on behalf of conservative Islam and successive governments succumbing to the pressure despite their liberal disposition. Fourth, the external strategic dilemma of Pakistan had its own impact on making Pakistan autocratic. The needs of peripheral capitalism, the confusion over the role of Pakistan in the Muslim world in the West (where Iraq and Iran were to become its US sponsored partners) and the conflict with India in the East led it into the US strategic calculations. Its economy and military gained from Pakistan's then emerging American connections. These factors created conditions for its authoritarian character. Both the internal and the external dynamics made the civilian leadership Janus faced. These civilians were militarist in looking for solutions to legitimacy crisis.

Let us look at the post- Zia civilian leadership to discover a similar pattern.

Benazir Bhutto and Nawaz Sharief: *In the Shadow of Military*

After a decade-long stint of Zia's martial law and Junejo's emasculated civilian government Pakistan witnessed the emergence of the daughter of the East from the ashes of Bhutto's martyrdom. She emerged as a star into the crescent of Pakistan's top power structure. The Movement for Restoration of Democracy (MRD) that PPP and Altaf Hussain's MQM and G.M. Sayeed's group and other smaller groupings had forged to oppose Zia's Martial Law forced the Army to go to the barracks despite its sprawling corporate presence in the power structure. The internal dynamics of Zia rule had made its own contribution to the emerging crisis. Arif says there was a power struggle between Junejo and Zia in which the former was the looser in 1988 and Zia was unaware of his sudden demise that year. On the power struggle Arif notes "While Zia found power slipping from his grasp, Mr. Junejo found himself politically hamstrung by the label of being hand picked nominee of an autocratic ruler."[106]

Two subsequent regimes of Benazir and Sharief were under the control of the Army and so could not survive the tussle they started with it. The nature of civil-military relationship remained intact in favour of the Army even though both the leaders tried to change it for their own narrow partisan interest to survive in power. The change they attempted was not aimed to build abiding civilian institutions or norms of democracy. They were meant for perpetuating personal rule. This is an interesting though fruitless aspect of the civilian rule. The civilian prime ministers come to power after their compact with the Army and the US and then later try to grow out of that compact in vain.

Benazir's Government: *Symbol of Subordinated Constitutionalism*

Benazir's Government came about after she made a trip to Washington and met up with the Military chief. As a woman leader and Prime Minister she had a lot of goodwill and for Sindh she also meant a vindication of the feeling that the wrongs on Bhutto have been redeemed. It is this dimension of her experience that remained with her as the most significant to such an extent that Ziring believed that "...she could not rise above it."[107]

Described as a 'democrat' who appeals to feudal loyalties, and, a shadow crossing her face when her father's misdeeds are mentioned to her. Benazir described the environment of her own rule thus "So much has happened. After I won the elections, I was of the naïve view that an electoral victory would end the hardship, the trials. But this wasn't true. During the time I was prime minister, I lived under the shadow of a strong military, a holistic president, an entire constituency that Zia had built; extreme right wingers, religious bigots, and politicians bred during that era of military dictatorship. They had one thing in common: they were dead set against allowing me to rule."[108]

At the time she took the oath the Generals, the mullahs and President Ishaq Khan were more important. Before her swearing in ceremony, for 13 days the President consulted persons including Nawaz Sharief. On the 14th day Robert Oakley told the President that the US wanted that Benazir should be made the Prime Minister.[109] Right from the beginning she was hamstrung. She had conceded to the military that the nuclear programme, the Afghanistan policy and the anti-Indian insurgency were not going to be within her purview. She could not even control the ISI.[110] In order to appease the Islamists she took to 'chador' (covering her head with a white cloth). To begin with she had the support of Aslam Ali Beg, the Army Chief, who had decided to hold fair and free elections through which she came to power and symbolised the urge for constitutional rule.[111]

The issues she confronted were many. She had a confrontation brewing in Punjab where Nawaz Sharief was present and who had developed relations with the President. She had the President to look after who was a Zia supporter during the period when he was with her father. The President had powers of dismissal under Article 73 that she challenged and that she wanted to repeal and restore the original provisions of the Bhutto constitution. There were problems in Punjab, Balochistan and Sindh that she had to look into and put the economy on the upswing. In her political dealings she could not forget the assassination of her father. Consensus building was the need of the hour but as days passed the political turmoil increased.

She has been described as a Peronist like in Argentina.[112] She is alleged to have wanted to build a dynasty rule on the pattern of India's Nehru family. She released hundreds of prisoners. She withdrew cases against political exiles. She released various categories of women prisoners, old pensioners, and generally commuted death sentences of convicts into life imprisonment. She liberalised the media. She wanted to repeal of 58th amendment to the 1973 Constitution.

Her confrontation in Punjab led her into conflict with the President. Continuing instability in Sindh made G. M. Sayeed call for independent or autonomous Sindh. Another movement Siraiki Quami Movement sprang up and demanded a new province from the merger of Multan, Bhawalpur, Dera Ghazi Khan, Dera Ismail Khan and Jhang divisions. Her uncle Mumtaz Ali Bhutto broke from the PPP forming the Sindh-Baloch-Afghan front. In Afghanistan Wali Khan's ANP drifted from the PPP. Hamid Gul, President Ishaq Khan and Nawaz Sharief conspired against Aslam Ali Beg and Benazir relationship. Nawaz Sharief introduced a no-confidence motion, and, disagreements surfaced between the President and the Prime Minister on appointments and retirements of high-ranking officers and soldiers. Still she won the no-confidence motion.[113] She was left with few friends to such an extent that she made her mother, Nusrat, a minister and father-in-law a minister and the chairman of Parliamentary Public Accounts Committee. While she was abroad visiting some

Muslim countries, President dismissed her under Article 53(b) on the grounds that she had lost the capacity to govern, demonstrated an inability to stem domestic violence and had nurtured nepotism. Jatoi was asked to become the care taker Prime Minister. Cases were filed against Benazir and her husband Zardari. Officials arrested them.

Unlike her father Benazir was not a radical in economic policy and moved in the direction of liberalisation. She had encouraged non-government investment in industry. Her economic reform was linked to exchange rate policy and removal of subsidies in agriculture. A three-year period for stabilisation and adjustment measures was a sales tax and lowered tariff. She could not denationalize or liberalise. Military spending continued to grow. She was ousted on charges of corruption, nepotism and misrule.[114] Benazir's rule was long on expectation and short on delivery. She could not address the social issues. The women's lobby was disappointed. Neither a liberaliser nor a socialist she was. She was hemmed in by the power of the Army, America, Allah and the President. Her symbolisation of constitutional hopes was subordinated to the interests of the Army. Her foreign policy and her control over the bureaucracy and the Army were minimal. She admitted to Mary Anne Weaver that she could not as a political leader do anything for the women.[115] A dipolmat quipped to Mary Anne Weaver that Benazir was bound to come back to power but quipped he was not sure if she could rule. The choices before her were wasted. As he said "She wasn't able to focus, and moved things forward, or to control situations. May be she will pick better people next time. It's her streak of loyalty that kills her; she always goes back to what people have done in the past—how they served her father, how much time they spent in jail—rather than considering what they could do in the future. She therefore failed to tap an enormous pool of brilliant young intellectuals and technocrats who could have turned this country around. Instead she relied on feudal landlords, who catered to her illusion that it was her birth right to rule. She is one of the most bewildering women I've ever met; one moment she is utter charm; the next moment she is so antagonistic that she comes perilously close to impertinence. But she is not a sulker, she is a battler and a survivor, and that's not all bad."[116]

To sum up the authoritarian aspects of Benazir's regime we need to notice the following. Before she became the Prime Minister she was part of a four-point deal. It included a PPP commitment to support Ghulam Ishaq Khan for President, retain foreign minister Yakub Khan for "continuity in foreign policy", uphold the accord with the IMF on the economy, and not to meddle in internal Army matters like transfers, promotions, retirements of senior officers. After the removal of the government from Office in August 1990 the PPP was the first to moot the idea of "a constitutional role of the Army"[117] Benazir's regime and prime ministership remained a junior partner to the interests of the Army and America. The US Ambassador was present at the time of this accord.

Nawaz Sharief: *Proximity to the Army and Liberalisation*

The Prime Ministership of Nawaz Sharief was another unmitigated disaster in terms of a civilian regime cutting loose from militarist autocracy. Hussains say "regarding relations of Nawaz Sharief with the army, in this key responsibility he is a Pakistani politician with a difference. His level of intimacy has probably without precedent for a politician before becoming prime minister, save perhaps for Prime Minister Zulfiquar Ali Bhutto who also enjoyed a cordial and intimate relationship with the brass before becoming Prime Minister. Three facts testify to past intimacy between Nawaz Sharief and the army."[118]

The three facts are that he started his political career during the martial law as finance minister in Punjab and never opposed the Army rule in Pakistan or the then martial law. Second, Nawaz Sharief forged the IJI for the 1988 elections with the help of the Army. Third, in his 20-month battles with Benazir Bhutto when she was in office the Army supported him.

The 1990 elections had two party blocks, viz PDA which had PPP at its core vs. IJI which included Nawaz Sharief's Pakistan Muslim League (Nawaz) though there was the triumvirate of Nawaz, Junejo and Ejaz -ul Haq, the son of Zia -ul Haq. Jatoi was with IJI. Another party that was originally with the PPP was with this group namely MKM. The two blocks fought elections in three major provinces, viz Punjab, Sindh and NWFP. In Balochistan the picture was more complicated. It was not polarised. It was an isssueless election. The major issue was misdeeds of the PPP vs.

the unconstitutional dismissal of the Benazir Government. The IJI got 37.16 per cent votes and the PPP got 36.38 per cent while the difference seat wise was much more.[119] On the basis of the 1988 and 1990 elections it was theorised that there was a possibility of civilian rule and partyisation taking place.

The period of 1991 to 1993 witnessed Nawaz Sharief's rule in which Pakistan's economy was liberalized. He reduced the role of the State, denationalised and implemented de-regulation, intervened less in industry and agriculture and showed readiness to embrace liberal trade and investment and offered tax and tarrif incentives. This led to the maturing of the new breed of industrialist and traders and a smaller entrepreneur and many others in the urban centre's middle classes.[120]

In foreign policy also he faced many challenges. Afzal Beg had criticised the US Iraq policy. Afghanistan crisis had to be resolved. Contacts with Saudi Arabia and Kuwait had to be established for reinforcement of oil. Developments in Central Asia were intriguing. Importance of Sino-US relations was underlined since the US was less inclined to support the Muslim world.[121]

By 1993 the Government had to resign along with the President, Ishaq Khan, since many sex and economic scandals exploded on the political scene. The critical issues that rocked the Government were orientation of the State towards students, teachers and education. More employment opportunities were needed. Government announced the scaling down of annual growth rate. A Commission was appointed to go into affairs of the Cooperative Finance Corporation. BCCI was involved in a scandal. The Pakistan Industrial Development Corporation was involved in mismanagement. Since the regime depended on foreign borrowings external debt kept mounting. Sharief attempted to placate by taking some Islamic measures like bringing forward Shariat legislation. Once the regime resigned, Qureshi was put in charge. He cleared the stables for getting the IMF loan.

Benazir: *Liberalisation Continued and Corruption Scandals*

In October 1993 Benazir returned to form the government. She continued the policy of liberalisation. She became unpopular because of her 'Misdeeds and her alignment with higher echelons of the bureaucracy and the economic elite'.

She had made friends with President Leghari but he ousted her in November 1996 since the corruption cases of the husband came forth and Benazir started to loose her popular base. The Interim Government of Miraj Khalid was installed.

Nawaz Sharief Back Again: *Concentration of power and control of the Army and the Supreme Court and opposition to Musharraf*

By the time he came back to power in February 1997 economy was in crisis. GDP dropped to 3 per cent from over all 6 per cent. There was 2 per cent of industrial growth rate but not in the manufacturing sector. There was huge deficit of bu lget to the tune of 8 per cent though the IMF prescription was 4 per cent. Overseas remittances of Pakistanis were declining. The Balance of Payment was in the negative to the order of 4.4 per cent. There was 2.5 per cent economic growth rate. Trade deficit was at $3 billion. Heavy spending on defence continued. In 1997 it had debt of more than $51 billion (30 billion to foreigners). Debt servicing had then consumed more than 50 per cent of total taxes collected and about 35 per cent of budget spending. Pakistan was net exporter of capital and depended on creditors.

Therefore it adopted a strategy to attract foreign creditors. The details are that FDI was $800 million in 1996 and as much as 5 billion was committed to power sector. Denationalisation was stalled. Low savings rate was imposed. Rs. 135 billion defaulted bank loans and by 1995 nationalised banking had collapsed. Smuggling took a heavy toll and black money went to construction business and cars.

The social sector remained far behind. Low literacy rate averaged 35 per cent. High fertility rate averaged 5.5. There was absence of women from much of work force. Education attracted meagre spending. Income inequality increased. Future was bleak on the brink of bankruptcy with such a rentier economy.[122]

Nawaz Sharief's handling of the Kargil episode brought him in conflict with Musharraf and prepared the ground for the fourth coup. In foreign affairs the Pakistan Army has heightened sensitivity on its Afghan and Kashmir policy. Nawaz Sharief, a businessman, was propagated to have entered the sugar deal with India and has now claimed that the Lahore peace process would have solved Kashmir. This process was on while Musharraf was planning the Kargil operation. Sharief's diplomacy with the US made the Pakistan military to give up on Kargil and this led to the events to oust Nawaz Sharief. A brief account of it is in order since this lays bare the dynamics of the authoritarian character of Nawaz Sharief's regime and how the military attempted to stop him in his tracks.

Lets us look at how the two civilian prime ministers were not allowed by the Army to act in foreign affairs. Owen tells us of this "Neither Benazir Bhutto nor Nawaz Sharief was allowed to formulate her or his own policies. During her first administration Benazir Bhutto had wanted to go to India to meet Rajiv Gandhi but the military establishment was so strongly opposed to the idea that she abandoned her trip. It was much the same story ten years later when, in February 1999, Nawaz Sharief invited Vajpayee to Lahore. In doing so, he faced opposition not only from the Islamic radicals but also from the army, Jamat-i. Islami displayed its displeasure by organising thousands of activists to rampage through the streets of Lahore during Vajpayee's visit."[123]

Musharraf refused to go to Wagah border where Nawaz Sharief received Vajpayee. Musharraf-Nawaz Sharief problems indicate the attempt on the part of the latter to accumulate powers in his hands by political manoeuvrings, constitutional change and executive fiat on the one hand and to marginalise his opponents inside and outside the Army and Bureaucracy, on the other hand. He also was identified with the economic crisis of Pakistan and a corrupt political culture with a growing restive opposition and no one squeaked when he was removed in 1999.

As for his relations are concerned Hasan-Askari Rizvi has noted three things. These are (a) the Sharief government's personalized and whimsical governance by appointing trusted personnel or non-entities to key positions so that there was no resistance to the decisions made by Nawaz Sharief in consultation with a small group of advisors hailing from the Lahore/Islamabad area. This he did through manoeuvering, constitutional amendments and executive fiat. (b) He turned his attention to the Army and upset the delicate balance in his favour that the Army would not tolerate. His attempt to change the Army Chief and determine appointments and retirements raised the eyebrows in the corps commanders who finally sided with Musharraf when the chips were down and Musharraf was in Sri Lanka. (c) He started cultivating certain officers by exploiting the Punjabi ethnicity. He was also critical of the Kargil operation though the operation was launched with his approval and he was in the know of it.[124] Veena Kukreja says this about Nawaz Sharief's rule "Nawaz Sharief's authoritarianism resulted in struggle between autocratic civilian rule and benign military dictatorship."[125]

The characteristics of the civilian regime show that they were second cousins of the military rule. The first cousins were the Junejos and Jamalis. Second, they all came to power with the help of the military beginning with Liaquat Ali as Suhrawardy alleged about Liaquat Ali. Third, the social compact that they represented were continuance of the basic class structure or governing elite from within that class constellation in which business was the junior partner. Third, each one knocked off his propogated political platform to accommodate societal conservatism. Fourth, each one-showed tendencies of vitiating rule of law, whatever was there. Fifth, each one attempted to concentrate. State power in his or her hands. Sixth, each one followed the policies of private capitalist development with or without social concerns (if adopted they were of secondary importance. Seventh, each one compromised with the military to come to power and remained within confines of the parameters laid by it. Whenever each one attempted to set out of it he or she earned the wrath of the Army and conservative religious forces. Eight, each one pandered to the orthodox vision of Islam. The rock bottom of their strategies was to seek Islamic legitimation in the electoral process. Ninth, each one faced the wrath of the masses since they were left in the lurch. As a result the human development index is one of the poorest though economists like Burki expected the country to graduate to a middle level country and Iftihkar expected the civil society to help the transition of the Pakistani State to democracy. Tenth, each one remained within the framework of the peripheral imperative and helped in shifting the economic policies to the neo-liberal agenda in the face of globalisation. Eleventh, it is wrong to look for democracy in Pakistan since that was not on the agenda. The legitimation process is marginal to the political compacts that each ruler arrived with America, Army, Bureaucracy and forces of Allah, who in any case were significant actors in creating opposition to the civilian ruler with the help of pliable politicians and ISI.

The lineages and linkages of the Army are therefore significant aspects of the Pakistani State. We turn to an examination of militarism in this part of South Asia to understand militarism's significance. Could this be the ugly face of the Punjabi-Pashtun identity? Or since in the Magreb region, there was no other modernising agency except the Army, should we look at the Pakistan Army as that modernising agency?[126] In case Pakistan's case is closer to the Magreb region and not the West Asian region then the traditional way of looking at civil-military relations in Pakistan would be off the mark. Zia's Islamisation negates this view about the Army.

Militarism is a new phenomenon that drew attention since 17th century and in more focused manner in the later half of the 20th century in the context of modern Nation States even though Machiavelli had underlined the need of a standing army in place of a mercenary one. In opposition Rousseau talked about free people's militia, Karl Marx stuck to this idea for his communist society. Lenin and Trotsky, since October 1917 till April 1918, opposed the idea of the standing army. Liberation movements, like in China developed a coalition of civilian and military leadership under civilian supremacy as in China. Sudan in its early years did not have a standing Army but developed it in the context of tribal warfare. Indian national movement did not pay much attention to forge coercive tools of independent India. The Congress did not pay much attention to work in the British Indian Army during the freedom movement and focused only on the political variable.

Internal Dimension: *Economic Change or Political Change*

Alfred Vagts talks about militarism. He looked at militarism as meaning to exercising an influence over civilian Government policy. By that standard we may notice that societies as far apart as India and the US would fall in that category since in both cases military does influence decisions related to security. Yet in both countries there is political neutrality within the framework of Huntington's professionalism. He maintains that political neutrality is assured in the nation states like in Britain and the US by objective control, education and constitutional responsibility.[127] In the context of the 18th century, however, it was perceived to be detrimental in the pursuit of democracy under the broad umbrella of progress. Subsequently the idea of harmony made the military superflous. It was considered that industry and commerce would do away with the need of military expenditure and militaries, which were a relic of ancient regimes. Militarism therefore got linked with both economic reform and political change.

In its twentieth century version it further got linked with military industrial complex both in the US and the Soviet Union. This negated the distinction that Spencer made between industrial and militant type of society. He also believed that the former would replace the latter. Liberals and Marxists both focused on the internal dimension. In the US especially the concept of military industrial complex was not regarded as a reality. It was considered as a cognitive category. Therefore the Americam society was variously described as Military Establishment, Weapons State, Pentagon capitalism and simply as State Monopoly capitalism. So fierce was the concern about the nature of the US State that the writings on Civil-Military relations began after President Eisenhower made his famous remark about the dangers of a military-industrial complex. Huntington, Morris Janowitz, Perlmutter went into the question of the nature of the power elite and all of them agreed that there was no militarism in the US.[128] Earlier on Schumpeter related militarism to atavistic factors of the feudal era.

Herbert Spencer developed the idea of an industrial society and a militant type of society to say that in the former the militarism has no place but it does have a place in the second variety. This argument subsequently does not hold credibility. Liberal societies do develop a military-industrial complex and do promote militarism in Third World States through military aid, trade and arms races in the 20th century. In fact Miles Wolpin's[129] argument is that both the local elites out of appetitive politics and metropolitan capital get together to promote militarism in their societies for repression internally. This is close to the Garrison State thesis of Harold Lasswell. Lasswell suggests that since in the context of the nuclear weapons external wars are rare it is only intra-state conflicts that would place decision making power in the hands of experts of violence and militaries will be armed. This fits into the New Left thesis of the repressive role of the peripheral states. We noticed that a Peripheral State like Pakistan works with the peripheral imperative and State power is dominated by the military. Schumpeter's atavistic thesis is worth exploring given the distorted nature of the Pakistani polity owing to emasculated growth of modern elites that occupied the Pakistani locale between the collapse of the Mughal Empire and the rise and decline of the British empire. Here one could draw interesting parallels with Japanese militarism as a result of the Meiji revolution there. The point is that both the lineages and the Pakistan's existential structures' linkages with metropolitan capitalism can go a long way to explain militarism of Pakistan's State.

Further we must notice that militarism is also linked to the level of political culture. In his famous book S. E. Finer suggests that militarism can be linked to the level of political culture. These are mature, advance and low. He suggests that militarism does not arise in mature political culture like the ones in the US and Britain. It has not much chance of rising in advanced ones as in the USSR. It however has the possibility of arising in the low political cultures. In case of India he considers that it has a developed political system and has high political culture and low possibility of militarism.[130] The Pakistani political culture is low, corrupt and lacks any viable democratic content. Lawrence Ziring said in 1997 that Pakistani political culture is corrupt and that its political process is anything than democratic. He says, "The vast majority of Pakistanis are a gullible congeries of factions, clans and tribes and their manipulation by traditional, as well as contemporary power brokers remains the central focus of the political experience."[131]

External Dimension: *War*

In the hands of some continental writers militarism got linked to external politics, especially in Bismarkian Prussia. To a Jesuist monk militarism was "the centralising tendencies of his time, rearmament to the utmost and the mobilization of all national resources for the purpose of maintaining a large army were essential features of a type of modern militarism to be observed in the 1860s and Napoleonic France"[132]

Karl Leibenecht related militarism to political economy. Engles and Wilhelm Leibnecht related it to promotion of arms races. To quote Wilhem Liebnecht "...the history of militarism was identical with the history of political, social, economic and, in most general sense, cultural tensions between states and nations and with the history of class struggles inside the individual states and national entities."[133]

To this he added naval and colonial militarism to underline the role of armies in wars. In this case Leibnecht had ignored the fact that he was writing in the context of Germany which was not a clear-cut case of capitalist dvelopment but a case of feudal-monarchical type of society. A generalisation covering the whole of the capitalist process was covered by Rosa Luxembourg who embedded militarism in the process of accumulation that served to develop nationalism and to conquer colonies like India. One needs to notice that Kipling's prototype of the hero in the NWFP was the soldier administrator and not the civilian administrator. Lenin also mentioned the internal and external functions of militarism.

Military Way and Militarism: *Post War Thinking*

Vagts describes militarism to imply "a tendency to extend dominion'. He makes a distinction between a military way and a militarism. By the first it means that the army exists for itself and not for war. Military way is "marked by a primary concentration of men and materials of winning specific objectives of power with the most efficiency; that is, with the least expenditure of blood and treasure. It is limited in scope, confined to one function and scientific in its essential qualities."[134]

"Militarism by contrast offers a vast array of customs, interests, prestige, actions and thought associated with armies and wars and yet transcend the true military purpose."[135]

Vagts thus brings forth the control of military by civilian authority in the military way and pervading militaristic tendency in militarism in the context of the inter war period of the present century. A significant theme that he further concentrates on is the relationship between militarism and society. In 1941 Lasswell talked about the increasing role of the specialist. Let us not forget that the First World War was of the chemistry man and the Second World War that of the physicists. The role of the second had raised the nuclear spectre. To this he suggested a business state, i.e. the old dichotomy appeared between civilianism and militarism. Garrison State thesis became part of the propaganda against the German policies of war and in 1962 against the Soviet State.

Discussion on Third World

The post-war discussion about the armies raised a new dimension about looking at the armies. These were to distinguish between armies that do and do not represent militarism. Huntington assigned to the armies a progressive role while the Marxists denied that role. Here again the army society lineages were significant. If these were with the radical petty bourgeoisie then radicalism would come about in the initial phase of national liberation and not in the subsequent period. As we notice in case of Pakistan the Army did not play such a role before independence. It also was not recruited from radical petty bourgeoisie. In any discussion of the militaries in the Third World the hegemonic role of the US cannot be disregarded. This hegemony has to be seen especially in the context of the Cold War. Since Pakistan's economy was embedded in peripheral capitalism its Army was ensconced with the US within less than a decade. Since its position externally was thus made significant it was able to dominate the internal politics by way of getting economic and military aid, especially when it has been in crisis.

Conceptualisation of Civil-Military Relations: *Garrison State, Professionalism, Corporatism, and Praetorianism*

Two significant themes emerge that need attention. First what is the relation of the Army with the society and what is the relation of the army with civilianism. On the first Morris Janowitz and Jacques van Doorn write extensively. On the latter there have developed many conceptual categories. These categories are Garrison State thesis, Professionalism, Corporatism and Praetorianism. Apart from Garrison State thesis and Professionalism that we have looked into above we need to focus on the other two categories. Corporatism is related to Professionalism.[136] Those who study the continental armies accord to them the character of corporatism. It briefly means that the military as a modern organisation is highly professional. By professional is meant individual and collective. Individually it means develop a professional behaviour and develop efficiency. By behaviour is meant imbibe the ethos and values of the organisation through peer group emulation. By efficieny is meant develop technical skills through training and exercise. Organisational professionalism is meant the development of organisational interests and the capacity to influence policy for their achievement. In other words it does not imply political neutrality that Huntington implies in his discussion of professionalism. Rather it implies an enlarged political role.

Praetorianism refers to the personal guards of King Augustus in Rome in ancient times for suppressing internal dissent.[137] They were payed from his personal coffers and were used against internal dissent. Weber identified Praetorianism with Sultanism of Turkey and advanced agrarian societies where soldiers were payed from the Sultan's personal coffers.[138] Praetorianism was linked to the colonial context in Latin America and South Asia. In Latin America it had to do with *mestizos,* the local chieftains called Caudillos who became mercenaries in defence of the landed classes or the monarchy.[139] Thus they developed a mercenary character. Huntington talks about praetorianism in society where a viable middle class does not gel and the students riot, the rich bribe, worker strikes, mobs demonstrate and military coups.[140] In Latin America modern dictatorships are related to the 19th century chieftains, i. e. men on horseback, of the aboriginal population. Further Praetorian armies have been divided into two kinds viz, ruling kind and the arbitrator kind, the latter returning to the barracks as quickly as possible.[141] Both have eight characteristics each. Morris Janowitz maintains that armies also civilianise their rule.[142]

We notice that the category of professioanalism as efficiency can be applied to Pakistan. The category of corporatism can also be since it has developed various foundations to serve its economic and social mobility interests as well as its influence on the defence budget. It is praetorian for it is available for suppressing local revolts, Stephen Cohen calls it civic action.[143] It is praetorian Army also since it is available to the US interests for a price, which cannot be 'pea nuts' (an expression used by Zia on the quantum of aid offered by Carter in 1979). It is further Praetorian Army of both the barrack and ruling kind. It ruled for ten long years from 1979-89. It withdrew since it allowed a civilian government for a decade. Further it is an Army that civilianises since it allows for civilian administration under its own rule. The Ayub and Musharraf phases are two examples of it.

There is however no clear indication of what constitutes militarism. So far it has been related to pre-capitalist and industrial societies and Berghahn suggests that militarism linked with technological society may be of the third kind.[144] It is possible that the two may be linked to produce militarism in the Third World countries. This should imply persistence of atavistic roots. These roots get strengthened by colonial administration and economy. The integration of this economy in the independence phase is with international finance capitalism as a peripheral economy. The involvemeent of the Third World State in the external war-like thrust of the hegemonic power out of choice and necessity. Thus both the internal and the external dynamics may stand in a symbiotic relationship. Further it is also possible that this symbiosis may come in the way of transition of the Third World State from a colonial imperative to self reliant mode and reorientation of the militarism to military way. The case of Pakistan is as complex as this is.

Lineages: *Since the Collapse of the Mughal Empire*

We must note that even though we go into the atavistic sources of military profession there is no doubt that the colonial settings brought about a basic transformation in the new military establishment. This is a part of the modern bureaucratic machine. It was during the pre-British feudal-monarchical period that new elite formation did not take place and certain tendencies of warfare developed to which we shall return to look for lineages.[145] They were however nowhere near the kind of military force that the British created. In the exercise to look for lineages we note that this exercise does not discover the linkages in order to underline the nationalist and expansionist motives of the society that get translated into militarism as happened in case of France. The nation in arms theory is not supported here.[146] We go into the exercise for a simple reason that the British recruitment policies in Asia and Africa they favoured certain sections of society and this in turn impacted upon the structure that they created. Further this also impact upon the new power structure after independence and created its own dynamic of fission. In Africa we notice that the Army was recruited from certain tribes called 'warrior tribes' which caused tribal imbalances in their representation in the Army in Kenya, Ghana and Nigeria.[147] In India the British recruited the Military from 'martial races'[148] Khalid B. Sayeed says about the British recruitment policy,

"Recruitment to the British Indian army was largely confined to the northwestern parts of India. This policy was also influenced by the fact that the British thought that future attack on India would probably be launched the Russian through the passes that lay in the North- Western Frontier. In this way also was the theory of martial races developed. These martial races were the Pathans, the Punjabi Muslims, the Sikhs, the Rajputs, the Dogras, the Garhwalis and the Mahrattas. All these races lived in the northern and North-Western part of India with the exception of the Mahrattas."[149]

Why were they called martial is difficult to say. There is nothing in the cultures of peoples or their natures that make them warlike or militaristic. This is true of the Punjabis, Pathans, Bengali, the Japanese, Germans or Italians as it is of the European colonial officer active in this region or the Americas. This could be situational. Conjunctures of factors and causality may lead people to resort to arms or be aggressive. Inter-imperialist rivalries or colonial expansion created such conjunctures with in less developed regions of the world. Therefore we will cover historical terrain to discover if such situations existed that made people of these regions warlike. The modern Pakistan Army is recruited from four districts of northern Punjab, namely Rawalpindi, Campbellpur, Jhelum, Gujarat and two districts of former Frontier Province, Peshawar and Korhat. Sixty per cent of the Army consisted of the Punjabis; 35 per cent of the Pathans and the others constituted the remaining five at the time of independence.[150] Sindhis and Bengalis were not considered to be fit for recruitment. Baloch tribes were recruited in small numbers.

Dewey rejects theories of peripheral capitalism and the difference between civilian elites owing to the common social roots of the Army and the civilian leadership and the Army striking roots in six or seven core villages of Punjab. He refers to the Punjab tribes in the Salt ranges, like the *Tiwanas* (Nawaz Sharief is a Tiwana)[151] who ruled the Salt ranges on behalf of the Mughals. The other tribes of Pathan origin in order of importance were *Yusufzais, Khattaks, Afridis* and *Bangash*.[152] The martial castes or tribes lived at strategic internal routes and the Mughal Army recruited them, used them, played each other off to contain them. These were brought under the rule of the Ranjit Singh as Sikh 'misls' that fought off local revolts. They created a confederation of guerilla bands and these became powerful. This confirmed the military supremacy of the misl of Ranjit Singh. The revenue official and chieftains emerged from the *misldars*. Plunder was as much Ranjit Singh's policy. Multan, Peshawar and Deras were the regions of operation. The British also played off these chieftains in a similar fashion during the first and the second Afghan wars and Anglo-Sikh wars.

In terms of political economy of the region since the late Mughal period and the adoption of the British, Imran Ali refers to the British policies of canal colonies, of recruiting areas, development of entrepreneur-peasant bourgeois and corrupt bureaucracy. Peasants revolted against the Mughals. Banditry was the order of the marauding population. Sikhism as a religion of Khatri castes was for peaceful purpose to begin with but in the hands of the last two gurus, Tegh Bahadur Singh and Govind Singh, it became identified with these marauding people. Ranjit Singh's *misl* was based in Phul and Maler Kotla on 'biradries' and feudatories of displaced Muslim nobility. These regions were attacked by the Turks of Central Asia. The Muslims had Central Asian origins rather than Turkish origins. After the Anglo-Sikh wars the British followed policies of development and accommodation. The development policies led to commercial activities in the hands of retired officials, unemployed graduates and departmental officials. They developed Salt Range cantonments and Canal colonies in West Punjab.[153]

The transition from the phase of Ranjit Singh to that of the British and the survival of the local Chieftains, who became part of the martial races, and, in martial areas is described by Andrew J. Major.[154] He points to the cunning of the chieftains. They showed their capacity to run with the hare and hunt with the hound. This they did when the palace intrigues in the post Ranjit Singh phase began. These factional activities continued and the chieftains played one against the other both inside and outside the court. The same thing they did with Sikh and the Dogras in the conflict. Repeated it with the British and so both opposed and supported them by some members being with them and others with the chieftains that opposed them.[155] The British rewarded those who remainded with them. This is true of them during the first and the second Anglo-Sikh wars. The story of Harsukh Rai gives a glimpse of how he came over to the British. Finally, how the British rewarded him and made him Extra Assistant Commissioner. Similar is the story of the Tiwanas of Shahpur. The Dogras and Punjab chieftains had their rivalries. The Dogras played their cards well and were able to get Kashmir finally from the British. Similarly one Jawahar Singh exhibited sufficient cunning and was rewarded by the British to such an extent that he became one of the wealthiest families of Punjab. Since the chieftains had the psyche of having honour and increasing it to make an impact on one and all, the British exploited this by conferring the titles to thirty six chieftains in two darbars. Tiwana maliks were rewarded and asked to raise soldiers to help the British. The British associated many of these with administration and land in the form of peasant proprietorship. This led to the creation of zaildars. This is the process from Ranjit Singh's misls to Punjab's chieftains. This was also the base of the politics of the Unionist Party.

The situation in provinces as a result of British policies could best be described as one of emasculated nationalism. Colonial conquest introduced cash crops that established prerequisites of capitalist production.[156] At the same time capitalist relations were curbed. This happened because of the policy of perpetuating feudal survivals and supporting local exploiting strata which were rooted in the out-of- date pre-capitalist system, because it is this strata (semi-feudal landlords and moneylenders) that were the major stronghold of the British rule. Colonial yoke with land tax also arrested the consolidation of the Punjabis into a bourgeois nation. This happened despite the fact that cash crops were grown-cotton and wheat during 1887-1921.The moneylenders were Khatris, Aroras and Agarwals.

The Punjabi bourgeoisie was nascent. It retained its relations with the landlords and the moneylenders. He identifies the ethnic origins of this class " ...Punjabi bourgeoisie arose largely from the local landlords, either Hindus or offspring of the Hindu castes of traders and moneylenders, while in the central Punjab these were members of the proprietory top crust of the Sikhs community.

"The Muslims of the Punjab turned to enterprising activity later than the Hindus. In the beginning of the twentieth century the Muslim entrepreneurs could be counted on the fingers of one hand. In the following decades the wealthy Muslim Punjabi landlords preferred to invest above all in the field of circulation, intermediary trade, banking and money lending. It is only during the Second World War when a favourable economic situation arose in the Punjab that members of the proprietary top of the Muslim community took an active part in enterprising activity also in the fields of industrial production. This circumstance contributed to the more fierce competition for a "place under the sun" between different sections of the nascent bourgeois class."[157]

Further hurdle in the consolidation of this class was that the British had inculcated the business from Bombay, Rajasthan and Gujarat. Bohra from Gujarat and Bhatias from Rajasthan were active in Punjab. This also prevented the growth of the proletarians who were mainly in the agricultural sector. These were from other parts of the country and not from Punjab.

Punjab was unevenly developed even in these terms and this had a negative effect on the growth of a single language throughout the province. Feudal survivals and religious ideologies were virile. Urdu and Punjabi had a contest and the former gained an upper hand even thoug the Punjabi dialects also gelled into one language.

"The Punjabi nation not only emerged later but also developed slower than the Bengali nation."[158]

British policies also hindered the growth of the Sindh bourgeois nation and its intelligentsia since its money lending and trade were tied to the colonial economy. The circumstances under which the national consolidation of the Pashtuns and the Balochs proceeded were much more complex than those of the Bengalis, Punjabis and the Sindhis. Administrative fragmentation, British colonial policies of keeping them isolated prevented capitalist relations to grow even of the level of Sindh. We noticed above that militarism in Europe got related to non-development in the economic sphere as much as in the political sphere. This brief survey shows that in the regions that came to form Pakistan different peoples were in motion of uneven change within the paradigm of feudal economy and relations tied to the colonial imperative. This led to the growth of the growth of pro-British partyisation, around highly centralised institutional rule that had a façade of parliamentary form but not content. So emasculated transition in a situation of aborted democratic institutionalisation led to the militarism in the region where a sufficient middle class did not emerge and the Congress influence had not taken place.

This brief survey of a long history shows that the political developments since the decline of the Mughals through the Ranjit Singh phase to the British colonial State the Punjab chieftains were caught in a situation where there was no possibility of the growth of new elites on their own. The development of fratricidal conflict in such a situation and the conscious British policy of preventing the growth of nationalism in the region prevented the development of middle classes. This accounted for the growth of militarism in the region. This argument is further buttressed by the fact that there was no growth of nationalism in the region that came to be Pakistan. The peoples of the Punjab, Sindh, NWFP and Baluchistan did not have the growth of the class that would go for either nationalism or democracy. There were no social classes that could be the base of Cromwell's revolution of the 1640s in England let alone Locke's constitutional oligarchy in defence of bourgeois property. In Bengal the situation was more developed in both the terms. But the artificial union of the West and the East was of uneven parts that later developed explosions along this faultline.

The post-independence Army remains predominantly Punjabi and regards Punjab to be Pakistan's core. Stephen Cohen says "Because the army draws its manpower from the peasantry, it believes that land reforms and social justice in the countryside (especially the dominant central province of Punjab) are vital to the state because they are vital to the army. Indeed, the army has long equated its survival, and health of the Punjab which provides most of the officers and other ranks, with the health of Pakistan."[159]

The Punjabi predominance has further led to the growth of multi ethnic compact within the military with Punjab at its core. Hasan-Askari Rizvi says "The significant majority of the army officers and other ranks hail from the Punjab, NWFP, and the tribal areas. These two groups (Punjabis and Pakhtuns) have not only developed strong mutual ties but have also established links with the civilian bureaucratic elite, both of whom have a similar ethnic background. The Punjabi-Pathan composition of the Army has been a source of strength which has *inter alia* contributed to enhancing the military's efficacy in politics."[160]

We notice here that despite the fact that the first generation of the Army leadership was trained in Sandhurst and the second in Pakistan the system of control over the Army and bureaucracy is rather feudal and not constitutional. From that perspective the Pakistan Army does not fit into the model of the objective control. The situation may be changing since the recruitment may not be only from the martial races. They have begun from the middle and lower middle classes. Would it lead to professionalisation or its decline, it is difficult to say. The control over them also would be in accordance with the training institutes for in house training of the Army and peer group behaviour rather than the Constitution. On the contrary since the Zia period and his constitutional amendments to Article 53 (b) and Musharraf's inclusion of the National Security Council in the decision making makes the Constitution subservient to the Army rather than the former establishing a control over the Army. If, further the Army is a source of social mobility then it is more like the Communist Parties of erstwhile existing socialist societies that did not fit into Huntington's definition of professionalism in political terms.

Military Regimes: *Common Points*

Traditional ways of explaining the entry of military regimes is to note the absence of the mass party, absence of a leader like Nehru, the factionalism in the Pakistani civilian leadership and dominance of the bureaucracy in the State structure[161] in the initial period and the mounting tasks of security that were to be performed beginning with partition and conflict in Kashmir. On subsequent developments in the Pakistani State's failure to become democratic, Malik says,

"The lack of consensual politics, enduring constitutionalism, and a properly agreed mechanism for transfer of power is reflected in the country's periodic phases of political instability. Such intermittent crisis, multiplied by an uneasy ethno-regional pluralism, have oftened allowed analysts to view Pakistan either a failed or a failing state."[162]

Yet we feel that democracy was not on the cards. It was only an elite conflict within a colonial-peripheral- imperative that did not entertain an Oliver Cromwell let alone Locke's constitutional oligarchy.

Hasan-Askari Rizvi in case of Ayub, Yahya and Zai-ul Haq's regimes, first defines what is militarism in Pakistan's context thus "The military established its hegemony assuming and consolidating power. The military established its hegemony marked by its dominance of core political and economic institutions and processes and monopolistic control over strategic policy issues. This also gave rise to 'militarism', making it possible for the military directly or indirectly to exercise 'a decisive influence upon Pakistan's domestic and foreign policies."[163]

Major concerns of the military that made it dominate the Pakistan State are listed by Hasan-Askari Rizvi. The military's interests in usurping power were six for Rizvi.These were paramountcy of national security on issues of nuclear policy, Afghanistan and Kashmir policy and generally its anti-India concerns. Second, overseas weapons and equipment programme with foreign policy implications. Three, Military autonomy and civilian non-interference in matters of the military whether it concerns core commanders for defence budget. Fourthly, it is opposed to any unilateral cut in defence budget by civilian leaders. Fifthly, improve service conditions and preserve the already obtained perks, pay and position in terms of service conditions. Sixthly, political views of the nation's politics.[164]

All the military regimes came in since they gave different interpretations of national interests. Second, they came in when their twin-civilian leaders were facing a legitimacy crisis. Third, each of the regimes went out at the time when their own legitimacy was at a low ebb. Fourth, they came in when the interests of the military were threatened. Fifth, they were fortunate owing to the change in the international environment and benefitted from the US and Western connection. Sixth, penetration of the civilian life. Seventh, they civilianised the military regimes with centralisation as the motto. Eight, they determined the course of economic strategy and if that was attempted to be changed, the Army came in, as happened in case of Bhutto introducing the state sector. Ninth, they determined foreign policy. Tenth they are responsible for fragility of the state.

Definition of National Interests: *Reasons for Intervention*

Ayub Khan, Ghulam Mohammad were together in determining that Pakistan should be one unit in West Pakistan.They rejected Bogra's constitution that had suggested a formula for federalisation. Ghulam Muhammad had asked Ayub to step in the context of sectarian conflict regarding anti-Ahmadi riots. Since agrarian reforms were not undertaken, corruption was not removed and economic development was not undertaken Ayub

Khan was requested to intervene. He intervened in national interest through operation Blue Bird' without firing a single shot.[165] Yahya Khan came to power when the struggle in East Pakistan was at a crescendo and he very much continued Ayub's policy and his martial law also aimed to contain Bengali politics. His holding of fair and free elections were to prove a disaster in the end.[166] Zia-ul Haq interpreted the Bhutto regime as one that had both internal and external disaster. Internally he pointed to the White Paper on rigging of elections and murder of Kasuri's father. 'Operation Fair-play' was in the context of Bhutto's ego and party considerations outweighing national interests.[167] Musharaff came to the fore since he developed differences over the Kargil operation. All the four Army Chiefs at the time of take over made statements to the inevitability of the adopted course to save the nation.[168] Ayub said on 8 October, 1958, "This is a drastic and extreme step taken with great reluctance but with the deepest conviction that there was no alternative to it except disintegration and complete ruination of the country."

Yahya Khan said on 26 March, 1969

" The armed forces could not remain idle spectators of this state of anarchy. They have to do their duty and save the country from utter disaster."

Zia-ul Haq said, "I was obliged to step in to fill in the vacuum created by the political leaders."

Pervez Musharraf said on 17 October 1999, "I wish to inform you that the armed forces have moved in as a last resort to prevent any further destabilisation."

Legitimacy Crisis: *Of the Civilian Leaders*

Ayub came to power at the time when internal turmoil had led to internal intervention of the military, e.g., in matters of anti-Ahmediya strife. The civilian leaders had not agreed to a constitutional structure owing to the games that Ghulam Muhammad had played by releasing Maamdoot and Daultana who attacked Bogra's formula incorporated in the Constitution particularly when Bogra was on a State visit to the USA. The party fights between the West and East Pakistan wings were at rising crescendo and both Bhutto and Awami League's Sheikh Mujib-ur Rehman were fighting it out. Zia-ul Haq came when Bhutto was faced with the PNA agitation and had failed to keep his promise of holding elections and instead visiting the Muslim countries at the time when the elections were to be held. Atleast that is how his visit was interpreted by the PNA leadership. Bhutto had also declared martial law in three cities. Musharraf stepped in since Nawaz Sharief was attempting to concentrate power in his hands, submit the Supreme Court judges under his control, replace Pervez Musharraf by his own ISI chief at the time when Musharraf was on a visit to Sri Lanka and because economy was in bad shape. President and Nawaz Sharief had to resign owing to the rape of Veena.

Illegitimacy: *Of the Military Dictators*

Ayub Khan was forced to retire since he could not contain student agitation and agrarian revolt despite his Basic Democracy and strategy of economic growth on the principles of Laissez Faire. His clientilist rule "...could not secure and utterly failed to cope with the participatory and distributive pressures mounted either by those who had been excluded or by the new socio-economic forces including the professional classes, the fast expanding labour, students, urban unemployed and the rural poor whose increase was many fold as a consequence of the regime's economic policies. The Bengalis of East Bengal were especially frustrated and felt that the power structure largely ignored their political aspirations."[169]

Further Ayub's foreign policy also came under shadow. This is true of his policy towards India. Not victorious in war—there was a stalemate—for some Pakistani scholars. With Soviet diplomatic initiative he met Prime Minister Shastri at Tashkent. Subsequently, Bhutto alleged that there was a secret clause in the agreement and campaigned against Ayub ferociously. Of course, he never revealed what this secret clause was. By this agitation he wanted to show that Ayub was not successful in the diplomatic front as well. Yahya's brief spell is marked by the major failure of the Army, and the dismemberment of the Pakistani State.

Similarly Zia-ul Haq's regime created conditions in which he first had to seek legitimation through fundamentalist Islamic measures. Failing this he had to civilianize the government by taking the help of Pir Pigaro from Sindh in nominating Junejo as the Prime Minister, then experienced the phase of tussle between

Junejo and himself and dismissed the latter. The strains on the polity were such that the Kalashnikov and drugs culture had created a period of endemic violence in Sindh. During his rule the shoots of civil society could be seen, especially in the area of gender discrimination connected with this Islamisation plan. His economic policy was nothing to talk about much since he laid emphasis on denationalisation, allowing the private sector to move on and rely on foreign aid. He engaged in denationalisation and introduced some Islamic principles on it. The Jamaat was at the core of this civilianisation. On the next dispensation Aijaz Ahmed says about Zia's coup "...the recent coup is structurally different from the previous two ones in 1958 and 1969; not only has the repressive apparatus arrogated to itself the tasks of political apparatus, it is also undertaken to transform the state in such a manner that the ultra-right shall now be propelled into a hegemonic position in all the basic structures of authority."[170]

Musharraf is considered in the tradition of both Zia and Ayub. He evinces the modernist image and took steps against some *jihadi* groups under the Western pressure owing to September 11. At the same time he immitates Zia in matters of civilianising drive. His strategy of referendum, continuation of Article 53(b) and ordering a Legal Framework order has attracted dissent and currently there are demonstrations against the LFO. The General retains both the post of the President of Pakistan as well as that of the Army Chief. The Opposition wants him to give up one of these. It is also reported that the Army is also not happy with him. Further against his wishes the Assembly of the NWF has passed some Islamic measures and he has come out against them. Most of Musharraf's promised plan of action on economic and social front have failed. The General may turn out more like Zia than like Ayub. He may believe that he can restore democracy but he also knows that pakistan needs the Army. He is living with this dilemma.[171]

Threat to Military Interest: *Internal*

The military realised that initial years' constitution-making, which was emerging to be successful, according to Allan Macgrath, made it unite with both the bureaucrats and the US. The bureaucrats had the leverage of controlling offices of the State like the judiciary and the government. Both Ghulam Muhammad and Justice Munir were an asset. So was Prime Minister Bogra with whom Ayub had gone to the US and was also keeping over him a watchful eye on behalf of Ghulam Mohammed. He became the Defence Dinister in the subsequent Bogra ministry after Ghulam Mohammad had succesfully aborted the new constitution and suspended the Assembly. When Bhutto started to interfere in the affairs of the Army by way of bringing it under civilian control the Army revolted. It also revolted since he was known to have met the corps commanders without the Army Chief knowing about it. Both Benazir Bhutto and Nawaz Sharief are known to attempt to amend Article 53(a) to curb the powers of the President and control the postings and attempt the removal of Army personnel. There was also an attempt to reduce the defence budget. In case of Zulfiquar Ali Bhutto, Zia replaced him. In case of the subsequent two civilian Prime Ministers, Benazir and Nawaz, the Army first attempted to destabilise them. These leaders also attempted to change the orientation of the foreign policy. Finally, all this led to a coup—in 1999.

US Connection: *Continual Strategic Considerations*

It is said that the US is not responsible for the military coups in Pakistan. Rizvi says, "However there is no evidence to suggest that the international factors, especially American connections, were decisive to the military's decisions to stage a coup in October 1958, although the US ambassador knew in advance of the impending change and Ayub Khan had good rapport with US administration. The same could be said about the coups in march1969 and July 1977."[172]

There is no doubt that the US preferred authoritarian regimes against the Iron Curtain. Second, the US made Pakistan an ally in its Cold War anti-Russian strategy. Kissinger used it as a launching pad for his Chinese diplomacy in the 1960s. The arming of Pakistan began with the visit of Ayub and Bogra to the US. When the US learnt that Ghulam Muhammad was opposing Bogra they increased the economic and military aid to Pakistan to support Bogra and Ayub. Third, along with the British delegation it helped the Pakistan Army against India on the issue of Kashmir in the UN. The Indians very early, during the days of Nehru, had taken a word from the US that the arms supplied to the Pakistanis will not be used against India.[173] This did not deter the Pakistanis from using these against India. Again when Zia was given the US aid Zia got a clause incorporated that the ISI will disburse the military aid and that the US will not have a say in this. That aid was also used against India. The Zia regime got enormous aid package. Along with the remittances of the Pakistanis from the Muslim World this aid package caused economic boom in the Pakistani economy. Third, currently once again the Musharraf government has benefitted from the US War on Afghanistan and managed to get multi-lateral debts written off. During Musharraf's visit to the US in June-July 2003 visit Pakistan further gained in U. S. economic aid. In this context most commentators say that the period of military dictatorships is one of economic success while that of the civilian governments is that of economic bleakness.

Further we may notice that Pakistan has been indispensable to the US interests in West Asia, Central Asia and South Asia. Member of the SEATO and CENTO it was required to play a role in West Asia. In the context of Soviet Central Asia it played the role of *tripwire*. In case of Central Asia it played the role of Frontline State during Zia and Musharraf's time. In the context of Cold War Pindi was part of Washington-Pindi-Beijing-Tokyo axis. Now that the cold war has ended and there is a reorientation of the Indo-US relations, even then US relies more on Pakistan as a strategic ally and admits that it is unable to put pressure on Pakistan to stop cross border terrorism. For the role that it plays in favour of the US strategic interests Pakistan is amply rewarded in economic and military aid and trade-traid, as it was earlier called.

After Ayub's coup the US realised that it could then deal with a more stable Pakistan. A Report of National Security Coordinating Board in the US said

"The political instability which was characteristic of previous Governments and seriously impeded the effectiveness of the US efforts in Pakistan has been replaced by a relatively stable martial law regime."

It further maintained,

"...In view of the present stability, even though achieved through fiat, the problem has changed from one of short terms urgency, requiring us reckon with individual politicians in one crisis after another, to one which allows the US to take a longer range view of Pakistan's potential ...because we recognise the potential accruing at this juncture from a stable political situation, we give special emphasis to assuring Pakistan's Government (General Ayub) of our sympathetic interests in, and support for, its proposed economic and social reforms."[174]

A Department of Defense Report in 1983 to the House Foreign Relations Committee said,

"The stability and security of Pakistan contribute importantly to meeting security objectives in South West Asia. As a frontline State resisting Soviet expansionism, Pakistan has incurred additional security responsibilities....Moreover Pakistan has provided refuge to nearly three million Afghans fleeing the fighting in Afghanistan....Our commitment to Pakistan's security is given both real and symbolic shape through the existence of our six year ($3.2 billion) programme of security and gap economic assistance and through our willingness to contribute to Pakistan's military modernisation.[175]

Stephen Cohen put the relationship thus, once in 1984 and again in 2002. He said of the relationship of the two during Zia's period

"Its survival is likely to be in part the result of super power rivalry and great power rivalry, a state of dependency uncomfortable for any state, but particularly so for one that has viewed itself as a rugged, tough and independent power."[176]

He said about US aid to Musharraf, after September11 attacks on the Twin Towers of the US.

"Pakistan's new geostrategic importance, and the realization that a failing Pakistan could pose a threat to the international community, has produced substantial economic aid-$I billion from the US alone..."[177]

Penetration in Civilian Life: *Militarisation of Administration*

Ayub Khan had replaced the civilian administrators by military administration from 1958-63. Chief Martial Law was above ordinary state institutions. The ordinances of Martial Law were above the ordinary law, even though an attempt was made to govern as closely as possible in accordance with the abrogated constitution. The CMLA was assisted by a secretary general and an advisory committee. These were military men. Country was divided into three martial law zones and each was under a Lt. General. Special and summary military courts were established. The military established the cooperative relationship with the civilian bureaucracy serving each other's professional and corporate interests. In all this,

"... the military commanders did not compromise their centrality to the martial law administration."[178]

About the period from 1963-68 after the new Constitution was introduced with its elected executive and Basic Democracy it was observed that,

"The new constitutional and political arrangement reflected the military's organisational ethos of hierarchy, order, discipline and attempted to regulate political activity; the democratic and participatory considerations were assigned a low priority. The continuity of key personnel and policies from military rule was more conspicous than the change."[179]

Yahya Khan concentrated power by remaining the CMLA, C-in-C and the President, unlike Ayub Khan. He had a three member advisory committee composed of the military men. A civilian cabinet that he appointed in August 1969 and continued till 1972 did not mean that power had shifted to the civilians. Like the Ayub government it subordinated the bureaucracy. Yahya Khan had faced a nasty situation for Pakistan, i. e., opinion against One Unit in the West, and the rise of Sheikh Mujib symbolising resurgent Bengali nationalism against the State of Pakstan. After conducting the fair and free elections, and, faced with the intransigence of Bhutto and Mujib, Yahya did not trust the civilian bureaucracy. K.M. Arif describes a fateful meeting in which Yahya Khan took matters in his hands and thus bid good bye to the civilian bureaucrat's views. Arif says of the Yahya option,

"This was not the genial meetings presided over by Yahya Khan during his turbulent tenure as the President of Pakistan. He told his exclusive audience that he had decided to personally control the law and order situation in East Pakistan. The presence of General Hameed in the meeting indicated that the military supported the decision.... The civil administration and the intelligence agencies were no longer trustworthy."[180] While in Dhaka he ordered the military option of operation Searchlight. Discussing the Pakistani responsibility for the failure at Dhaka, Arif blames the military as much as the civilian bureaucracy thus,

"If the politicians blundered, weakening the national political system, the military harmed the country no less with its repeated intervention in civil affairs."[181]

Under Zia-ul Haq the CMLA posted officer corps in key civilian positions in the federal and provincial governments. Zia team's key men retained their military and civilian offices—Chisti, Ghulam Hasan Khan, Sayeed Kadir, J.S. Mian, Rao Farman Ali Khan (retired). PSOs, i. e. Pakistan Service Officers remained junior partners. Despite the fact that Junejo asserted himself he lost out to Zia. During the Junejo period, military remained the strongest force. Hasan-Askari Rizvi says of this

"The current power sharing arrangement blends the authoritarian tradition with democracy. It allows the military share in decision making and in facilitating the electoral process and representative government. Political stability depends on a trouble free interaction between the civilian government and the military.... The military continues to be the strongest political force and it can veto Pakistan's transition to democracy."[182]

Civilianisation of Regimes: *Authoritarianisation as watchword*

Ayub Khan, Yahya Khan, Zia-ul Haq and Pervez Musharraf have indulged in providing a variant to their initial response of martial law administration or military intervention. Ayub Khan is held in repute for introducing the 1963 constitution and making Basic Democracy as his form of civilian rule. Yahya Khan had introduced a Legal Framework Order to keep power in his hands. The Zia-ul Haq regime amended the Bhutto constitution of 1973 to create a subordinate prime minister in the troika of power composed of the Army Chief, President and the Prime minister. The period of Pervez Musharraf is marked not by announcement of the martial law. It is also attempting to discover a civilian legitimacy for itself by holding referendums, like Zia did, holding of partlyless elections, again Zia's legacy, holding local elections like Ayub did. Further like Yahya Khan he has also suggested a Legal Framework.

Ayub Period

Army was emboldened by its performance in the anti-Ahmedia or adhian riots. It organised horse and cattle show and Ayub came to increasingly play an improtant role in the civilian administration before he took over. It is during this phase that in Lahore the slogans of Pakistan Army zindabad were raised.[183] After it entrenched itself it wanted to civilianise. President Ayub Khan held a referendum for the Presidency for himself for five years. He won this. He set up a Constitution Committee to make a constitution for Pakistan. Before this while in London in 1954 he had penned down his views on Pakistan in a document called 'A short appreciation of present and future problems of Pakistan.' In practical terms he ousted General Iskander Mirza finally to become the sole power centre in Pakistan. He established a Constitution Committee under Justice Shahabudin. It was given the task of uniting East and West, reconciling the theory of Islamic State with modern polity, frame a constitution of 1962. In the 1963 elections of Presidency Ayub Khan was chosen. The new Constitution was remarkable for its idea of Basic Democracy.

The Constitution was not universally hailed. Chief Justice Shahabudin and bar associations of Karachi and Lahore were not enthusiastic about it. Similarly intellectuals in Dacca were not supportive of it. After the Constitution was announced Akhtar Hussain was chosen the Chief Election Commissioner. Among the issues raise by the candidates there were no serious political issues. Some advocated the repeal of the constitution and universal suffrage. Foreign policy was also a low priority issue. Ascriptive considerations played a role especially of biradries. In Hyderabad two pirs, a qazi and a mir were chief contenders. D. I. Khan division saw the 'nawab's descendants' locked in the struggle. In Quetta and Kalt tribal affiliations played a dominant role. In Lahore biradries held the balance of power. Sindh and East Pakistan were an exception to this pattern. Basic Democracy was based on the feudal biradries of the village system and were not composed of the middle classes that he wanted should emerge in Pakistan. Instead out of the total of 156 Assembly members 136 that were elected under the Constitution belonged to the landlord class, the lawyers and businessmen. Those who were elected did not show respect to their fellow basic democrats and they were in a slight minority in the National Assembly. Electors showed no aversion for leaders of past regimes. Landlords, lawyers and businessmen were in a majority of those elected. They were 136 out of 156 Assembly members.[184] The premise on which the new leadership was built was the principle of leadership on the basis of merit. But soon it was replaced by leadership through organisation and the idea of party was introduced. In this Bhutto had a role to play.

The pattern failed for a simple reason that the new edifice was like a column based on a single column of bureaucrats supported by the armed forces.[185] Even the column of basic democracy did not deliver the goods of manufacturing consent. He started ruling through ordinances. These were related to banning of political parties. The first ordinance allowed the President to disqualify fronts or groups or parties to express opinion. The revolution of civilianizing the regime did not alter the following aspects of his military rule. His construct of the strong centre that controlled the legislatures; his dependence on the military; local bodies were not emancipated from bureaucratic controls. These were the weaknesses of the guided democracy that Ayub had tried out. We know that by the end of his tenure he did not achieve any political institutionalisation.[186] When the transfer of power took place it was unconstitutional. When the time came for transfer of power it was unconstitutional since Indo-Pak war had eclipsed Ayub's image. To quote K. M. Arif,

"The Indo-Pakistan war of 1965 eclipsed President Ayub Khan's political image".

Commenting on transfer of power from Ayub to Yahya he said,

" It was relevant to note that their bilateral deal was both unconstitutional and undemocratic."[187]

Zia-ul Haq attempted to gain civilian legitimacy. It was also a failure. Like Ayub Khan he went in for a referendum. Like Ayub Khan he tailored the Constitution. The Bhutto constitution made in 1973 was amended by Zia to dilute the role of the Prime Minister and his cabinet and give more powers to the President by amending Article 53(a). He continued as Army Chief. Elections were held to the local bodies. Strictly regulated nonparty elections were conducted. The coopted civilian leaders were installed in March 1985 but martial law was not lifted till December.[188]

Commenting on the referendum and the exercise in gaining legitimacy Craig Baxter says that this strategy totally failed. On the referendum Craig Baxter says,

"The principal element in the failure of referenda to confer legitimacy on either Ayub or Zia-ul-Haq is the absence on the ballot of any alternative to the person or programme of the ruler asking for confirmation. What would have happened had the voters recorded a resounding negative vote in the referendum in December, assuming such a result would have been announced? Possibly Zia would have resigned, but another military officer probably would have replaced Zia and reversed any of the minimal political gains that Zia had granted up to that point. Zia has taken the favourable vote as a mandate for his own presidency for a new period of five years. This, too, is unwarranted conclusion and could be upset if the new national legislative body is permitted to function as a parliamentary group which can actually exercise powers to amend the constitution."[189]

Further he points out that the issue of centralisation of power by amending the constitution has taken the political system of Pakistan to the Viceregal stage. Zia had further created the National Security Council that would have played an extra constitutional role. Baxter predicted then that one of the scenarios of the Zia period would be a civilian facade with an active military role. This has happened subsequently with the Junejo Government. That government was finally dismissed by him in 1988 before his death in the aircrash.

After a decade long authoritarian civilian rule Pakistan returned to the rule of Pervez Musharraf. He followed the model of both Ayub and Zia. Kukreja says of his approach that he is more inclined towards Zia than Ayub. She says

"He opted for institutionalised technocratic politics, building on the models of both Ayub and Zia.

"General Musharraf has announced plans to set up a two tier system to run the country—a National Security Council comprising of the armed forces' chiefs and civilian members of the government which are to work as a supreme administrative body, assisted by a group of advisors to help in running the country's day to day affairs."[190]

The course of Musharraf's process of civilianisation of his rule was to first discard the earlier civilian leadership either as inefficient or as with malafide intentions of murder, conspiracy, corruption and subversion. Second to instal himself in the power structure as the President, without relinquishing his military office, he held a referendum. Third, he held controlled elections first to the local bodies. Then he held partyless elections. Fourth, he held the Assembly elections on partyless basis to choose

Jamali's Government by seeking support from the conservative *Ulema* through an ingenious system of qualification of a bachelor's degree hoping that in case they disobeyed he could get them challenged in the courts since they were holding fake B.A. degrees. He sacked sixteen judges who refused to take oath swering allegiance to the military regime.The courts already have a precedence of the earlier decision to support the military regimes on the doctrine of 'historical neccesity'. Court justified that take over. He bargained with Nawaz Sharief and agreed to his exile on the assurance that nobody of his family will be active in politics. He announced local bodies elections by 2000. The questions of the referendum were so cleverly worded that there was no possibility of any one saying no. [191] This was the same tactic as followed by both Ayub and Zia. He combines in his person the posts of the President and Army Chief and the opposition wants him to give up any one of them. He has further integrated the National Security Council in the decision making structure which the other military rulers had not done. For this he had announced the Legal Framework Order, a tactic that Yahya Khan had followed successfully to retain power in his own hands.

This survey of the attempts on the part of military rulers to seek legitimacy through the electoral process suggests that the authoritarian political system have patently failed despite the civilisation. This is true of the civilian leaders as well since both leaderships can be viewed as authoritarian. Arif says on this authoritarian nature of the existing alternatives,

"The military dictators were not the sole spoilers of the democratic order. Many elected leaders in the country were in fact democratic in name but autocratic in their conduct and behaviour."[192]

The fact that Pakistan have developed a tension within the power structure manned by cousins, namely, military backed authoritarian-civilians and domineering military authoritarians who form the backbone of the system is no surprise. At another level both kinds of regimes find it difficult to deal with the tension between regimes and fledgling political parties which are by and large of the conservative variety except for a short interlude of Bhutto's populism that also slumped to conservatism. There is, thirdly, nothing in the electoral system to give any hope of democracy.

Economic System: *Peripheral Economy*

Pakistan has had two distinct phases in its economic history. It has predominantly been a foreign aid based economy with economic growth as a watch word, and, for a short interlude of 1972-75, during a longer Bhutto phase, has had focus on strengthening the State sector and social development. During the initial strategy called Mehboob-ul Haq and Gustav Papanek strategy laissez fairie was followed.[193] The alternative to this free market approach, or laissez fairie economics was Bhutto's nationalisation policies with considerations for the social sector. Burki praised these policies of economic liberalism while Hamza Alavi criticised these as part of peripheral capitalism. Burki praised the economy with having four positive aspects, namely competent civil service that Pakistan inherited from the British period. This service performed well in the river water disputes between India and Pakistan, according to him. It helped in resettling the refugees. It managed natural disasters like floods and crop failures in that period. It, however, failed to evolve a social consensus on policy planning. Second advantage was the continuation of the private sector economy and not to build a public sector or planning that India did. The third strength mentioned by him is the fact that government allowed private sector to operate in the whole economy, i.e., a small group of farmers and businessmen. It is of course disputed whether the economy had the advantage of capitalist farmers as claimed by Burki. The fourth advantage that he talks about is the economys openness with the foreign economies.[194]

We must in the beginning note that the reformed Mahbub--ul Haq now takes the position that the economy that he preached earlier neglected the human development index. Second, that the economic reforms that Burki praises even for 2000 in the direction of privatisation and liberalisation are a continuation of an economy that perpetuated dependent feudal-capitalism in the service of both the US and the Pakistan military. This therefore is the backdrop to the contemporary sources of Pakistani militarism apart from other factors of geostrategy. The economic policy of Ayub was carried forward by Yahya Khan, Zia did not tinker with it except in the area where Bhutto had tried to change it by nationalizing industry and introducing genuine land reforms in his early phase. Benazir Bhutto remained a conservative leader. Nawaz Sharief behaved like a modern businessman and opted for mounting debts from western lending agencies. Musharraf, like Zia, had a windfall by Pakistan again becoming a Frontline State and getting economic and military aid as it began in 1954. The first US aid package was announced in 1954. All the civilian and military leaders of Pakistan have allowed the defence budget to spiral. So, the defence budget, the comprador economy with feudal lineages within the peripheral imperative, and the corporate character of the military penetration in the economy with its four foundations and social welfare schemes are the roots of militarism and authoritarian civilian governments of the Pakistani State.

The economic phases of Pakistan's history are subdivided as (a) 1949 when the focus was on private sector and the market; (b) 1958 begins with the Ayub period and is identified with private sector and economic management; (c) 1972 is related to the Bhutto period where public sector and state economic management was added; (d) Zia period when the economic system was not disturbed. Only denationalisation was done. Bhutto's nationalisation was reversed and private business was asked to come forward; finally (e) 1992 which marks the period of liberalisation.[195]

During the Ayub period William Rushbrook tells us that the economy was on the upswing. The infrastructure was restored by setting up development Board, Planning Commission as part of Colombo Plan, and his priorities were agriculture, transport, commerce, industry and mining, fuel and power, and social uplift schemes. His period witnessed improvement in the exports of basic commodities, like cotton, jute, wool, hides and tea. Jute and cotton mills multiplied. Export oriented economy also meant the need to start mills for processed goods. These were ready-made garments, serges, knitting yarns, cotton goods, domestic hardware, furniture and spare goods. This further led to the light industry around Lahore, Rawalpindi Peshawar roads and Karachi lead in pharmaceuticals and plastic. Small scale industry developed in carpets, printing ink, leather goods, home handicrafts, soap, boot polish, paints and varnish, rubber boots, shoes, cycles tyres and tubes. Ford Foundation gave technical expertise and the West gave capital. Ayub's ministers praised him as creating conditions where the balance of payments was favourable, arresting inflation, encouraging exports, and conserving resources.[196] This miracle was not because of any process of primitive accumulation even though Burki thinks that Ayub's Green Revolution did create a class of capitalist farmers. The reason for this position is that the land reforms commission suggested a land ceiling of 500 acres of irrigated lands and 1000 acres of non irrigated lands. It was an individual ceiling and not family ceiling and so the ceiling reform did not touch the landlords and the biradries. Peasant proprietorship did not develop. Since internal resource mobilisation could not take place the economic development was on the basis of foreign capital and the economy developed in accordance with that requirement.

The land reforms that were introduced by Bhutto also did not lead to structural transformation and to internal resource mobilisation. The latter part of his rule alienated landlord and businessman, radical and conservative. During his period economic performance was not good. In contrast the performance of Ayub and Zia's regime was better in all the sectors, e.g., in agriculture, manufacturing and exports. On the Zia period John Adams says,

"Zia's luck was good on the economic front after 1977. Remittances expanded, and aid continued to flow in, rendering the balance-of-payments gap manageable. The weather was good, and pests were absent. Some serious attention to input prices and input availability created favourable conditions for farmers. Pakistan became self-sufficient in food and has recently exported wheat to Iran. Even a sluggish international economy did not deter Pakistan's exports. Agricultural and small-scale exports rose rapidly."[197]

But by 1984 the GDP fell to 4.5 per cent from 6% in 1982-83. Agricultural output fell by 4.6 per cent. Cotton crop suffered the most. By 1984 the ambitious sixth five-year plan was scaled down. The Islamisation of the economy was another negative aspect. Further he was able to focus on both the interest groups and mass demands better than Ayub could.

The time Musharraf came to power the problems of Pakistan were that the economy was in a mess, poverty was extreme and there was mounting debt burden.[198] We noted above the dimensions of this situation and the windfall that Musharraf has had owing to the recent war on terror. Iftikhar H. Malik spells them out thus,

"Pakistan's economy throughout the 1990s suffered from a handful of significant distortions that should have been redressed many years before. First, the tax base remained meagre, consisting of approximately half a million of people out of a population of 140 million. Second, most budgetary allocations were devoted to such nondevelopment sectors as debt servicing, defense, and administration costs, leaving almost nothing for development. Third, the country was slow to introduce structural reforms and overhaul its financial system to make it transparent. Finally, the country had massive external debt; at 32.5 billion, it accounted for 61.33 per cent of the gross domestic product (GDP)".[199]

Economic Bases of Militarism: Priority of Internal and External Security Concerns and Military's Corporate Interests

We noticed above that the Pakistan militarism is embedded in the structural imperative of peripheral capitalist economy and its pre-modern lineages. Its economy's structural internal roots are the failure of the civilian and military regimes to carry out structural reforms in agriculture. Secondly, the bureaucracy that came to occupy levers of power at independence and later in company with the military bureaucracy as a junior partner did not allow for the growth of an independent role of the business class. The expansion of the manufacturing sector dependent on State initiatives remained ineffectual to unite with the business class to influence the formation of a viable business class and develop its independent role. Thirdly, the educational system languished badly, remained enmeshed in poor quality and suffered from Pakistan Studies which were a product of Zia's right wing Islamisation programme for it did not promote criticality, creativity and change as values of thinking. In place of this attitude to change, archaic social and economic ideas, as enshrined in the Shariat laws against women, modern economy and modern values of social equality and social science research proliferated.[200] Absence of determinant old and new petty bourgeoisie, i.e., the shopkeeper and the professional, independent of the military family conditions, account for the growth of militarism. The existence of a middle class, as we notice in case of India is no guarantee of revolutionary change. It can be split into revolutionary and reactionary wing. But if it is accompanied by a viable business class it can align with the liberal and democratic reform project as did the Congress, while the Muslim League failed to do.

Political economy of defence proliferated owing to the predominant control that the military exercised over the regime types. In fact the whole of the State structure increasingly came under its sway. Not only matters of defence and foreign policy but its economy and social relations. This is the reason for what Ayesha Jayal calls political economy of defence euphemistically. She says,

"Pakistan's military has been able to translate its dominance over the state structure to become deeply entrenched in the political economy. Military regimes in Pakistan have rewarded senior officers in the defence establishment with top positions in the state structure as well as semi-government and autonomous organisations. In addition, Pakistan's military dominated state has its each step awarded its principal constituents with land grants, defence contracts, permits, licenses and ambassadorial appointments."[201]

The military has direct interest in Government's economic and industrial policy. Army has intervened in political conflicts among political parties, among politicians, among provinces, in situations of turmoil since that hurts the Army most. The obverse of it is that it does not allow any civilian authority to interfere with issues of importance to the military- like those of democracy, civil-military relations and interests of defence personnel is correct as well. The right wing Zia regime increased the influence of the military in the decision making in a more consistent and extensive manner than ever before. The army officers, in and out of service were inducted into key civilian posts in government, semi-government and autonomous institutions. Those officers who were Brigadiers and above were posted as secretaries in the federal and provincial offices or were made high officials in corporations and government bodies and paid handsome salaries. They came to occupy positions in higher central Superior Services on a regular basis. The most common groups selected for their induction included the district management group (formerly CSP), Foreign Service and Police Service.

The military regime not only rewarded the officers with foreign postings but also alloted agricultural land to officers of armed forces under various schemes, i.e., border areas, gallantry, military welfare and ghori pal.The Punjab Government allotted about 450,000 acres of land to 5,538 military personnel during 1977-85. Similarly agricultural land was allotted to service personnel in other provinces, especially in Sindh. The budgetary allocations also have marked a steady rise. Rizvi notes the rise of budgetary allocations during Zia regimes and says that its rate of increase "was higher than that of the Bhutto period."[202]

So entrenched were the interests of the military that the civilian governments after Zia's could not interfere with their interests in the polity. During her first government Benazir Bhutto soured her relations with the military over a number of issues, viz. she did not want the officers discharged in the wake of Bhutto's assassination to be punished, officers did not like her interference in military and organisational matters. She made an unsuccessful attempt to retire Admiral Iftikhar Ahmad Sirohi, Chairman of Joint Chief's of Staff Committee, in 1989. The Government was not allowed to interfere with the retirement and extension of the military officers in June-July 1990. During her second Prime Ministership the Sindh imbroglio created strains in the relations between the government and the army. During the period of Nawaz Sharief government, General Janjua pointed in a corps commanders' meeting that the government tried to corrupt the Army.[203] Not only this, the Army under Musharraf has come to believe that democracy is through the military dictatorship.[204] We also notice that during his regime the US doled out aid to Pakistan to take it out of the economic mess that it was in. The recent rip of the US by Musharraf in 2003 has meant further economic aid. The economic largesse come to it for its relevance in the region's strategy that gets played out at intermittent intervals since the Second World War ended.

Political Revolt: *Provinces and the People*

The literature on political revolt suggests that people revolt either out of a feeling of crunch or a feeling of poverty. Crane Brinton takes the position that the English and the French Revolutions, and, the US War of Independence took place since the ancien regimes were poor. The new societal forces felt a feeling of crunch. They felt the ancient regime to be anachronistic.[205] Allied to this thesis is the Weberian view that it is values that bring about revolutions.[206] The adverse comparison of the internal with the external factors, and, the emergence of the local insurgent elite groups was responsible for revolutions. This is the position of Theda Scokpol.[207] Eric Wolf theorises that in the twentieth century the peasants revolted owing to their dislocation caused by the spread of the market forces and commercialisation.[208] The peasant revolt was successful for him as well as for Hamza Alavi owing to the independence of the middle peasant.[209] A variation of the thesis of Brinton and Weberian argument is that it is relative deprivation that is reponsible for rebellion.[210] The theory of relative deprivation is based on the psychologists view that frustration leads to aggression. In contrast to this tradition of theorisation is the Marxist theorisation that it is the absolutely poor, the proletariat that revolts with the help of the peasantry and the middle classes.[211] The Mao strategy focusses on the role of the peasantry and especially its poor sections.[212] Chalmer Johnson underlines the nationalist aspirations of the peasants in the case of China.[213] It is therefore possible to suggest that revolts are possible either as a result of single class or multiclass composition and orientation lead by either the poor or the rich. The revolt could take the form of nationalist or the social cause. Most of the colonial countries experienced the multi-class compositions and single-class orientations either of the rich or the poor.

In the provinces of Pakistan we notice that the revolts are multi-class as evidenced by the revolt in East Pakistan. It has also taken the shape of Sindhi, Baluch or Pakhtun nationalism against the Punjabi dominance. Within Punjab it has taken the shape of sectarian conflict against the Ahmediyas or there were differences among the east and west Punjabis. Sectarian strife has taken place among the various provinces as well. The Mohajir-Sindhi conflict, the conflicts involving the Pathan and the Mohajir, and the Sindhi in Sindh are notorious for their irrestible ferocity and persistence. The ferocity of the Baluch and Pakhtun nationalism was invited the use of the military and the launching of conspiracy cases by the State under Zulfiqar Ali Bhutto. In 2003 Baloch unrest is reported again.

The revolt in the provinces was linked to the very manner of the creation of Pakistan, the administrative measures taken thereafter and the compulsions of politics. The Two Nation Theory, propounded by Jinnah, was faulty since India had gone through the processes of composite culture. Instead of religion linguistic identity was a major issue. By the early 20th century Congress had to take note of the demand for linguistic recognition and not for religious division. The latter demand picked up gradual momentum in the wake of the British Reform Acts and Jinnah's response to constitutional reforms, especially by 1940. The two problems plagued Bengal since 1905 when it was partitioned by Lord Curzon and in response to the Congress extremist propaganda was annulled in 1911.

East Pakistan: *Centrifugal Tendencies*

The bringing of East Bengal into West Pakistan was unnatural on many counts. First, Pakistan became a State with non-contigous territory. Second, East Pakistan had Hindu landlords unlike the Western Muslim landlords. Third the base of Muslim League was among the peasants in East Pakistan and not among the landlords as in West Pakistan. The character of the Muslim League was therefore different and more radical in the East than it was in the West. In the East and West Muslim League could not increase its influence without the help of other parties: Sikandar Hayat-Jinnah Pact and not even after the death of the leaders of the Unionist Party could it form a ministry. In East Bengal also the Muslim League had to seek an adjustment with the Krishak Praja Party.

Bengali nationalism was matured in comparison to such sentiments in other provinces of Pakistan. The Muslim League had its first session in Dhaka in 1906. In the Objectives Resolution much later the demand for sovereignty and autonomy for provinces was made. Hussain Suhrawardy said,

"Each of the provinces in the Muslim majority areas should be given the right to choose its future Constitution or enter into a commonwealth with a neighbouring province or provinces."[214]

This desire for autonomy of the provinces, the fact that East Pakistan was more numerous than the western part, and, that the eastern part was linguistically more homogenous than the western went against the idea of one State. One of the leaders of

Bengal, Abul Hashim, had contested the idea of one state at the Delhi convention in 1946.[215] During Jinnah's time the language issue raised its head and Jinnah's visit to Dhaka pushed the matter under the carpet but only temporarily. Jinnah had announced in Dhaka that Urdu was to be the language of Pakistan. Not only did this reverberate opposition later on the language issue in Bengal, but also in Sindh, Balochistan, NWFP and among the Punjabis and Sirakis. As we have noted above it became the language of power and elites and not of the peoples of Pakistan. Again in 1952 in the wake of the speech of another Bengali but pro-Pakistani leader, Nazimmudin, there was disturbance in Bengal. By 1954, Bogra announced that the Bengali language would be provincial language along with Urdu but it was too late. Macgrath says

"Language is an emotional issue which cut across class lines and mobilised a broad base of the population. Language issues had served to separate Hindus and Muslims in pre-independence days. After independence, this issue served to separate, with the same degree of virulence, the Bengalis and those from the provinces of West Pakistan."

The issue of incorporation of the Hindu population of the province and the powers of the province in any constitutional set up were issues that were debated during the initial period of Pakistan's history in Bengal. After the Objectives Resolution and the Interim Report were introduced.[216] East Pakistan opposed it. Liaquat Ali had to withdraw the Report. The objection of the Bengalis were to the keeping of the single language as also to bi-cameral legislature that would have given them only one place despite their numerical superiority and since the Houses will have an equal say it would give to the West an unequal importance. In Dhaka the *Dawn* described the Report as a 'shameless conspiracy' and a 'fatal stab'. Maulana Bhashani went to the extent of raising the idea of Bengal becoming the colony of West Pakistan.[217] East Bengal opposed the Constitution of 1954.

West Pakistan and the East Pakistan had economic disparity with possibility of growth more in the West. As always East felt itself to be ill-treated. In the First Five Year Plan it got only Rs. 171 against 720 to the West in non-developmental funds. For developmental funds it had 100 as against 400 crores of the West. This inequality of treatment remained in the second, the third and fourth plans till 1970 as well. The aid from abroad was similarly disproportionately distributed. The effects of inter-regional and international trade were to the disadvantage of the Bengalis. These contributed to the transfer of resources to the East. The East Pakistanis kept demanding decentralisation of economic control and removal of disparity and the Ayub measures were too inadequate and too late. The PIDC was bifurcated along provincial lines and more resources were allocated. Bengalis had a meagre representation in the Army and the Bureaucracy and it is well known that Ayub had a distrust of their military prowess as much as those of the Hindus.[218]

As far as the three elites of Pakistan are concerned, viz, political, bureaucratic and military the initial Bengali equality during 1947-58[219] gave way to decrease in the role of the Bengali effectiveness in decision making. In the subsequent decades the situation reversed. Callard says of how this happened "Whether through Bengali ineffectiveness or the Machiavellian methods, wiles of their opponents (West Pakistanis) Bengali influence had never been decisive."[220]

The three leaders that came to dominate politics in Pakistan were laid back drunkYahya Khan, wily Bhutto and mobster Mujib.[221] It is Mujib who won hands down in the last elections. It is Bhutto who wanted to prevent him from becoming the Prime Minister despite the fact that he was the leader of the largest party. It was Yahya Khan who had conducted the freest elections till date. The three were unable to contain the centrifugal tendencies in Pakistan. This led to the break up, despite the Pakistani Army's intervention, to its defeat and surrender to the Indian Army at Dhaka, cashed in by Bhutto, as he had done at the time of the Tashkent summit against Ayub and now against Yahya.

Sindh: *Restive Cauldron*

Mohajir, Sindh, Pakhtun and Siraik politics make for uneasy mix of provincial matrix and mayhem uncontrollable by the Army. The souring of relations between Mohajirs and Sindhis by 1975 were caused by three factors. First, was the political role of the bureaucrats. Second, a feeling of frustration among the people of Sindh caused by the inefficient operation of the One Unit system. Third, an "unfair role played by some public officials, political leaders as well as others, Mohajirs and Sindhis."[222] The beginnings of the Sindh-Mohajir conflict can be traced to the demand for Urdu as a State language made by the Mohajirs. The second reason was that the Ayub regime feared that the urban Mohajirs may not vote for him in Basic Democracy in the Urban areas.[223] G.M. Sayed, the father of Sindhi nationalism, and a pir himself, said that Zia's Punjabis dominated over the Sindhis.[224] The Bhutto regime had raised hopes of the Sindhis owing to his being a Sindhi wadera. His rule had disillusioned them since it brought nothing to their aspirations. In fact the radical Sindhi youth got disillusioned first owing to his compromises with the landed classes. Benazir Bhutto's regimes did not do anything for them either.

Sindhi nationalism has its own causes in political economy, clevages of the society and political alienation.[225] Its complications began with the arrival of the refugees from India—both from Gujarat and the United Provinces. These were better off sections of society and brought with it technical expertise and business acumen. The Mohajirs demanded Urdu to be the national language. This led to festering of language wound in Sindh. Since Urdu was adopted they found themselves disadvantaged among, what Hamza Alavi called, the salariat. In the decades after the 60s the Sindhis were faced with another wave of influx from the North-West that led to ethnic turmoil owing to the conflicts among the Mohajirs and Pakhtuns, and, Pakhtuns and Sindhis. During Zia's regime the Mohajirs had also become a deprived community. His foreign policy had led to the Kalashnikov-drug culture. In Sindh the culture of Kalashnikov combined with ethnic strife took a very violent turn. Business of transport had also come under the influence of the Pakhtuns. Even a small accident in a mini bus plying on the roads lead to communal mayhem. By the 1980s the incursion of the Punjabis in the lands connected with the Sukkur Barrage complicated the situation. The politics around scarcity led to dacoity. Lamb describes this thus,

"In a corrupt society where so many have to struggle just to stay alive, dacoity with its rich pickings becomes understandable. When dacoits first progressed from stealing animals to abducting people, they restricted themselves to highway robberies. The first reported kidnapping was in 1979.The victim was the son of Rafi Kachelo, a supporter of Bhutto. As arms flooded in from the war in Afghanistan, kidnappings became more common."[226]

During the period of Zia the Mohajir Quami Movement (MQM) of Altaf Hussain made a beginning in 1984 as a result of the official policies. The Mohajirs had supported the Muslim League after the partition. After the latter's decline they supported the Islamist parties. They kept their distance from the PPP but were near the PNA. During Zia's regime the alliance broke down because of Zia's attempt to Punjabise and Islamise the political system. It performed well in local elections in Karachi and Hyderabad in 1985 and 1987. Its failure to make a mark at the provincial and national level has led it to adopt a strategy of alliances with either the PPP or the PML. In 1988 provincial elections it won 26 out of 100 seats. It formed the government under an independent dispensation. It could not retain its alliance with the PPP for national elections since the latter did not keep the promise agreed to. In 1990 it supported the IJI and went close to Nawaz Sharief. It boycotted the national elections and gained 27 seats in the provincial assembly. In 1997 elections it won 28 seats out of 108 seats.

The weakness of the MQM is that it has not been able to penetrate the rural scene and so cannot form a government on its own. Power sharing with other parties has not worked. The dynamics of the Sindhi and *Mohajir* conflict is that it's rising aspirations have pitted against the established ethnic nationality of the Sindhis. It has also drawn the Punjabis into the conflict and so complicated the picture.[227] The MQM has followed both legal and extra legal methods and have been called by the pejorative term terrorist/fascist. In 1992 its changed it name to Muttahida Quami Movement from its original Mohajir Quami Movement. Despite its weaknesses of leadership and its style there is no denying the fact that it is popular among the lower middle class and middle class youth. The *Mohajirs* have demanded compensation from the government for the loss of lives as a result of the military operations against them. The amount is to the tune of 60 billion rupees. Musharraf, himself a *mohajir,* has to show up his strategy of dealing with the ethnic conflict in Sindh. The conflict has not yet acquired secessionist tones. If it does there would be a question mark on the future of Pakistan, according to Rajat Ganguly.[225] There is no doubt that in order to solve the problem of Sindhi nationalism, decentralisation, accountability and distributive justice should inform the political system. In the wake of the MQM making a political headway Malik says Mohajir homeland is not possible even though Sindh will remain a 'Beirut' and MQM movement will not be able to attract other ethnic groups.

"Its continued territorial and electoral confinement and narrow franchise, besides its occasional lapses into highhandedness, would only add to its contradictions."[229]

There is no denying the fact that the MQM is a significant force to reckon with. If it becomes a province level force it might make or break governments. If it is able to develop a pan- Pakistan existence it could pose serious possibilities to Pakistan's continued existence in its present form. There is no denying the fact though while there is plurality in Pakistan there is no pluralist society or democracy since Pakistan is a segmented society. A mass political movement on values of modernity might ignite the spark of uniting the various segments and elites.

Punjab: *Leviathan's Core has Seraiki Demand*

Punjab, despite the numerical strength of the Muslims from United Provinces, has been the backbone of the Pakistani State in terms of its ruling classes, political, bureaucratic elites, military officer corps, its salariat, political system and its sectarian conflicts. It has dominated the political system and made and unmade leaders in and out of office. Ghulam Mohammed, Mamdoot, Daultana helped in subverting the Constitution that was framed by 1954. It is in Punjab that the strife against the Ahmediyas took place and this provided the military to establish its military rule even before Ayub regime was established. Zia-ul Haq gave to Pakistan a taste of conservative Punjabi's Islam. Nawaz Sharief's role in Punjabi and Pakistani politics has resulted in his permanent exile. In Punjab the single unit scheme was thought about and implemented. This moved against the State of Pakistan. It is Zia's attempt to Punjabise the Sindh after the Sukkur barrage that complicated the ethnic situation in Punjab. It is in Punjab that the land legislations floundered. It is against the Punjabi domination that Bengal revolted. The ideology of Islam and the idea of making Urdu to be the national language has played havoc. It is Punjab's lineage and linkages that militarism in Punjab breathes. Waver says of this ethnic dominance.

"The Pakistan Army was always, and remains Punjabi dominated: periods of military rule have generally seen a growth of Punjabi influence. Although there are no official figures, it is estimated that 65 per cent of officers and 70 per cent of other ranks are Punjabis. That compares with the province's 56 per cent share of population. Pukhtoons from the NWFP, with 16 per cent of the population, constitute a 22 per cent of officers and 25 per cent of other ranks. The Mohajirs have generally been over represented in the officers' corps and underrepresented in the lower ranks. Despite somewhat half hearted to correct these imbalances, the Sindhis and the Baloch have severely been under represented."[230]

Under Ayub the Punjabis gained at the cost of the Mohajirs to such an extent that most Mohajirs voted against Ayub in the 1965 presidential elections. Zia-ul Haq, the devout Punjabi, has provided one of the most right wing regimes to Pakistan. During his tenure the Punjabis entered Sindh in millions to habitate the lands near the Sukkur barrage. His Islamisation of the Pakistani society is more a response to the right wing Jamait and not perhaps to the Punjabi ethos since Punjab has had the tradition of the *pirs* and not *Ulemas*. In this it is more like Sindh. But being the backbone of the military and its regimes it must share in the responsibility of the conservative Islamist ideology that Zia imposed on Pakistan and changed the political idiom of political discourse. Waseem divides Zia's Islamisation programme into three categories, viz. punitive (the Hadood Ordinance), reconstruction of the economic system ('zakat' and 'ushr') and general Islamisation of the morals, education, and science (Islamic theory of knowledge) in its most conservative form.[231] That this is qualitatively different from the other attempts to Islamise is noted. Very early Maulana Mahdudi had attempted to talk about Islamic State. The early leaders recognised Islam but not a theocracy as is evident by both the enumeration of the Objectives Resolution and the arrest of Mahdudi in the context of anti-Ahmediya riots. The Ayub Constitution did not go beyond reiterating general principles of Islam. Yahya Khan's regime was too brief for this. Bhutto's populism took him to both radical and conservative direction. The latter came closer to the demands then being made by the Islamist groups. Benazir Bhutto bought peace by wearing the 'chador'. Nawaz Sharief joined up with the IJI agitation. Musharraf's attitude towards it is ambivalent owing to the compulsions of domestic politics and requirements of being a Frontline State.

Islamic stance has been used to control sectarian divides. It has been used to contain movements in the provinces. Islamisation has been attempted to control political unrest, to seek legitimation as did Ayub and Zia, to formulate a set up of a presidential kind and a means of transition to an authoritarian government.[232] It has served as a means to identify with the rest of the Muslim world. It has been used to further goals like the 'Islamic bomb', membership of military pacts and be relevant to the US in the latter's over all strategy in the region. It has been very effectively used for Mujahedeen support against Afghanistan and for aiding organisations active in Jammu & Kashmir. Yet it has its limits. First, the early leaders of Pakistan were not religionists even though they were communalists. Second, these very leaders were not interested in creating a revivalist Islamic ideology. Third, they were not interested in sectarian conflicts. Fourth, at the time when Zia was getting his Islamic laws passed the people in Junejo's Assembly were opposing and violating them in favour of the local pirs. In the whole of Pakistan the role of pirs cannot be ignored. Let us note that Zia had to rely on Pir Pagaro for selecting Junejo as the Prime Minister. Fifth, Islam could not prevent the break up of Pakistan into two. Sixth, Islam has not been able to prevent the assertion of nationalist sentiment among various ethnic groups of Pakistan despite Army being used from time to time. Seventh, like the role of Christianity in 16th century Italy, the role of Islam in Pakistan is to prevent the emergence of a Pakistani nation. The Army's spirit of the 'ghazi' and 'jihad' and the State ideology of 'jihad' may not be sufficient in the face of a serious political revolt to produce nationalism. The Punjabi-Pakhtun dominance may not be enough to bring about a new social compact among the emerging elites in its various regions. Internally therefore the Punjabi dominance may be its Achilles' heal, especially if it is abandoned by foreign powers once it ceases to be of use to them. For example, Czar was abandoned by Western powers during the First World War. The Pakistan Siraiki Party has said that Punjab is composed of two languages, viz., Punjabi and Seraiki. It demanded that Siraiki should also be given the same status as Punjabi has in the province. Further we may also notice that though the East Punjab's population has adjusted in the West but there are differences among them, perhaps insignificant currently.

Balochistan: *Saudi Sheikhs Hunting Ground for Bustards and US' for Airfields*

Balochistan and the NWFP have been a thorn for the Pakistani State. Despite their desires for independence preceding the creation of Pakistan the Baloch nationalist cause for autonomy/independence, despite its radicalisation through Patrice Lumumba University, has been suppressed by the massive use of military force by the Pakistani State. The last to do so was Bhutto. The revolt started with the Baloch objection to the One Unit scheme in 1958. It was possible for the Pakistani State to defeat Baluchistan since the Baloch never could gain international support, they were internally divided on political, ethnic and ideological grounds. Baluchis, even now under Musharraf's Pakistan, complain of Punjabi colonisation since they supply Pakistan's sixty per cent needs of gas. Akber Bugti has been coopted through a fleet of Toyotas. But other leaders are contnuing to fight.[233]

Balochistan was in the eye of the storm by 2001. Three of the four air bases that Musharraf offered to the US are in Balochistan—in Pasna, Shamsi, and Dalibandin. It is alleged that a few thousand Al Qaeda agents have slipped through Balochistan. Balochistan sits astride the oil lanes of the Gulf. Squeezed into the triangle where Pakistan, Iran and Afghanistan meet, it is geopolitically and strategically the most important part of Pakistan. Baloch's onyx and marble were shipped to Karachi for finishing, and its natural gas was piped to industrial belts in the Punjab and the Sindh, returning in cylinders to Balochistan. In Turbat which is the centre of the Makran coast black money prospered. Drugs and Kalashnikovs proliferated.[234] The US and China is busy developing the Makran coast. The former is building roads. Balochistan could become another Beirut or Afghanistan. Qataris and Saudis came for hunting the houbara bustard. No Pakistani law operates here since the Saudis are financiers of Pakistan's sectarian missions and its attempt to spread Wahhabi fanaticism. The Arabs eat the houbara for sexual prowess. Though this does not happen.

Pakhtoons: *Moderate and Unspectacular*

Abdul Ghaffar Khan is the symbol of Pakhtun pride and desire of independence. The demand for 'Pakhtoonkhwa' was made very early. It includes areas of Balochistan and Afghanistan that had Pakhtun population. Greater Afghanistan was called for by every government of Afghanistan. Jinnah failed to kill the demand.Pakistan imprisoned Abdul Ghafar Khan. After 1979 the Pakhtoon demand diminished. Under Wali Khan the movement has been mute and not spectacular. The Pakhtoons are an active community in Karachi and send remmittances and have developed a direct interest in the continuation of the Pakistani State.[235]

Peoples Revolt: *Wretched of the Earth*

The peoples of the territories that compose Pakistan have stagnated for too long. They were first part of the colonial imperative and then peripheral imperative. The colonial imperative meant that they lost their own world without gaining a new world. A new economic structure attached to colonial exploitation was introduced that did not benefit the ordinary man or even the elites. No new elites came into existence. They suffered this strange tragedy that people of Hindustan had suffered under the British colonial rule, as had been noted by Marx. This is one region where peasants had not revolted. Barrington Moore said that the peasants of India did not revolt owing to the ideology of Gandhi.[236] Kathleen Gough took the position that the Indian peasants did revolt. If they did not it was owing to the British policies or post-colonial state rather than to the village structure. She said,

"I would argue that the limitations of the peasant revolts have sprung more from broader province and the colonial and post-colonial state than from the caste system or from peculiarities of village structure."[237]

Bengal, Bihar, UP, Gujarat, Andhra and some parts of Punjab witnessed revolts by the peasants on partial demands in India. There were Wahabi and Farazi[238] and Santhal and Moplah rebellions. The princely states of India or Indian India did not witness either a peasant revolt or a nationalist revolt. There was no Gandhian ideology present here. It was also not a case of passive revolution.

The British rule had seen to it that the peoples of the regions composing Pakistan did not revolt by creating a social support base. The Muslim League had no base in any of the provinces that formed Pakistan and had to rely on the local parties. There was no mass movement for Pakistan apart from the mobilisation strategy involved in the Pakistan resolution. Even this did not create a mass movement in a province like Punjab. In fact, it is the changed policies of the British that created a base for the Muslim League. Jinnah's communal stature, the dynamics of constitutional reform and the British interests that created Pakistan. This artefact started its journey with the support of the landed elites, bureaucracy and the military in the context of partition and surrounding security considerations. The Leviathan of this artefact has not been able to hammer out a popular compact for its governance. As a result there have been either simple crime on the rise (lumpen form of revolt against poverty in urban centres) or robbery as part of political culture or creation of terrorist groups as part of Islamic ideology or outright corruption as an instrument to rob the public exchequer. We also noticed the spread of drug and Kalashnikov culture after 1979. The conflicts among the elites are known for their intrigues. (in the 1950s, attempts of the military regimes to tame civilian puppets; 1980s and 2002, the junior position of the Prime Minister in the troika of power that came to exist by the 1990s) and the decade long struggle among the three offices of the President, Prime Minister and the Army Chief, causing immense damage to the polity's economy and political process. Authoritarian State has not helped in solving the issues of personal security of the common people-girl child, education, women, health for the poor despite the fact that during Zia's period rich opened hospitals but for the elites.[239] This has given hope for the emergence of the civil society, as we noted above.

The autonomy of the State is brought out by the fact that in every crisis it is able to retain the traditional power structure and to that extent the voice of the people is weak or manipulated. The various military regimes have been able to come to power by destabilising civilian regimes and the people have not revolted against the change. The obverse is also true. The people have revolted against the military regimes as well. It is well known that right wing protests have been made recently against Musharraf's policy of banning fundamentalist outfits. This is only the culmination of the process of revolt in the Pakistani polity. The revolt against the Ayub regime is well known. Then there was the revolt against the Yahya regime. The Zia regime's life line was cut short by his undue departure in the air accident, the real reasons may also show up its anti-Zia aspects. The Zia regime had problems with Sindh. Its Islamisation had opposition from the various sects and peers. His Afghan policy gave economic dividends but at the same time led to the proliferation of the drug-Kalashnikov culture and criminalisation of public life, university campuses apart from raising the barometer of sectarian violence. The regime has successfully managed to sniff out radical voices of the likes of Faiz Ahmed Faiz and others.[240]

Counter-Elite: *Dim and Distant*

Minus the US aid and strategic support the Pakistani State has put a question mark on itself. A negative or an affirmative answer can be found out from the following considerations; health of the Army in terms of its personnel, training and Islamisation since now the new recruits at all levels belong to lower middle classes. Second, it has to be seen how far the business interests take it to a position of developing a viable economic class and a professional middle class that will develop and deepen the democratic ethos. The revolt of the people as and when it comes, through sectarian or social faultlines will cause it a basic explosion. It is in that sense that the people of Pakistan have yet to do what the people did in storming the Bastille-engage in political participation against the State's ideology of fundamentalist Islam and divide people around sectarian lines. The issue for the spark could be poverty, elimination of corruption, democratisation of state structure, liberal Islamic dispensation (Musharraf has only mutely voiced it), and end to the manipulation of the elites for a civilian or a military regime. This process is currently going on on the issue of the LFO announced by Musharraf and the attitude of the alliance of restoration of democracy. Pakistani politics has to move out of its elite chess board game. Spontaneity, with all its limitations may throw up its leaders beyond the present pale of Bhutto-Sharief parties' conservatism. The nadir of the fragile State needs peoples participation to avoid its demise. The use of Islam has not made it any stronger. A democratic Pakistan is possible once the people develop a counter elite that can deal with both the ruling elite that does not want to give up power and the people seeking change. Theda Skocpol's analysis and the analyses of transition from feudal authoritarian rules suggest this. Currently this may come through the youth, revolutionary elements of the civil society, grass roots leaderships of both the tribal and agrarian populations and the provincial leaderships. Lastly let us not ignore the Army. In case of change of circumstance when the socio-economic conditions deteriorate beyond the pale of morally defensible a section of the Army officer corps may be motivated by changing the peripheral bondage and acquisitive propensities of the military elite. The argument is borrowed from the first revolt in Czarist Russia in Battleship Potempkin. In this revolt the leadership of the revolt came from the officers belonging to Russian nobility. In Pakistan the class interests of the estates and the petty bourgeois exist in the Army. They are in harmony today. Tomorrow may be another day. A counter elite to civilianising and militarist authoritarianism is a must. Even staunch supporters of Zia, like K. M. Arif have voiced the need for democracy in Pakistan. In the present struggle between Musharraf and the MMA, it is reported that more and more former military officers are pitching in on behalf of the Opposition. This can be interpreted in two ways. One, the Opposition presented by MMA may have the Military's hidden hand.[241] Second, this may be genuine. Third, the more representative Alliance for restoration of democracy may find some sustenance if these two, representing twenty per cent of the electorate do not arrive at an agreement. Let us not forget that the MMA is represented in Pakhtunistan and Balochistan and not in other provinces. The other possibility also exists. This is that the MMA may utilise ARD for its purpose now and make it irrelevant as happened to MRD in 1985's attempt to civilianize the regime. Even earlier the military kept in touch with civilian leaders to manipulate power. Ayub's links with Ghulam Muhammad are well known. In 1970 at the time of Yahya Khan who was faced with the issue of East Pakistan and the crisis of polity, Bhutto was in link with the top military brass jockeying for power. On this Mazari says,

"Through out this period Bhutto not only remained friendly with General Peerzada but he also carefully cultivated his links with General Gul Hasan and the new Air Force Chief, Air Marshal Rahim Khan. Bhutto, Rahim Khan and Gul Hasan used to frequently meet, often at their mutual friend Iqbal Shahban's place in Islamabad, and have lengthy convivial chats over drinks. Gul Hasan and Rahim Khan were coming to the conclusion that they now understood Bhutto and would provide support to him when the opportunity later arose."[242]

References

1. Nicolas Poulantzas, *Social Classes and Political Power,* New Left Books, New York, 1973.
2. Immanuel Wallerstein, 'The Collapse of Liberalism', *New World Order, Socialist Register,* 1992, edited by Ralph Miliband, Leo Panitch, London, The Merlin Press, 1992, pp.96-110.
3. Hasan Gardezi, *Jamil Rashid, Pakistan: Roots of Dictatorship,* Clarendon, London, Zed Press, 1983; Aijaz Ahmed, *Lineagaes of the Present,* Delhi, Kulika, 1996.
4. Volker R. Berghahn, *Militarism, A History of International Debate,* Cambridge, Cambridge University Press, 1981
5. Hafeez Malik, 'Dilemmas of National Security and Cooperation', in Hafeez Malik, edited, *Dilemmas of Security and Cooperation in India and Pakistan,* St. Martin's Press, 1993. p.1.
6. Stephen Philip Cohen, 'The Nation and the State of Pakistan', *Washington Quarterly,* summer 2002.
7. Antol Lieven, The Pressures on Pakistan, *Foreign Affairs,* January/February 2002.
8. *Dawn,* 12-06-03.
9. Emma Duncan, *Breaking the Curfew, A Political Journey through Pakistan,* London, Michael Joseph, 1989. pp. 221-224
10. Siara Suleri, *Meatless Days,* Colins, London, 1990
11. Christina Lamb, *Waiting for Allah,* Viking, New Delhi, 1991.
12. Mary Anne Weaver, *Pakistan, In the Shadow of Jihad and Afghanistan,* Farrar, Strauss, & Giroux, New York, 2002, p.55.
13. *Ibid.* P.108.
14. *Ibid.* P.259.
15. *Ibid.* p. 39
16. quoted in *Dawn,* 12-06-03.
17. Anour Abdel-Malik, *Nation and Revolution,* Volume 2 of Social Dialectics, Albany, 1981.
18. Owen Bennet Jones, *Pakistan, the eye of the storm,* London, Viking, Corgi, 2001, p. 238-40; Veena Kukreja, *Contemporary Pakistan,* Delhi Sage, 2003; Veena Kukreja, *Civil Military Relations in South Asia,* Delhi, Sage, 1991.

19. Iftikhar H. Malik, *State and Civil Society in Pakistan, Politics of Authority, Ideology and Ethnicity,* in association with St. Anthony's College, Oxford, Macmillan Press Limited, 1997.
20. L. F. Rushbrook Williams, *The State of Pakistan,* London, Faber and Faber, 1966 (Revised), p.130.
21. *Ibid.,* p. 131.
22. Ian Talbot, 'The Unionist Party and Punjab Politics, 1937-47," in D. A. Low, edited, *The Political Inheritance of Pakistan,* New Delhi, London, Macmillan, 1991, p. 95.
23. Mohammad Waseem, *Politics and the State in Pakistan,* Islamabad, National Institute of Historical Research, 1994.
24. *Ibid.* P.1.
25. *Ibid.* P.67.
26. *Ibid.* P. 132.
27. *Ibid.* P. 449.
28. *Ibid.* P. 450.
29. Mohammad Waseem, 'Causes of Democratic Downslide' *Economic and Political Weekly,* November 2-9, 2002, New Delhi, p. 4538.
30. Allen Macgrath, *The Destruction of Pakistan's Democracy,* New York, Delhi, Oxford University Press, *Karachi, Oxford,* 1996, p. 218.
31. *Ibid.* p. 231.
32. William L. Richter, 'The 1990 General elections in Pakistan,' in Charles H. Kennedy, edited by, *Pakistan 1992,* Boulder, San Francisco, Oxford, Westview Review, Lahore, Islamabad, Karachi, Pakistan Book Corporation, 1993, p. 28.
33. Lawrence Ziring, 'Dilemma and Challenge in Nawaz Sharief's Pakistan' in Charles Kennedy, edited by, *Pakistan 1992,* Westview, Boulder, San Francisco, Oxford, 1993.
34. William L Richter, *op. cit.*
35. *Ibid.*
36. Lawrence Ziring, *Pakistan in the Twentieth Century, A Political History,* Oxford, 1997. pp. 550-600.
37. *Ibid.*
38. *Ibid.* p. 585.
39. Veena Kukreja, *op. cit.*
40. Owen Bennet Jones, *op. cit.* pp. 54-55.
41. Iftikhar H. Malik, *State and Civil Society in Pakistan, Politics of Authority, Ideology and Ethnicity,* Oxford, St. Anthony's college, 1997. p. 5.
42. *Ibid.* p. 8.
43. *Ibid.* p. 9.
44. *Ibid.* p. 178.

45. Mushahid Hussain and Akram Hussain, *Pakistan, Problems of Governance,* Centre for Policy Research, New Delhi, Konark Publishers, 1993, p. 55.
46. *Dawn,* 12-06-03.
47. Anita M. Weiss, "Pakistan: Some Progress, sobering challenges" in Selig Harrison, Paul H. Kriesberg and Dennis Kux, edited, *India and Pakistan, First Fifty Years,* New York, Cambridge University Press, 1999, p. 151; Anita M. Weiss, "The transformation of the women's Movement in Pakistan", in J. Henry Korson, edited by, *Contemporary Problems of Pakistan,* Boulders, San Francisco, Oxford, Westview, Islamabad, Karachi, Pak Book Corporation, Lahore, 1993, pp. 92-106.
48. Lawrence Ziring, *op. cit.,* p. 614
49. Veena Kukreja, *op. cit.,* p. 302.
50. S. Akbar Zaidi, 'Politics of Opportunism', *Economic and Political Weekly,* November 2-9, 2002, New Delhi, p. 4540.
51. S. H. Hashmi, 'Foreword', in Charles H. Kennedy, *Bureaucracy in Pakistan,* Karachi, Oxford, New York, Delhi, Oxford, 1987, p. xiii.
52. Tariq Rehman, *Language, Ideology and Power, Language Learning Among the Muslims of India and Pakistan,* Oxford, 2002, p. 47.
53. Charles Kennedy, *op. cit.,* p. 193.
54. Karl Manheim, *Ideology and Utopia,* Routledge & Kegan Paul, 1948.
55. Gunnar Myrdal, *Asian Drama,* New York, Pantheon, 1968.
56. Charles Kennedy, *op.cit.,* p. 209.
57. Mushahid Hussain and Akram Hussian, *op. cit.,* pp. 11-15.
58. Sarkar Zaidi, 'Dismal state of social sciences in Pakistan,' *Economic Political Weekly,* August 31, 2002, pp. 3644-3663.
59. Tariq Rehman, *op. cit.,* p. 60
60. Mushahid Hussain and Akram Hussian, *op. cit.,* pp. 18-20; Hasan Askari Rizvi, *Military, State and Society in Pakistan,* London, Macmillan Press Limited, 2002, p. 233.
61. Omar Noman, *The Political Economy of Pakistan,* 1947-85, London, New York, KPI, 1988, p. 21.
62. *Ibid.* p. 40
63. General K. M. Arif, *Working with Zia, Pakistan's Power Politics,* 1977-88, Oxford, 1995, pp. 250, 404, 413.
64. Shaheed Javed Burki, 'Economic policyAfter Zia-ul Haq,' in Charles H. Kennedy, edited, *Pakistan 1992,* San Francisco, Oxford, West View Press, 1993.
65. Quoted in I. N. Mukherjee, 'Economy and Democratisation in Pakistan', *World Focus,* 286-287, April-May, 2002, New Delhi, p. 26.

66. I. N. Mukherjee, *ibid.*, pp. 26-27.
67. Tariq Ali, *Can Pakistan Survive, Death of a State,* Penguin, 1983. P. 189.
68. Hamza Alavi, 'Class and State,' in Hassan Gardezi and Jamil Rashid, edited by, *Pakistan: The Roots of Dictatorship, The Political Economy of a Praetorian State*, Zed Press, London, 1983, p. 59.
69. *Ibid.*, p. 56.
70. *Ibid.*, pp.62-63.
71. *Ibid.*, p.64.
72. Peter Evans, Dietrich Reuschemeyer, Theda Skocpol, *Bringing the State Back In,* Cambridge, Cambridge University Press, 1973; Nicolas Poulantzas, *fn.1*.
73. Ralph Miliband, The State in Capitalist Society, The Analysis of The Western System of Power, London, Melbourne, NQ, Quartet Books, 1970, pp. 10-11.
74. Antonio Gramsci, *Prison Notebooks,* USA, International Publishers, USA, 1973.
75. in Margaret and Theda Skocpol, 'State and Structures and the Possibilities for "Keynesian" Responses to Great Depression in Sweden, Britain, and the United States', in *fn.72*.
76. Karl Marx, *Eighteenth Brummaire of Louis Bonaparte,* Progress, Moscow, 1973.
77. Hamza Alavi, *op. cit.*
78. *Op. cit.* pp. 44-55.
79. *Ibid.* p.56
80. *Ibid.* p. 71
81. Hasan N. Gardezi, 'Feudal and Capitalist Relations in Pakistan' in Hasan Gardezi and Jamil Rashid, *op. cit.*, p. 37.
82. Alfred Vagts, *A History of Militarism,* New York, Meridian Books, 1959; Jacques Van Doorn, edited by, *Armed Forces and Society, Sociological Essays,* Mouton, The Hague, Paris, 1968; S. E. Finer, *The Man on the Horseback, The Role of Military in Politics,* London and Dunmow, Pall Mall Press, 1962; Morris Janowitz, *The Professional Soldier,* The Free Press of Glencoe, 1960; Volker R. Berghahn, *Militarism a History of International Debate, 1861-79,* Cambridge, Cambridge University Press, 1981; Samuel P. Huntington, *The Soldier and the State,* Cambridge, Massassuchets, Harvard University Press, 1957.
83. The Pickering Masters, *The Reception of Locke's Politics,* Pickering and Chatta, Vols. IV &V, 1999.
84. K. M. Arif, *op. cit*.
85. Robert Dahl, *Polyarchy,* Participation and Opposition, New Haven, Yale University Press, 1982.

86. Jospeh Schumpeter, *Capitalism, Socialism and Democracy,* London, Allen and Unwin, 1943.
87. Immanuel Wallerstein, 'Collapse of Liberalism', Ralph Miliband and Leo Panitch, ed. *Socialist Register,* 1992, pp. 96-110.
88. C. B. Macpherson, *Life and Times of Liberal Democracy,* Oxford, OUP, 1933.
89. Allan Mcgrath, *op. cit.,* p.45.
90. *Ibid.,* p.55
91. *Ibid.,* p.71.
92. *ibid.* p. 80.
93. *ibid.* p. 137.
94. Mohammad Waseem, *op. cit.,* p. 138.
95. Allan Macgrath, *op. cit.,* p.221.
96. Sumit Ganguly, *Conflict Unending, India-Pakistan Tension since 1947,* New Delhi, Oxford, 2002, p. 5.
97. C. Dasgupta, *War and Diplomacy in Kashmir,* Sage, New Delhi, 2002.
98. Aijaz Ahmed, 'Democracy and Dictatorship', in Hassan Gardezi and Jamil Rashid, *op. cit.* p. 98.
99. Mushahid Hussain and Akmal Hussain, *op. cit.,* p. 129.
100. *Ibid.,* p. 130.
101. Mushahid Hussain and Akram Hussain, *op. cit.,* p. 130.
102. Waseem Mohammad, *op. cit.* p. 341.
103. K. M. Arif, *op. cit.,* pp. 69-70.
104. Quoted in *ibid.,* p. 69.
105. Allan Macgrath, *op. cit.,* p. 33.
106. K. M. Arif, *op. cit.,* p. 237.
107. Lawrence Ziring, *Pakistan in the Twentieth Century, op. cit.,* p. 511.
108. Mary Anne Weaver, *op. cit.,* p.187.
109. *Ibid.,* p. 191.
110. *Ibid.,* p. 191.
111. Mohammad Waseem, *op. cit.*
112. *Ibid.*
113. *ibid.,* p. 511.
114. Mervin G. Weinbaum, Pakistan; Misplaced Priorities, Missed Opportunities', in Selig Harrison, Paul H. Kries-berg and Dennis Kux, *op. cit.* pp. 89-106.
115. Mary Anne Weaver, *op. cit.,* p. 193.
116. *Ibid.* pp. 193-94.
117. Mushahid Hussain and Akram Hussian, *op. cit.,* p.102.
118. *Ibid.* pp. 103-104.
119. William L. Richter, *op. cit.,* p. 37.
120. Mervin G. Weinbaum, *op. cit.*

121. Lawrence Ziring, 'Dilemma and Challenge in Nawaz Sharief's Pakistan' in Charles Kennedy, *op. cit.*
122. *fn. 118*, p. 103.
123. Owen Bennet Jones, *op. cit.*, p. 283
124. Hasan-Askari Rizvi, *Military, State and Society,* Macmillan, NY, 2002, pp. xv-xvi, 226-27.
125. Veena Kukreja, 'Pakistan's Fourth Military Regime' in Asha Gupta, *Military Rule and Democratization,* Deep and Deep, 2003, p.60, New Delhi.
126. Morris Janowitz, *The Military in the Political Development of New Nations,* University of Chicago Press, Chicago, 1964, pp. 18-23.
127. Samuel P. Huntington, *op.cit.*
128. R.E. Lapp, *The Weapons Culture,* New York, 1968; F. Cook, *The Warfare State,* New York, 1962; S. Melman, *Pentagon Capitalism,* New York, 1970; C. Wright Mills, *Power Elite,* New York, Oxford University Press, 191956. Paul Baran and Paul Sweezy, *Monopoly Capitalism;* Morris Janowitz, *op. cit.* Samuel P. Huntington, op. cit. Samuel Adamsky, *The Military Establishment,* Boston, Beacon Press, 1964.
129. Miles Wolpin, *Militarism and Social Revolution in the Third World,* Asmun, Allanheld, 1981.
130. S.E. Finer, *op. cit.*
131. Lawrence Ziring, *fn 36,* p. 613.
132. Volker R. Berghahn, p.10.
133. *Ibid.*, p. 22.
134. Quoted in *ibid.* p. 34.
135. *Ibid.*, pp. 78-81.
136. Bengt Abrahamson, *Military Professionalisation and Political Power,* Groteborgs offsettryckeri, 1987.
137. Frederick Watkins, 'Praetorianism', *Encyclopaedia of the Social Sciences.*
138. Max Weber, *The Theory of Social and Economic Organisation,* New York, The Free Press, 1944, pp.346-53.
139. Eric R. Wolf, and Edwar C. Hansen, 'Caudilla Politics: A Structural Analysis', in Amos Perlmutter and Valerie Plave Bennet, *The Political Influence of the Military, Comparative Reader,* Yale University Press, New Haven and London, 1980, pp. 212-215.
140. Samuel P. Huntington, *Political order in Changing Societies,* Yale University Press, New Haven 1968, pp.194-97.
141. David C. Rapaport, 'A Comparative Theory of Military and Political Types' in Samuel P. Huntington, edited, *Changing Patterns of Military Politics,* The Free Press, New Haven, 1962, pp.390-91.

142. Morris Janowitz, *op. cit.*
143. Stephen Cohen, *The Pakistan Army,* New Delhi, 1984.
144. Volker R.Barghahn, *op. cit.*
145. Morris Janowitz, 'Armed Forces and Society: A World Perspective', in Jacques Van Doorn, edited by, *op. cit.* p. 25.
146. Jacques van Doorn, 'Armed Forces and Society: Patterns and Trends', in Jacques Van Doorn, *ibid.,* pp. 45-46
147. M. J. V. Bell, 'The Military in New States of Africa' in Jacques Van Doon, *op. cit.,* pp. 259-60.
148. Stephen Cohen, *Civil Military Relations In India, Pakistan and Bangladesh,* Mimeographed.
149. Khalid B. Sayeed, 'The Role of Military in Pakistan', in Jacques Van Doorn, *op. cit.,* p.275.
150. *Ibid.*
151. Clive Dewey, 'The Rural Roots of Pakistani Militarism' in D. A. Low edited, *The Political Inheritance of Pakistan,* Macmillan, 1991, pp. 265-66.
152. *Ibid.,* p. 276.
153. Imran Ali, 'The Punjab and the retardation of Nationalism' in D. A. Lowe, *op. cit.,* pp.29-49.
154. Andrew J. Major, 'The Punjabi Chieftains and the Transition from Sikh to British Rule' in D. A. Lowe, *op. cit.,* pp.53-85.
155. *Ibid.,* p. 61.
156. Yu V. Gankovsky, *The Peoples of Pakistan,* Moscow, Nauka Publishing House, 1971, p.180.
157. *Ibid.,* p. 187.
158. *Ibid.,* p. 193.
159. Stephen Cohen, 'The Nation and the State of Pakistan', *op. cit.,* p.113.
160. Hasan-Askari Rizvi, *op. cit.,* pp. 4-5.
161. Ayesha Jalal, *Democracy and Authoritarianism in South Asia,* New Delhi, Cambridge University Press, Foundation Books, 1995.
162. Iftikhar H. Malik, 'Pakistan in 2001, The Afghan Crisis and the Rediscovery of the Frontline State', *Asian Survey,* 42:1 p. 205.
163. *fn.* 160, p. 8.
164. Hasan-Askari Rizvi, Civil-Military Relations in Contemporary Pakistan, *Survival,* Vol.40, No.2, summer 1998, pp. 99-100.
165. William L. Rushbrook, *op. cit.* p. 187
166. Mohammed Waseem, *op. cit.,* p. 228; Mushahid Hussain and Akram Hussain, *op. cit.,* p.3.
167. K. M. Arif, *op. cit.,* pp. 93-94.
168. Quoted in Owen Bennet Jones, *op. cit.,* pp. 269-270.
169. Hasan-Askari Rizvi, *fn.* 159, p.8.

170. Aijaz Ahmed, *op. cit.*, p. 121.
171. Owen Bennet Jones, *op. cit.*, pp. 288-90.
172. Hasan-Askari Rizvi, *op. cit.*, p. 7.
173. Sumit Ganguly, *op. cit.*
174. M. S. Venkataramani, *The American Role in Pakistan,* 1947-1958, New Delhi, Radiant, 1982, p.6.
175. Quoted in Rakesh Gupta, 'Pakistan's Dependencia Militarism and Aggression', in V. D. Chopra, Rakesh Gupta, *Nuclear Bomb and Pakistan, External and Internal Factors,* New Delhi, Patriot Publishers, 1986, 121.
176. Stephen Philip Cohen, *fn.141,* p.135.
177. Stephen Philip Cohen, 'The Nation and the State of Pakistan', *op. cit.*, p. 118.
178. Hasan-Askari Rizvi, *State, Military and Society in Pakistan, op. cit.*, p. 85.
179. *Ibid.*, p. 101.
180. General K. M. Arif, *Khaki Shadows, Pakistan, 1947-97,* Oxford, Oxford University Press, 2001, p.115.
181. *Ibid.*, p.137.
182. Hasan-Askari Rizvi, *fn.*159, p. 16.
183. General K.M. Arif, *fn.180,* pp. 11-13.
184. Karl von Vorys, *Political Developments in Pakistan,* Princeton, Princeton Centre of International Studies, Princeton University Press, 1965, pp. 230-38.
185. *Ibid.*, p. 254.
186. *ibid.* p. 298.
187. General K.M. Arif, *fn 180,* pp. 94,95.
188. General K.M. Arif, *fn.* 63.
189. Craig Baxter, 'Conclusion: Legitimacy for Zia and his Regime?' in Craig Baxter, edited, *Zia's Pakistan, Politics and Stability In A Frontline State,* Vanguard, 1985, p. 112.
190. Veena Kukreja, *fn 125,* p. 68.
191. Veena Kukreja, 'Musharraf Style Democracy in Pakistan', *World Focus,* April-May 2002, April-May, New Delhi, p.17.
192. *fn.*180, p. 327.
193. Mahbub ul Haq, *Strategy of Economic Development: A Case Study of Pakistan,* Oxford University Press, 1968; Gustav F Papenek, *Pakistan's Development: Social Goals and Private Incentives,* Cambridge, Massachussets, Harvard University Press, 1967.
194. Shahid Javed Burki, 'Pakistan's economy in 2000; Two Possible Scenarios' in J. Henry Korson, edited by, *Contemporary Problems of Pakistan,* Published in Cooperation with the American Institute of Pakistan Studies, Boulder, San Fransisco, Oxford, Westview Press, Pak Book Corporation, Lahore, Islamabad, Karachi, 1993, pp. 6-7.

195. Shahid Javed Burki, 'Economic Policy after Zia ul Haq' in Charles H. Kennedy, *op. cit.*
196. L. F. Rushbrooks William, *op. cit.,* pp. 160-90
197. John Adams, 'Pakistan's economic performance in the 1980s: Implications for Political Balance,' *fn.194.* p. 54.
198. Veena Kukreja, *fn.125,* p.74.
199. Iftikhar H. Malik, *op. cit.*
200. S. Akbar Zaidi, 'Dismal State of Social Sciences in Pakistan,' Economic and Political Weekly, August 31, 2002, pp. 3644-3661, *Economic and Political Weekly.*
201. *fn.*161, p. 142.
202. *fn* 178, p. 172.
203. Hasan-Askari Rizvi, 'Civil-Military relations in Contemporary Pakistan', *Survival,* Vol. 40, No. 2, 1998 Summer, p. 105.
204. Iftikhar H. Malik, 'Pakistan in 2000, Starting Anew or Stalemate', *Asian Survey,* Vol. Xli, No. 1, January-February, 2001, p.112.
205. Crane Brinton, *Anatomy of Revolutions,* Prentice Hall, 1953.
206. Seymour Martin Lipset, *Young New Nation.*
207. Theda Scokpol, *States and Social Revolutions, A Comparative Analysis of France, Russia and China,* Cambridge, Cambridge University Press, 1979.
208. Eric Wolf, *Peasant Wars in the Twentieth Century,* Penguin, 1976.
209. Hamza Alavi, 'Peasants and Revolution', in A. R. Desai, *Peasant Struggles in India,* Bombay, Delhi, Calcutta, Madras, OUP, 1979
210. Ted Robert Gurr, *Why Men Rebel,* Princeton, Princeton University Press, 1970.
211. V. I. Lenin, *State and Revolution,* Moscow, Progress.
212. Mao tse tung, 'Hunan Report', Franz Schruman,and Orville Schell, *Republican China, China Readings,* Penguin, 1968, pp.125-137 ; Edgar Snow, *Red Star Over China,* Pelican, 1973, pp. 183-85.
213. Chalmers Johnson, Revolutionary Change, Boston, Little Brown, 1966.
214. Quoted in Owen Bennet Jones, *op. cit.* p. 149
215. *Ibid.,* 151.
216. Allen Macgrath, *op. cit,* p. 85.
217. *Ibid.,* p.76, 77.
218. Mohammed Waseem, *op. cit.,* pp. 263-68.
219. Mohammad A. Quddus, *Pakistan, A case Study of Plural Society,* India, Macmillan, 1981, p. 110.
220. Quoted in *ibid.* p. 110.

221. Owen Bennet Jones, *op. cit.,* p. 147.
222. Afak Haydar, 'The Mohajirs in Sindh: A Critical Essay', in J. Henry Korson, Jr, *fn. 194,* p. 112.
223. *Ibid.*
224. Mary Anne Weaver, *op. cit.,* p. 73.
225. Iftikhar H. Malik, *op. cit.,* p.119.
226. Christina Lamb, *op. cit.,* p. 126.
227. Teesta Ghosh, 'Ethnic Conflict in Sindh and Its Impact on Pakistan', Rajat Ganguly and Ian Macduff, edited by, *Ethnic Conflict and Secession in South and South East Asia, Causes, Dynamics, Solutions,* New Delhi, Thousand Oaklands and London, Sage Publications, 2003, pp.107-109.
228. Rajat Ganguly, *ibid.,* p. 10.
229. Iftikhar H. Malik, *op. cit.,* p. 254.
230. Owen Bennet Jones, *op. cit.,* p. 116.
231. Mohammad Waseem, *op. cit.,* pp. 380-86.
232. *Ibid.* pp. 387-89.
233. Owen Bennet Jones, *op. cit.,* p. 135.
234. Mary Anne Weaver, *op. cit.,* pp. 105-06.
235. Owen Bennet Jones, *op. cit.,* p. 140.
236. Barrington Moore, *Jr. Social Origins of Democracy and Dictatorship,* Boston, Beacon Press, 1966.
237. Kathleen Gough, 'Indian Peasant Uprisings', *Economic and Political Weekly,* New Delhi, Special Number, 1974, pp. 1391-1412.
238. Narhari Kaviraj, *Farazi and Wahabi Movements,* New Delhi, PPH, 1983.
239. Mahbub-ul Haq, *Social Development in South Asia,* Karachi, Oxford, 1998.
240. Tariq Ali, *op.cit.,* p. 9.
241. Mohammad Waseem, Politics of Manipulation, *Dawn,* 18-08-03.
242. Sherbaz Khan Mazari, *A Journey to Disillusionment,* New Delhi, Oxford, 1999, p. 167.

3

Russian State

The Russian Federation, became a successor State of the Soviet State and continued its membership of the UN Security Council. It slided from Soviet Union's super power status to great power status, which it is finding difficult to retain. Yeltsin visualized[1] a western-style State, democracy and economy.[1] Under Kozyrev, his Foreign Minister, Russia's orientation was towards Westernization of Russia. Ruslan Khasbulatov wanted Russia to be a parliamentary democracy with a mixed economy on the pattern of Scandinavian countries.[2] Khasbulatov had moved from a defence of Perestroika to radical democracy, like that of Yeltsin and from there moved towards a position of mixed economy and a Welfarist State. Gennady Zyuganov viewed Russia to be a Eurasian Power, more in the tradition of the Soviet pattern with political and democratic restructuring[3]. He considered Perestroika as spelling disaster for Russia. They differed on domestic and foreign policies and stateness of the Russian State. Political power for Yeltsin was to perform the instrumentalist function, like in Adam Smith, to extract surplus labour and appropriate it through economic growth. For Khasbulatov Power had the role of promoting social welfare, with economic growth and social cohesion. For Zyuganov power was to aim at increasing the Stateness in order to prevent social and economic chaos and national secession. The latter two were very critical of Yeltsin's political and economic approach and wanted Russia to deal with external issues independently. In internal matters they wanted to use the levers of State power, in the context of a power vacuum since state, national, military and CPSU structures had collapsed and Gorbachev had ceased to matter.

The ontos of Russian State belies the earlier hopes of liberal democracy and capitalist economy. Its plutocracy and political institutions have hardly held any promise of economic stability political democracy, national unity and viable State. Its political class, divided on ethnic economic and political lines suffers from mafiaisation of the market and irresponsible and uncivil behaviour in State Duma[4] . Unmindful of its future project and recognising the promise of Szelenyi's new managerialism[5], we look at the anatomy of the new State in terms of its economic policy and functioning of its political system. Russia is in search of its identity.

This chapter looks at the issue of democratic identity. Recognising the merit of the analytic (Lucien Pye-Verba) and the syncretic (Dittmer and Kim) analyses in comparative politics of identity, the chapter goes beyond these and searches for identity in terms of collective consciousness, political and social emancipation. Territorial decision-making (Pye-Verba) and determination of national essence (folklore, myths, rituals) and national purposes of the states in external relations (Dittmer and Kim) are useful but not adequate theoretical considerations to look for democratic identities, particularly in societies that have undergone a process of post-feudal development, either under the framework of capitalism or socialism. A comprehensive analysis, at that a cultural analysis, could focus on emergence of individual and collective consciousness as it exist (e.g., multi-ethnic or multi-religious or multi-cultural) as opposed to, say Great Russian or Great Han or Great Hindu. Marx's analysis is on The Jewish Question and Economic and Philosophic Manuscript could be used to flesh out this approach.

Political emancipation in societies, particularly with reference to post-Communist and liberal societies has its limits. Both these societies are moving in the direction of marketisation, development and democracy within multilinear processes of capitalist development. Democracies face greater vulnerabilities since political emancipation is not an insurance of social emancipation. The articulation of dissent emanating from the limits of political emancipation may be anti-systemic. It may take as it often does, the form of ethnic, communal religious mobilisations. There are movements based on the right of nations to self-determination in most societies. Such movements can be a hindrance to the consolidation of democratic identity if those take terrorist forms. They cut at the fragile, limited, evolving and tenuous political process, as in Russia. In countries that are more advanced in terms of democratic process at the electoral and political level, violent and terrorist forms have been continually disrupting these processes since the last decade. Gurr and Harff's theory of ethnic conflicts in world politics is relevant since it focusses on the political variables of such conflicts, and suggests that democratic absorption is the solution.

Such challenges could very well be inimical to the consolidation of democratic identity since at the level of the state it may give rise to national security concerns—legitimate or otherwise. This chapter examines the dialectic of Russia's quest for identity and its symbiotic relationship with the demands of coercive apparatus of the state in the wake of porous borders, arms smuggling, crime, secession and mafiaisation that market has meant, particularly in Yeltsin's Russia. It is claimed that this approach to analyse democratic identity is relevant for India, Russia, and with suitable modifications, China. Russian being, political emancipation, nascent but evolving civil society, limits of political and social emancipation, tensions based on old and new social contradictions, threats to national security and the orientation of the defence doctrine to national security concerns have made scholars describe the state as clientilist or predatory.

That the breakdown of the Soviet Union and the withering away of the Warsaw Pact powers led to a multifaceted crisis is beyond dispute. Crisis as an expression is being used not in the sense of a breakdown. It is being used as a "decisive moment", which is composed of elements of danger and opportunity. It is a moment of danger in that the basic problems cannot be systemically resolved, but may give rise to new ways of resolving the breakdown. The multifaceted crisis of Soviet fragmention implied a power vacuum expressing itself in crises of political, economic, military, spiritual and national identity. The crises offered an opportunity to examine issues of identity anew in the form of the Russian Federation, or the parameters of the ethnic Russians, Russian people or multinational citizens of Russia. There is increasing literature on the inadequacy of Marxist praxis, on the one hand, and the assertion of a non-Marxist, if you please, an anti-Marxist, (read anti-Soviet) in the case of Russian identity, on the other. In this search of post-Communist identity, here and elsewhere, the globe is defined in terms of the self as against the other. The writings of both Francis Fukuyama and Samuel P. Huntington are an assertion of not only the self but of historically, a superior identity.[6] In both cases, the self is held aloft as against the other. In the case of Huntington, the distinct fundamental unity of the Western (read liberal in Fukuyama's lexicon) is maintained by the Western capitalist world. Anything that poses a challenge becomes a "faultline" in Huntington's terms. Traditionally, in the case of Russia, the Slavophil and the Westerner represent this distinction of the self from the other. Currently, the discussions on Russian's identity take the form of a debate between Eurasian identity vs Western identity. Another way to seize the opportunity offered by the crisis is to look at the limits of this view and offer a critical evaluation of the processes at work in terms of current transitions that are afoot in the region of the erstwhile USSR as elsewhere. The limits of this global unity of the new world order are brought out by the analyses of the volume of the Socialist Register[7]. Since the search for post-Communist identity is an issue of active politics in the entire erstwhile Soviet region and Eastern bloc, appropriate theorisations are being evolved for analysing this phenomenon, particularly in the Russian Federation for reasons of its unprecedented nature. The dimensions of this uniqueness could be both external and internal. In both cases, the issues of identity are not restricted to national identity alone. They cover a whole range of issues in the political spectrum. In order to specify the search, we look not at the issue of ethnicity but the issue of democratic identity. The reasons for this are that the search for democratic identity is more basic. The search for other identities may emanate from limitations of this identity. The limits of democratic identity in terms of lack of human emancipation may lead to communal, ethnic, revivalist and irredentist assertions of identity giving rise to national security concerns in response. Yeltsin wanted to project Russia in terms of a democratic identity, both internally and in foreign policy orientation. So does Putin.

Theoretical Considerations

Collective identities have been formed, transcended and reformed in history. Benedict Anderson's analysis of collective identity shows how culturally communities have imagined and formed progressively on the basis of religious texts, ideograms, dynasty, cosmology, and print capitalism followed by the colonial state[8]. Identity collectives coincided with the State with the breakdown of feudal identity that got dissolved into the atomised individual alienated from the rest, on the one hand, and the abstraction of the State, on the other. The State assumed either the form of a Nation State or that of a multinational state. The problems of defining the national issues forth in a number of theoretical axes. A traditional definition of identity is provided by Sidney Verba and Lucien Pye in the Social Science Research Council series on Comparative Politics. It says national identity is the "set of individuals who fall within the decision-making scope of the state."[9] Dittmer and Kim find the Verba-Pye view as analytically useful but inadequate since it does not go beyond territory, class, ethnicity/nationality, and historical/cultural exclusiveness. It can be empirically validated but cultural/ linguistic plurality and non-coincidence of language boundary with territory makes the definition less useful.

Russia cannot be defined in terms of such a coincidence even if one may concede the predominance of the Russian language of the Russian Federation. Dittmer and Kim call this an analytic definition and find that this definition cannot "deal with those periods in a nation's history when there is pervasive uncertainty about boundary questions, either geophysical demarcation of frontiers or inclusion of marginal subgroups."[10] They reconceive national identity as "the relationship between nation and state that obtains when the people of that nation identify with the State. It is not a property or an aspect of that nation or state, which would force the differentiation between state and national identity, depriving the concept of the unity we have characterized as fundamental."[11] Dittmer and Kim posit national identity in terms of what the purposes and essence of the State are. These purpose of the State are to be related to the external dimension and the roles that they perform. An identity is "a repertoire of such roles. Roles have to be seen in terms of national identity is the state and that the state defines itself by what roles it plays—by self-categorisation in alignment with positive reference groups and in opposition to negative reference groups—by its performance in the international arena[12]. "The states' foreign policy behaviour would be marked by assimilation into the national identity of a sense of expansive and sometimes aggressive self-confidence. In the case of States that had traditional great power image and face current underdevelopment, the foreign policy behaviour may be ambivalent and express a sort of national inferiority complex.

The essentialist aspect is laid bare by myths, rituals, ceremonies, and folklore that relate how the nation came to be and what it stands for. An example of the Dittmer and Kim theoretical projections into the terrain of the Russian reality could very well be another work called Russian's Future where essentialist and foreign policy roles are examined.[13] A similar work on post-Communist identity in countries of Central and Eastern Europe in terms of their foreign policy (with cultural analysis as its axis) is provided by Michta.[14] For Russia, Shenfield suggests that the search for Russian cultural identity can be explained in terms of four ideal types, viz, Neo-Soviet, Archaic, Statist and Liberal. These have to do with territory and foreign policy.[15] Blum discusses Russian foreign policy in terms of liberal, statist, national-patriotic perspectives in order to encapsulate the contemporary tendencies in the political spectrum of the Russian Federation. He concludes to say that "foreign policy bears on the problems of ethnic separatism and Islamic fundamentalism by identification and support."[16] This does not explain Russia's position on the Missile Technology Control Regime (MTCR), Nuclear Non-proliferation Treaty (NPT), human rights, terrorism, ecology, etc. It further does not relate the Russian opposition to such streams of primordial identities to the cosmopolitan character of the Russian being as it exists and to more secular, and pragmatic concerns of geo-politics.

The political dimension of this cultural specificity transforms itself into the Wilsonian-Lenin application of solution to the problems related to the logic of either secession or autonomy implied in the right of nations to self-determination vis-à-vis imperialist domination. At the cultural and societal level, self-determination could express itself into merging of groups, particularly in terms of secular or homogenised multicultural identities without recourse to secession. In this sense, the event in Chechnya may make sense of a different order. On the face of it they validate the Pye-Verba analytic approach. But the events connected with the use of force against the Parliament in the

Autumn of 1993, cannot be understood in the absence of an attempt to look for a more comprehensive theoretical consideration of which identity relates to development and participation. A more comprehensive approach could be developed with reference not just to myths, folkfore, rituals and other symbolic contents of identity that Dittmer and Kim emphasise. Analyses of the processes bearing on Russian multi-ethnic identity, evolution of political freedom, political and electoral process, inadequate social emancipation leading to violent tensions, and State responses to them, would have existential and prognostic value.

How did the Russian model consciousness come about? What is happening in terms of formation of civil society? How is it relevant for identity in terms of current politics? Is neo-patrimonial society sublated, subsumed or transcended? What is the strength of electoral and political process, given old and new process of modernization? Such issues have a bearing on another set of issues, namely legitimacy that participation in electoral and political process involves. Each one of these, i.e., participation, electoral process and political process are as closely connected with identity as the issues of development, integration and international relations are connected with it. Are these to be understood in specific societal terms or in terms of macro process of unilinearity of the expression "Globalization"? Raising of such issues is as much cultural as it is social or political. It is much more comprehensive definition of culture. The word culture is a contested term. It has at least six usages. It denotes artistic, literary and narrowly defined cultural activity. It denotes intellectual activity. It denotes concepts in sociology and anthropology. It denotes a way of life. It denotes human productive activity. It denotes transformative approach. A way of life that is industrial and transformative like the struggle for capitalism or socialism would be subsumed in the term culture. In this sense, culture could be looked at as cumulative societal norms, values and practices. Since Russian society is struggling to change its way of life away from its Soviet past in the direction of capitalist social development and political democracy, a cultural analysis need not restrict itself to an examination of narrow cultural symbols for specifying the Russian search for democratic identity. It could include values of self and other, of development, market democracy and legitimacy.

Capitalism with democracy is on the agenda of debate with regard to change in the Russian Federation. Since it is possible to talk of multilinear development of capitalism in the same society, there is a scope of consensus and dissensus being equally strong leading to a stalemate which may warrant the use of force. The Yeltsin-Khasbulatov-Rutskoi conflict involving use of force against the White House in 1993 autumn can be understood in these terms or in terms of traditional political culture conceptualized as "neo-patrimony of the state". That event raises issues of political emancipation in the Russian society. Hidden below it is the issue of social emancipation of the Russian peoples. Democracy and development could become the analytic essence of Russia's search of identity as it is in India.

It would be a little ironic that the post-Soviet changes may as well validate the analyses of Marx with regard to capitalist states for Russia is passing through a savagery of capitalism that the 19th century had witnessed. Marx's works on the Jewish question and Economic and Philosophic Manuscripts raise the issues of identity in terms of the rise of capitalism where the self is atomised and the other becomes an enemy. Marx's view on the growth of the civil society and the problem of alienation can be fruitfully used to understand Russia's search for post-Communist identity since the present Russian political class is interested in development, marketization, democracy within the parameters of either 19th or 20th century versions of capitalism.

Falling back on Marx's writings to flesh out an approach for an understanding of Russia's search of post-Communist identity is consistent with a quest for cultural examination since Marxist tradition is a contribution to cultural studies. Raymond Williams says, "there is the effect of his general position to human development which can be taken at least as the outline of a general cultural theory"[17]. Such an approach is also consistent with prevailing social contradictions in Russia.

On the Jewish Question, Marx develops the problems of the separation in modern politics of the individual from society, and of the state and civil society[18]. The distinction is not upheld in Marxian argument since it insisted on class rule. It was used by Gramsci for conducting a political struggle. The significance of the work lies in that it relates the issue of political emancipation with human emancipation in a society that has alienated human individual through political democracy, on the other. He regarded political democracy as a great step forward and "the final form of universal human emancipation within the prevailing order of things for man was regarded as sovereign. "Real democracy could find fulfillment once development through socialism had taken place, as a negation of capitalism. According to him, the rights of the universality of the State. These rights reflected the social essence of man in abstract form and in case they were sought to be achieved in practice, they would require human emancipation. In contrast, the rights of man in general only reflected the contradictions of a bourgeois society. According to him the rights of man "....are nothing but the rights of a member of a civil society, i.e., the rights of egotistic man, of man separated from other men and from his community. Individual liberty and its application from the basis of civil society. It makes in every man see in another man not the realisation of his own freedom, but the barrier to it."[19] The economic basis of this estrangement is worked out by Marx in his Economic and Philosophic Manuscripts where it shows how the working of 19th century capitalism led to the disadvantage of the species being and the community got dissolved into the atomistically existing individuals, or, as Gramsic says, at times composed of homo economicus. Hoare and Smith make the same point thus, "And Gramsic too at times adopts this usage...." and to quote Gramsci thus, "Every social from has its homo economicus, i.e. its own economic activity."[20] Marx hinted at the divorce between the State and the Civil Society and later in the German Ideology found the linkage between the two in the modified concept of State dominance.[21]

Gramsci, who theorises the connection in power terms through hegemony, also provides a modified version of civil Society as composed of organisations and not just atomistically existing individuals. It is through the linkage between State and the Civil Society as worked out by Marx and Gramsci that one comes to a discussion on democracy and through it to the meaning of democratic identity that Yeltsin's Russia is looking for. In Yeltsin's Russia, analyses using civil society only want to see how far it helps State's policies of capitalism. The state in the capitalist society, at least in the most advanced ones, looks for hegemony over the civil society.[22] Hegemony is achieved through the legitimation process in which organisations of civil society play a significant role to perpetuate the system in a way that appears to be non-socialisation, role of political parties, the incorporation of left wing parties as quests in power, the Church and institutions maintained by it, the freedom of the Press, the media's apparent neutrality the propagation of the idea of national interests by the press, mass media, educational institutions, youth organisations, ex-soldiers association, specifically nationalist organisations, the Churches, business, its association and lobbies are the elements of the civil society that help in perpetuation of hegemony in a non-partisan way.[23] What are called the ideological apparatuses are the non-coercive means for the perpetuation of hegemony of capitalism. Civil society is not for revolution.

Since political democracy, in all its versions in the life and times of liberalism[24] cannot overcome the boundaries of the market society, the value of participation remains a distant dream, and leads to the growth of a security state (read national security state for the contemporary period). Marx recognised this possibility thus, "security is the highest social concept of civil society, the concept of police, expressing the fact that the whole of society exists only in order to guarantee to each of its members the preservation of his person, his rights, and his property..."[25]. In the contemporary time, the collapse of the Cold War has not negated the need for a national security state, by both the advanced and advancing capitalist state, in China. New issues have cropped up on which Marxist sociology needs extensive research. These are issues that give scope for political articulation of dissent. These new issues are the issue of gender, student movement, and ethnic identity[26]. Marx's ideal of restoring humanity to man in a participatory community is possible only if the marginal groups govern themselves after overcoming the limits of underdevelopment and the *raison d'etre* of a national security state. Russia's search for identity is a search for a democratic identity and is stymied by the need and reason of a national security State. Parallels can be seen in India and China, though less so in India for it has a strong democratic ethos and a reasonable working political process. In China, given the inexorable consequences of capitalist marketisation in the forms of various "pollutions", the assertion of the State is underlined. Even here the party attempts to incorporate new groups to "thwart or limit the possibility of alternative political ideological definitions" arising[27].

Russian Being

What is being done is to replace the German philosophical being with unity of being with consciousness and looking at the unity of the Russian beings as unity of heterogeneous external influences. This would help us in steering clear of the romances of little identities, on the one hand, and the pathos of regarding Russian being as only Great Russian identity, on the other. The evolving Russian being in beings is the focus. Whether life is mimetic[28], illusory or eternal, or both, it does raise the issue of the self and the other. In Dosteavsky's *Brother's Karamazov,* some children ask Aliocha: "Karamazov, is it true what religion says, that we shall see one another again?" And Aliocha answers: "Certainly, we shall see one another again, we shall joyfully tell one another everything that has happened."[29] Historically, it is possible to construct the Russian Being in beings in terms of unity of the self with the other, i.e., Russian with the non-Russian, Slav with the non-Slav, pagan with the orthodox, as a prelude to the modern multi-racial and secular Russian being, as it can be for the Indian and the Chinese. The Russian Constitution of 1993 recognise Russian people to be multi-ethnic.

Russian history is marked by the process of the inter-mixture of both the drive of the Russians as a frontiers people and the subjugation of the Russians by others like the Mongols. Throughout Russians history the drive of expansion into new frontiers and the necessity of co-mingling have led to the evolution of the Russian identity. A frontiers people[30] with drive of conquering timber, trade and fur frontiers co-mingled with other people to acquire a habitat which was largely Eurasian in geographic terms. The Russians, Finnish, Tartar, Bashkr Siberian tribes, and Mongols came together to form the Russian Federation.

Russian nationalism in the West European sense because has not emerged. Looking at the Russian history as part of the whole (a la Toynbee), Obolensky underlines seven phases of Russian history that have external influences. These are (a) Russia's conversion from Slav paganism to Byzantine Christianity, which began on a large scale in the late 10th century; (b) the Mongoloid from 1240 to 1480; (c) growth of Moscow autocrats in opposition to the Khanate or the Golden Horde; (d) the ecclesiastical schism of the old Believers in the seventh decade of the 17th century; (e) the Westernising reforms of Peter the Great in the first quarter of the 18th century; (f) the liberal of Alexander in the seventh decade of the 19th century; and (g) the Bolshevik Revolution. The point of this narration is that these phase s "illustrate Russia's close dependence on the outside world; for none of them is fully intelligible unless we view it against the background of one or several civilizations more extensive than Russian herself."[31] Just like the Western Christian world, so also the Golden Horde left its imprint on the Russian being. During the period of Ivan the policy begun in the mid-15th century of granting lands to renegade Tatar princes and taking them into frontier service, a policy of assimilation which continued to be a main feature of Russian relation with Tatar and other people. "The land of the Khanate of Kazan Tatars, the heirs of the Volga Bulgars, were equally composite, including various Tatar-Finnish peoples in the mixed forests and the middle Volga. They also took long to subject fully or to assimilate, and their main river valleys were not solidly occupied by Russian... till about 1650."[32] During the period of great schism, Nikon, the servent of Anti-Christ declared, "I am a Russian..... But my faith and religion are Greek". The Westernisation of Peter the Great was also aimed at changing the mindset and the appearance of the Russian apart from reforming State and Society. It was a veritable cultural revolution.

Kavelin, who was influenced by Hegelianism, said that the spirit of the individual broke up the primeval Russian view of man's relationship with his community subsequent to the death of Manomakh in 1125, under the influence of Ivan the Terrible and Peter the Great. It meant that the Russians acquired a civic consciousness that was not entirely determined by their environment and indistinguishable from that of their fellows[33]. Obolensky is unable to place Russia either as a Western or a Eastern entity. The split between the Westerners and the Slavophils was resolved in Alexander Herzen's famous image of two-faced Janus or the two-headed eagle, which looked in different direction's, East and West, but in whose breast there beat the same heart. The intellectual life of the first half of the 19th century was liberal under the influence of the French utopian socialist thought. In Chernyshevisky, rationalist scientific, tradition dominated given the social transformation that was afoot in Czarist Russia in the direction of the 1861 reforms, the consciousness that was transcended by the community oriented consciousness in terms of the socialist understanding of the Russian being. The labour and peasant consciousness of the need of reform, as Isaacs Deutscher called it, the agenda of "dual revolution" subsequent to the emasculated socio-political reforms of 1861, led to the socialist consciousness as is evident by the October Revolution. The need for it was underlined by Alexander Herzen when he said that the fight against Czarist absolutism will lead to socialism.

The species–being argument was integrated into the struggle for enunciating a different view of the Russian being in the form of the fatal and in many ways flawed view of the Soviet man[34]. The core of this view was an instrumental view of consciousness that was to lay the basis of an integrationist view of Russian consciousness, as different from the traditional way of Russian assimilation. The instrumentalist view of the Soviet man was not very different from the rationalist view of the liberal man except that the shift was from the atomised individual to the integrated individuals with a cosmopolitan outlook. The cosmopolitan core of the Russian being, with suitable modifications, continues to be the basis for the post-communist search for identity with greater emphasis on political, and less on social emancipation. It incorporates the self and the other through the hoary and recent past as an ideal. Against this background, the movement for session need to be approached for the purposes of assimilation and integration. In the Russian case, the self and the other are not on antagonistic terms. There is the co-mingling initiated by patrimonial, the book, Slav script, development of the language, intermixture of races, co-existence of religions, class formation and historical evolution of a continuously expanding territory and the modernity project of the Soviet State. The nuances of these can be seen in such expressions as ethnic Russian, multinational Russian citizen of Russia and the Russian people. It is this compositeness that can and is being abused as Russification and revolts against it, as in case of India, the compositeness of India as emphasised by Nehru is being described as a myth or pseudo. Both in India and Russia, the composite being has been the object of abuse. In case of the latter Chechnya provides the exercise.

The issue of the individual and the other would lead to a discussion on the civil society since the community of the self and the other will become the basis of social intervention since the new Russian Constitution recognises the Russians "multi-ethnic people." In India and Russia, the Hindu or the Russian need not be determining element. Perhaps in China the Great Han is neither. In India, the Constitution calls India, Bharat not Hindu.

Civil Society

Feudal civil society dissolves into atomistically existing individuals in the bourgeois society for Marx. It is imbued with economic organisations for Gramsci. The latter believes that the State also helps in the formation of the organisations of society. He however, warns against the organisations becoming statolatory or ones that worship the State.[35] These, therefore, need to be agents of mediation between the State and the individual in defence of the society against capitalism. In case of Russia, the existence of organisations from the point of view of anti-state is denied by Miluykov, the Foreign Minister in the first Provisional Government, since the social orders in Russian history "...have always been subservient to the aims of the state"[36] . Therefore, the gentry, the nobility and the bourgeoisie were of no use since they were dependent on the State. Paul Milukov suggests that the Russian cities were nothing more than garrison towns and administrative centres rather than foci of trade and manufacturing. The organisations that did exist were corporative associations at the provincial, town or village level. These associations were collectively responsible for the conduct of their members, and for townsmen and peasants they performed fiscal disciplinary functions. These forms of social organisations encouraged these groups, which formed the bulk of the population, to negotiate directly with the government rather than to seek common cause against it.[37]

From the vantage point of looking for alternatives to the State, Russian history does, offer some periods when the State did rely on the autonomously existing institutions in the society before the October Revolution. This suggests that the Russian society showed significant and substantial signs of indigenous movements for democracy. In the Kievan period, in the 10th and the 11th centuries, assembly of clan elders i.e. the vetche, and the popular assembly in the towns existed. Both fell victim to the power of the territorial princes. In the 17th century, at the beginning of the Roman period, when royal authority was weakened, the Czar ruled in conjunction with a quasi-parliamentary gathering of leaders of the Stande, or the status groups known as Zemskii sobor.[38] And yet the Czarist state, with the aristocracy and the bureaucracy, in the name of order and tranquility, sparked these off and tyranised the people below. Between the higher orders and the people below there emerged new groups of intellectuals, who were granted education and who found the gap between what was said and what the reality was, rather too much. In the 19th century, these new circles of young Russians shared a "profound feeling of aversion for official Russia, for their environment, and, at the same time, the urge to escape out of it- and, in some of them, a vehement desire to change the contemporary state of affairs"[39] . The opinion against the state expressed itself in liberal and Marxist trends or put differently, in the trend of democracy and/or socialism. On the fringe were the official bureaucratic hostile reactions. A counter elite was emerging and the violent politics of the People's Will.[40]

The post-revolutionary phase was concerned with the issues of democracy and the role of autonomous struggling organisations that the struggle of workers, peasants and soliders had given rise to, namely the Soviets. The role of the Soviets has been an issue not only before April 1918, as Neil Harding implies[41] , but from time to time subsequently. The Lenin, Khrushchev and Gorbachev periods attempted their renewal while the Stalin and the Brezhnev periods bemoaned their incapacity and wanted to activate them. There is no doubt that Lenin's one-man management imposed its limitations on trade unions specifically, and democracy generally got emasculated by Democratic Centralism. Despite the limitations of one-man management and the practice of the Party boss in the industry and the trade unions, the latter continued to enlarge their role in the arena of welfare measures with regard to leisure, health, holidays and local injustices. Greater autonomy was provided to regional-level leaderships at the party level. That there was institutional pluralism is recognised by the structural-functional analysis of the Soviet system[42]. The Gorbachev reform led to the growth of association of the tertiary sector: soldiers, miners, women and other strata on issues of ecology, of political reform, peace, gender and other older issues like media reform, electoral reform, and of artistic activity[43]. That this was interpreted in terms of Lenin by Gorbachev is well known and also the fact that the problematic of emancipation is linked to the theoretical axes of routes to political and social democracy. That reforms were subtantial in terms of creation of a viable civil society is reflected in the response to the State constitutional coup. The new institutions were too incipient to have played a concrete role in opposition to the coup. They did, however, help in creating a new atmosphere, sometimes intense and at other times waning. Subsequent researches into the Gorbachev phase and in initiating this process of change may reveal the possibilities of an objective assessment of Gorbachev since we are too close to this phase of change to conclusively prove if his motives in initiating restructuring and openness were suspect. It may, therefore, be too early to call him a democrat, though he can easily be described as a *crisis* leader against Statism.

Political Emancipation

The August coup created a power vacuum[44] and offered an opportunity to the new forces to overcome the limitation of the Soviet system by laying down the fundamentals of social change and political institution. There was bound to be a struggle between the old and the new groups and organisations. Yeltsin says that the democratic restructuring was hindered by this post-coup struggle. The desire to be identified as a democratic country internally and externally and the impediments to it have been articulated by Yeltsin since the summer of 1990[45]. The constitution of democratic Russia (expressions used in the constitution) gave to the country a strong President and described the Russian people as multinational. At the same time, it looked at the society in the terms of the individual per se for in Article 7 it described the Russian State as aiming to create conditions for ensuring a worthy life and free development of the individual along with the system of social services. The enumeration of the rights—human and civil—mentioned right to life, liberty, freedom, privacy of the communication (part of liberty), equality before law, rights of property, freedom to dispose off the abilities to the labour and sectional security rights. Most of these rights, like the rights to property, declared by the 1936 and 1977 constitutions, were more formal than real. In the present case freedom of contract to act under it was emphasized.

The rights guaranteed are both a reaction to the negative aspects of the Soviet past and simultaneously a preparations for the operation of the practices of the capitalist market society. The Soviet practice of "compulsory distributions of the entire labour force of the country by the central economy authority which will distribute this force according to needs of an overall government economic plan is rejected". (Trotsky's expression).[46] In the agricultural sector, practice of "Ural-Siberian" method and forced collectivisation are the negative backdrop to the present emphasis to free labour for the market. Whether the market operation will be in its 19th century version or the 20th century version of the capitalist development will determine the real meaning of the social security rights that are incorporated in the Constitution. In the version of 19th century capitalism, these rights will be formal.

The emergence of a political culture that would support the framework of the Constitution will depend upon the evolution of the political and electoral process, the partyisation of interest aggregation and the legitimacy of the governing institutions like the presidency and the parliament. It is in this as in the other areas that the Yeltsin remark that the period of transitions is full of contradiction is relevant. He was referring to the dissensus between the Presidency and the Parliament with regard to the force of capitalist change. A similar view with regard to contradiction in federal relations was also articulated. He informed the Congress of People's Deputies, "confrontation between various political forces and the lack of desire or ability to find a compromise are becoming a powerful break on the reforms"[47]. To the Federal Council, he said, "let us face it, in Moscow, as well as in the regimes, there are forces which are hindering ...the implementation of the federation treaty"[48] . The constitutional position of the Federation treaty is below the position of the Yeltsin decreed Constitution. Yeltsin had been tireless in his indictment of the "conservative forces", implying the old order forces in the current contradictions. What is equally, if not more, serious is the incapacity of the reform forces to provides for stability and reform. At the national level, the splintering of the Democratic Russia Movement since its inception in 1990 and the personalised leadership of the fragments are no abiding support bases against the mafiaisation that market life has meant. Both of them, at the regional and the national level, are unable to match their adversaries—old and new communists. To console oneself, one can only hope that "crisis is progress", as a Russian scholar does[49].

As for the institution of the Presidency and the Parliament, "The constant struggle for control of the institutions, and of subsequent policy outcomes, led to the stalemate that paralysed both the government and the parliament",[50] and has led to the use of force and charge of conspiracy among the anti-coup forces. The Parliament has not been able to develop consensus building institutions and procedures like parties, committees and factions. This is a situation that detracts from incentives to members to be consistent. The forces of democratic reform were unsure both of the specificity and the speed of reform. This was balanced by the emergence of the populist parties like the Zhirinovsky nationalist detachment in the earlier elections (1993) and the decline of the strength of the democratic groups behind Yeltsin. To believe that democratic Russian forces behind Yeltsin were going to be institutionalised was a pipe dream. With this dream, there was the lingering doubt about the possibility of success of the strategy of the shock therapy that Yeltsin wanted to pursue, even if we kept in mind that the 1996 elections to the Presidency were to be decisively predictable in favours of Yeltsin, if the 1995 Parliament elections results are taken as an indication against the possibility of Yeltsin's victory.

The electoral process, and the development of the electoral law and crystallisation of vote banks has not yet reached a final shape given the amorphous nature of the political institutionalisation and/or consensus building. The electoral law, nominating procedures, campaign regulations, and delineation of constituencies had been done but needed yet to crystallise. The election system was rather complicated.[51] It may have introduced a conservative bias for Smyth,[52] but it surely was not conducive to create homogenised voting which is a base under normal circumstances, let alone in times of crisis. The countryside had voted this time for the communists, who are for marketisation, but not for the shock therapy that Yeltsin had been pushing. Smyth maintains that according to the law, one half of the Deputies are elected directly as voters choose one of several candidates to represent a given district. The other half is elected indirectly, through balloting for party states. This means that individual Deputies depend upon the percentage of the votes that the Party receives. The State Duma, which is the Lower House of the Parliament, is elected by two procedures. Out of 450 members, 225 are elected on the basis of direct territorial simple majority voting and the remaining 225 members are elected by countrywide single constituency in which there are Party nominations. Whatever the system of election, social cleavages are reflected and are not created by an electoral system. Smyth's assertion that there is a rather conservative and democratic division because of the system, is a rather misplaced search of the cause of the political divide. The divide has to be seen in the societal cleavages in post-communist Russia, where neither marketisation nor Westernisation of foreign policy has brought relief in the more apparent form of free political life. The existence of the Russian at the political level appears to be going ahead but at the social level, the rights enshrined in the Constitution do not mean a life of prosperity and community living. It may mean a non-terrorised, free living without the necessities of social life. This raises the issue of the multilinear process of marketisation or even capitalist development since the political ambit of declaration of sovereignty as related to individualised achievement and community, or individual well being and social cohesion.

Path of Social Development

The contradictions in the Soviet society were for anyone to see and infer from what the Soviets were doing and saying. The social contradictions generated by the Soviet type of development led to the growth of groups but not a cohesive social class. Social inequality among the workers on the basis of skills, social background and wage differentials and social distinctions among the agricultural workers created the need to have a new social compact under Gorbachev. During Brezhnev's period, the system came to rely increasingly on the new but pliable intelligence[53] that was increasingly articulating itself in terms of alternative policy choices. Subsequently, the Novosibirsk group of economist, the intellectuals who were advising different foreign policy choices like the institute of US and Canadian study, the policy projections of Nichole Ogarkov for defence acquisitions, showed emerging conflicting policy projections by different groups. As in traditional Russia, so in the Soviet period, it was the State that was a prime mover in matters of accumulations of capital for development and so the Soviet bureaucracy had its own distinct position from other sections and also its own in-house differentials. Individuals were incorporated in segmented formal and informal groups of the CPSU. These groups multiplied under Gorbachev. In addition to the normal societal groups, there emerged groups with nationalist orientations thus adding the dimension of open ethnic/nationalist articulation of inequality in the Baltic Republics and in Caucasia. At the same time, there emerged unprecented political groups of Army officials showing the heterogeneous character of the Army.

Yeltsin's Russia does not have a self-conscious classical capitalist class[54] though it has now the induction of private property, shock therapy and the withdrawal of the State implied in that therapy. It has a bureaucratic class as a substitute. Like the Soviet states, the Yeltsin state relied upon his chosen advisors, who had grown to more than 20000 officials with acquisitive and compradore features. The point is that the inequalities in the society cannot prevent the regionalisation of the economy, since these are not based on class homegenisation. The new organisation that mushroomed into thousands under glasnost were not viable organisations to provide for an argument in favour of pluralist (read American kind) democracy. In terms of Rutland's analysis, Russia is not ripe for any kind of democracy, in liberal, elite or Marxist terms. He concludes by saying that democratisation of Russia has a long way to go[55]. Russia may have its own version of democracy, a task yet incomplete.

Russian social emancipation is linked to the strategies that are sought to be pursued. The debate in the Russian Parliament between the government and the legislature shows that under discussion was the issue which strategy of capitalist development is appropriate for Russia. The difference of opinion has been on three issues viz., the role of the State, the correlation of various forms of ownership and the degree to which social issues were to be tackled in terms of social justice[56]. Khasbulatov preferred a social market economy to Prime Minister Gayder's strategy of market economy in which privatisation, liberalisation, stabilisation or demonopolisation were to accompany the strategy of containing inflation at the then rate of 25 per cent[57]. Gayder also commended the effort of the Russian government in getting loans from abroad. The government opted for a market economy while the Opposition asked for a mixed capitalist economy. A mix of both will bring in comparisons with India and China, with a liberalising and privatising the economy.

The Russian government appears to be pursuing an economic package that can be called a liberal economy and political package which ties the values of individual political freedom, personal responsibility, rights and liberties, freedom of choice and responsibility. This is a neo-conservative prescription[58] that takes one back to the 19th century version of capitalism and democracy wherein the state existed as an antinomy to the market. The resultant situation of this strategy then was, as it is now, more acute social contradiction. The loans available to the Russian government by the European Bank for Reconstruction and Development (EBRD) established in 1991 to help restructure Russia's economy, combined economic and political objectives which are to "promote multi-party democracy, pluralism and the market economics". (Article 1).

Given the fledgling, weak, and ineffective process of democratic politics from the standards of bourgeois democracy, and given the fragmented nature of democratic parties, the plurality of institutionalisation of social contradictions, outside the pale of communists of different hues, is bound to take the form that may go against the secular, multi-ethnic character of the Russian people, on the one hand, and the model of Western democracy, on the other. This, in turn, will make people go back to obsolete signs of cultural and historical identities in the face of crises that can not thus be solved. It is bound to give rise to an acute sense of deprivation and to political action.

Russian democracy will face the challenges emanating from assertion of a sense of deprivation—both absolute and relative—

in violent forms. During the period 1988-1991, the number of social and inter-nationality conflicts in the territory of the Soviet Union totalled 87. Between January 1988-1993, emergency was imposed on 26 occasions. In the Russian Federation, there are innumerable hot spots in Caucasia and TransCaucasia.

Challenges to the Democratic Identity

Three theories that have attempted to explain the emergence of ethno-political conflicts, namely, that of modernisation, historical-cultural roots and the instrumentalist may be useful in explaining the assertion of partial truths of the ethnic, religious and cultural roots of the new challenges that have emerged in the world, and particularly in the erstwhile Soviet Union. Tedd Gurr and Harff suggest a more comprehensive theory for explaining ethno-political conflicts in countries as far apart as Germany, Malaysia, Iraq, and Nicaragua[59]. Their thesis is "that a people who strongly identify with their ethnic brethren and who live in an autocratic political system with low international economic status, one that has used discrimination and intermittent violence to repress its ethnic peoples, are the most likely to challenge their oppressors"[60]. The strength of the thesis is that it takes into consideration the internal and external factors, and in the latter, its focus is on the political environment with the variables of sense of relative deprivation, leading to a sense of discrimination, group identity as evolved through history, leadership from elements that have benefited from the process of modernisation and those who have the capacity to provide group cohesion. The political aspect of the variables is related to the guarantee of political and civil rights for all citizens, effective constitutional limitation on the power of the executive, multiple political parties that compete for office and transfer of power by constitutionally prescribed ways[61].

In the Russian Federation, contingent danger of the social contradictions taking recourse to ethnic/criminal violent terrorist articulation are real. The causality has to be sought in the primacy of weak liberal and social democratic tradition, the absence of a social class/classes given by the liberal, neo-conservative, liberal social democratic economic strategy and more specifically, in the weak political institutionalisation and the equally weak political process that the present democratic restructuring shows. It must be kept in view that despite the role of a movement based on the right of nations to self-determination in building democratic polities and of building the edifice of socialist Soviet polity, it has the potential of the negation of democratic identities and their consolidation. The lack of political autonomy in the Soviet case after secession, the growth of the new problems in the Union Republic that emerged as a result of Soviet industrialisation and administrative distortions denying autonomy, led to a new ethnic articulation as in Nagorno-Karabakh. These and others could play a negative role in that it may chip away from the state security. This negative role of the principle of self-determination is highlighted elsewhere too. Amitai Etzioni feels that in the new international circumstances, the movements based on the principle of self-determination, more often than not, undermine the potential for democratic development in non-democratic countries and threaten the foundation of democratic ones. It is time to withdraw moral approval from most of the movements and see them for what they mainly are destructive[62]. Most of the countries that face these challenges in the form of severe violent-terrorist framework can not escape the international implication of it.

Though theorists do sanction the use of force for removal of inequality[63] as democratic violence, no State can ignore its illegality and therefore, will resort to force till force becomes counter-productive and, therefore, needs to manage the political variable in terms of media, public opinion, and all the other tools of hegemony listed earlier. In the case of Russia, given the weakness of the political dimension (in comparative contrast to India), there is the likelihood of the use of the national security apparatus for the restoration of political and electoral stability. The role of the Russian peace-keeping forces in the 'near abroad' and the Russian Federation can, and has, effected the desirable results from the angle of Moscow.

National Security Thinking

The attempt on the part of Yeltsin to quickly arrived at the CIS without the initial participation on the Central Asian Republics at Minsk was a damage limitation exercise in the wake of Gorbachev's failure to get the Union Treaty ratified on August 22, 1991, owing to the failed coup. The Ashkhabad and Alma-Ata endeavours to give greater coherence to the idea of a common military, economic and political space by including the Central Asian Republics and the facilitating consolations with states like Ukraine that have refused to join the military union of the CIS, were prompted by security threats emanating from porous borders[64], illegal and trans-border activities to undermine the Russian Federation by creating the problems of migration of the Russian diaspora. Apart from the external threats that the region's new emerging States faced, there was the problem of increasing threats to internal stability in the absence of the security protection that the Soviet forces had guaranteed[65].

The Russian Federation is equally afflicted with the problems of internal security. These problems are closer to the countries of the Third World and share very little of the security concerns of the Western advanced countries in NATO. The literature on security on the Third World concerns itself with the issues of political instability, societal violence and national fragmentation[66]. Russia faces them in the post-communist phase[67]. The new Russian military doctrine that has evolved since the publication of its summary draft version, underlined the danger of threats emanating from within and goes on to discuss the force structures necessary for meeting the new threats. The threats detailed under this head are the following: unlawful activities of nationalist, separatist and other organisations aimed at destabilising the internal situation within the Russian Federation and violating its territorial integrity through the armed force; attempted overthrow of the constitutional regime, disorganising the operation of organs of State authority and control, attacks on nuclear energy facility, chemical and biological plants and other potentially dangerous objects; creation of illegal armed formations; growth of organised crime and smuggling activities on a scale which threatens safety of citizens and of society at large; attacks on arsenals and arms store, enterprises producing weapons and special military technology and property, and on organisations, institutions or structures permanently equipped with weapons, with the purpose of capturing them; illegal dissemination within the territory of the Russian Federation of weapons, ammunition explosives and other means of performing acts of sabotage and terrorism; and illegal drug trafficking[68]. This threats can be classified into issues of internal stability, societal violence and national or ethnic disintegration. The interventions by the Russian State on these threats will give rise to a threat to the fragile but emerging co-relation of civil-military relations and the dangers of having national security priorities concerns as opposed to the democratic process in Russia as also elsewhere in the 'near abroad'[69]. It may now necessarily be the malaise of authoritarianism, of transition from neo-patrimonial regimes[70].

Yeltsin's Russia's democratic identity is conditioned by the limits of Russian specificity of political emancipation involved in the fragility of the democratic process afoot there. This limitation would increasingly be evident in the emergence of the new contradictions that are rooted in the savage capitalist policies presently followed. The form of these contradictions could be social, ethnic, religious and cultural with or without external linkages. The politics of these movements could be violent. Given the tradition of State intervention, and fragility of democratic political culture, Yeltsin's response could be strong armed, particularly if the movements have external linkages or if internally the going is tough. Two possibilities exist in such situations. One, either power gets fragmented; or two, it gets concentrated. In Russia, both are happening. The concentration of power is evident in that the new security structures are coming directly under the President. Under the new strains of transition, the Russian Army's fractionalisation is taking place. The regime has to increasingly depend upon the advice of the internal security chiefs[71]. At the same time, the leaders of the military districts are insistently demanding autonomy. This is happening in day to day administration as also in situations of conflict, or, to put it in other words, in the process of transitions full of contradictory pulls. It is possible that Russia may not be able to fully achieve its democratic potential and that the national security concerns and the increasing role of the specialists of violence will strain the linkage between development and democracy that the Western funding agencies are insisting on. The Russian economy reached its nadir in 1998, when the rouble was devalued in the wake of an economic crash, Yeltsin had to resign and nominate Putin. Similarly, the behaviour of some of the members of the Russian DUMA is singularly disgusting and undemocratic[72]. One member of DUMA, who was living with a few women, wanted to introduce a legislation on introducing polygamy. Another member beat up Priest member. The fight was attempted to be prevented by two women. It is documented that Zhivnovskey joined in and hurt a woman interventionist.

II

It was election time in the Russian Federation, with the Presidential elections being held on March 26, 2000 as a result of pre-ponement, after Vladimir Putin stepped into the Kremlin once Boris Yeltsin resigned prematurely, in the wake of a melt-down of Russian economy and polity that began in May 1998. A 110 strong Initiative Group composed of deputies of St. Petersburg Legislative Assembly, Sergei Mronov and Igro Matveyev, St. Petersburg Writers' Union Chairman Mikhail Chulaki, the Unity movement north-west division leader Boris Gzyzlov, St. Petersburg's State University Chancellor, Lyudmilla Verbitskaya, Mining Institute Dean Vladimir Litvinenko, as well as directors of the leading industrial enterprises such as Krishin Efteergsyntcz (Krisihi refinery), Glynozem (black-soil) Joint Stock Company and Lenteransgaz (Gas transportation company) supported his candidature.

The parties, he had the support of, were All Russia Movement of Yakovlev, Our Home Is Russia of Victor Chernomyrdin, Democratic Russia, Common Cause leaders, Peasants Party of Russia and Free Democrats. Ex-Prime Minister, Primakov made an announcement that the Fatherland movement will take a positive attitude towards Putin. The chances of Putin of consolidating further were bright while the support base of Zyuganov was already split. The Union of Public and Political forces (UPPF) a split away faction of the Patriotic Union of, Russia, held a congress and announced their displeasure at the hegemonic attitude of the communists, under the leadership of Valeriy Tarasor. Putin had the support of Trade Unions and Mufti Talagat Tadzhddin.

The long registration process showed that the list of original fifteen aspirants was getting reduced to eleven as the nomination process was coming to a close. The nomination process suggests that the shrinkage was due to factional fights, loss of original support base and corruption that investigations of original election papers that were submitted by candidates like Zhirinovsky. He was debarred from elections and had threatened to take the Election Commission to the Court. Zyuganov was as well asked to explain his possession of two flats and four Volkswagens, and his commercial bank accounts and wife's shares in the joint stock company. The two incidents show a coincidental prejudice on behalf of the Election Commission. Zyuganov continued to be a challenge to Putin. Owing to the performance of the Communists in the preceding elections to Duma in December, 1999, i.e., polling highest votes to the tune of 24-29 per cent and owing to the suspicion of Putin's proclivities, some political forces talked of impending dictatorship, especially in the wake of Putin's support to a communist for speakership of Duma.

The context of the last elections is Russia's descent into dismal anarchy since the introduction of the market, that has meant mafiaisation of economy, society and polity, with absence of strengths of pursuing a democratic path under the Constitution, which is patterned on the French. The winter of discontent that Russia witnessed during the failure of Perestroika had deepened beyond recognition. To take a shorter view of the descent, it can be traced back to August 1998 when the rouble was devalued owing to the growth of oligarchs instead of entrepreneurs. This meant that drift of power was towards (a) the DUMA and (b) the regions. The drift had been caused by dysfunctioning of the economy, high inflation, societal dislocation, budgetary collapse and the criminalisation of the military. Yeltsin charisma and authority touched its *nadir,* owing to his nomenclature, the role of his daughter, the corruption surrounding the family, and, significantly lack of German and Japanese support once Kohl and Hashimoto left their respective political scenes.

The Financial Mess

The condition of the Russian economy was revealed by the following data released by the Russian Economic Ministry, as reported by the end of January, 2000 (a) citizen's official money incomes in 1999 fell by 15 per cent in contrast to the previous year; (b) every third Russian was below the poverty line; (c) purchasing power of money fell by 20 per cent; (d) 2/3rd of the country's population experienced a drop in living standards in 1991; (e) pensioners and disabled became especially poor; (f) purchasing power of families with many children, single mothers, public sector workers and employees shrank by almost 1/4th; (g) the poor-rich divide is especially acute (40 fold) in Magadan, Kamchatka and Amur regions, Yakutia, Khabarvosk Territory and Moscow. These are the regions that are richer and where packages of mixed economy (read welfare) are in operation. Of course, every Russian family has alternatives sources of income, but, legal wages do not exceed more than 40 per cent of the overall composition; (h) finally the number of unemployed at the end of 1999 December were 8.65 million, i.e., down by 11.1 per cent from the figure of January 1999. Crime reached unprecedented heights with theft, robbery and contract killings heading the list of 1999.

This was the condition despite the fact that 1999 witnessed positive trends, i.e., 9-10 per cent growth in industry, 5 fold increase in positive balance of profits to losses, lower inflation rate, i.e., down to 38 and doubling of balance of trade from 15.1 billion to 29 billion dollars. However, economic recession continued and disintegration of Russia was the forecast for the first decade of the 21st century because the decline in the federal income was 19.4 per cent below the projected figure. This means that regional Governors have become powerful and their support to the Presidential candidate a deciding factor.

Regionalisation had not only caused Chechnya, but had also meant that regions pursue their own economic, diplomatic and foreign policies. There was a general failure of the Russian system owing to the non-intervention of the Russian State that had allowed the oligarchs to grow. In that context, Putin's popularity has taken an upswing because of Russian victory in Chechnya. Howsoever, you may judge it— from the perspective of State or that of human rights, the Russian State had asserted itself.

Candidates and Issues

Russian presidential candidates were faced with the tasks of building statehood, market and capitalism with a human, if not, a humane face. The election campaign shows that there is talk of banishing the oligarchs. They were compared by Putin with Lobbyists and Corporations in the US. However, he bemoaned the fact that their influence was not institutionalised, and also that institutions, including that of the Presidency were not above their influence. There was talk of privatising gas, electricity and rail monopolies. Putin opposed the dismembering of the Unified Energy System of Russia, Joint Stock Company Gazprom and the Ministry of Railways. There was a fuel and food crisis, especially in the North.

Given the threat of Russian State's deepening meltdown what route will Russia take with these Elections? Going by the programmes of some of the candidates, it is difficult to give an answer that will negate the dismal prognostications for the present decade. Zyuganov analysed the situation, attacks the oligarchs and suggested that national assets should benefit the people and not the former. He suggested the introduction of State monopolies in tobacco and *vodka,* which will help the budget to triple straight away, and the State would be able to guarantee a minimal of monthly payment of 1,000 roubles to each person. He suggested tax reduction, prevention of drain of hard currency to the tune of one to two billion dollars each month from the country. Primakov, who had announced his tentative support to Putin said the reasons for support to Putin are the latter's defence of the principles of Statehood, order, the development of the real sector of the economy, support for the domestic producer, a socially oriented economy, and the preservation of the State's territorial integrity. On the political front, Zyuganov suggested amendment of the Constitution to curtail the power of the President, increase those of the Duma and the Ministry, support to local self-government, creation of a Procurator General's Office and the support to courts that are paralysed by criminal cases because almost 10 million people are involved in latent or hidden crime.

The right wing parties' programme suggested a referendum (rejected by the Election Commission) on issues of property rights, immunity of legislators, making the army professional, and, for making amendments to the Constitution and limiting the right of the President to dismiss the government. They were, generally, for market society, individual rights and restructuring the regions. The last had to be seen in the context of various proposals being made to decrease the number of regions. For example, a Presidential candidate Tuleyev suggested that number of regions should be reduced and that the governors should be centrally nominated for a period of five years.

Putin's Agenda

Putin's views are significant and that have influenced the subsequent years, for, he won. His personality was little known, but whatever is known (through his earlier colleagues) of this 47 years old Leningrader, the Security Service officer, shows him to be a very private person, secretive, rarely thaws but with few, and is 'tough, cynical and ambitious' with colossal capacity for work; bit of a snob, and values technology for professionalism. The men whom he brought, after he came into Kremlin, show his bias towards Leningraders and security services background. These are Aleksey Pudrin, Dimitriy Kozak, Igor Sechin, Vicktor Cherkesov, Leonid Reyman, Sergei Ivanov, Yuri Shevchenko, Dro Tiry Medvedev, Vladimir Kozhing, German Gref, Victor Ivanov, Yuri Zaostrovskiy and Alexander Abramov. He praised these for their professional qualities. His elections campaign staff was headed by Dimitriy Medvedev— a Leningrader.

High on Putin's agenda and low on Western estimates of Putin has been the Russian Army's Chechen campaign. Putin decided to be in Chechnya because of security concerns. Rebutting the suggestion that he should not focus on the issue he said, 'I am absolutely convinced that we will solve no problems— neither economic, military nor social— in the conditions where the State is falling apart. Therefore, I believe that there is nothing unusual in the fact that we are now, currently, attaching such an importance and paying such attention to the problem of fighting terrorism. We must solve this problem once and for all. This is why I made the trip there'. He announced the successful completion of campaign in Grozny and gave directives for normalisation of social and political situation in Chechnya by supplying electricity to the Shali and Urus-Martan administration districts and to the whole of the Chechen plains not later than March 15 and return gas service to lowlands by 1st of March, as also the opening of schools and hospitals by then. He ordered that by September 1, 2000 schools, oil institutes and universities should open. In retaliation, Chechen leaders, like Ring-General, Vakha Assanov and Commander of Eastern Front announced the beginning of total combat operations in the entire State of Russia.

Commenting on the labour parameters, Putin said, "... it is now very important for both the State and the trade union movement to establish a civilized labour market,' by bringing in labour legislation to manage relations between the labour and entrepreneur associations, to work towards the development of the small and medium businessman as well as open the possibilities of new jobs. He supported the right wing's proposal for a referendum mentioned above. He supported property rights, opposed absolute immunity for members of Parliament, did not commit himself on the issue of dismissal of government and said that Russia should move in the direction of the professional army keeping in view the possibilities of the Statehood. He supported protection of the rights of citizen-patriotism and people's welfare, rights and freedom. He admitted that life of the ordinary Russian is very hard. He opposed the communists' demand for redistribution of property and intended to have pro-market reforms.

For the 'near abroad', he wanted that the CIS should integrate. In a CIS council meeting he discussed the free trade zone, which was not on the agenda and set up an "expert group" from among representatives of the Commonwealth countries to perfect free trade mechanisms. The Russian military doctrine is also in for further change and in this re-emphasis on the nuclear arms has been announced. Given the need for the State to assert itself with reference to domestic economic and federal turmoil, Putin will assert this in external policy as well. A foreign policy reorientation towards Asia and South Asia will dovetail his westernised slant in the context of NATO expansion.

What happens on the 26 of March when elections were held depended upon a variety of factors, namely, (a) alliance with regional governors, who are playing their own game of altering regional alignments, (b) alliances with the Russian Oligarchs, (c) levels of disruption of the electoral process, (d) winning over of the rival's support base and (e) international support. DUMA elections' pattern will not be repeated here. Putin's chances seemed better than Zyuganov's. The fight was between two parameters of State intervention: a little more than minimalist and less than maximalist. Putin seemed to be symbolizing this mixed ground and receiving lot of popular acclaim for that in Russia.

III

Putin's elections took place in the double context of globalisation externally, and the logic of it in the Yeltsin era, internally. Described as coronation, Putin's nomination to the Prime Ministership first and then to the position of the acting President on Yeltsin's premature retirement raised many contradictions within Russia that involved the Russian plutocracy and policy options. Putin's career will remain constrained by the existence of the political stranglehold of plutocracy- bordering on a shadow state. Owing to Putin's desire to win away the mass base of Zyuganov, the Communist candidate, in the last two elections to the Presidential Office, that desires welfarist state with a strong domestic and foreign policy.

Since the end of 1991 and the coming in of Yeltsin Presidency there has been a desirable expectation among the Russian elites of the introduction of the market economy on the basis of the neo--liberal agenda. This was belied by the reality of the myth of it. The optimists in the US administration along with the Russian policy makers, under Yeltsin, believed that it was necessary and desireable to integrate Russia in the Western capitalist market. The nature of Perestroika with its privatisation, liberalisation and voucher scheme had little to offer as a road to transition to the prescribed neo-liberal agenda. The Yeltsin shock therapy, i.e., monetary stabilisation, liberalisation and privatisation, known as Washington consensus, led finally to the debacle of the 1998 August meltdown in the economy and the festering wound of poverty into which the population had been since sliding. So the regime's aims of joining the market were belied. Says Rutland 'the regime set out along the yellow brick road which it hoped to bring Russia, sooner rather than later, to the market...appeared to furnish the emergent, and rather insecure, Russian ruling group with a ready made objective around which they hoped to unite the Russian people.' But 'the rhetoric of marketisation was merely a smokescreen behind which the old elite could ruthlessly set about looting the country's assets for its own private benefit.'[73] At the same time the Russian State has been flooded with funds but with no effect on the economy. This made the scholar prognosticate about Russia's incapacity in foreign policy to assert against the West. Walton describes it as a predatory state in the throes of a slide into a second rung power in the category of Japan and India. As such given the geopolitical compulsions Russia is not being able in the long run to offer any challenge either to the West or to China.[74]

The analysis of some others shows the Russian State to be a shadow State. By this is implied a relationship between corruption and politics. It is based on dejure personal rule. The concept borrows from Weber's patrimonial state where the patrimonial office lacks above all the bureaucratic separation of the private and the official sphere. Political administration is treated as purely a personal affair of the ruler and the political power is considered part of his personal property, which can be exploited by means of contribution and fees. The shadow states should be understood as 'private commercial syndicates'[75]. Some polls show that criminal structures exercise control and influence. In an opinion poll in 1988, 80 per cent of Russians said this. In another survey 46 per cent percent believed that the judicial system is fair now and then. Sixty-eight per cent reported that they would seek help of the police, courts and security agencies if their legal rights were violated. 16.1 per cent believed that Russian governments 'primarily benefited shadow economy and Mafia capital'. Moscow had in 1997 homicide rate of 18.1 per cent per hundred thousand residents well short of Washington's 69.3 per cent and was below 250 per 100, 000 in Lagos. There was the incidence of the high profile political assassinations: e.g., in December 1998 murder of Galina Starovoita, a military police officer from St. Petersburg, and the attempt on the life of Moscow's Deputy Mayor, Mayor Yuri Shantsev's. This analysis compares Russia with African states like Liberia where President Samuel Doe accumulated a fortune equivalent to half of Liberia's annual domestic income.

The second contradiction relates to the desire of Russia's transition to the democratic order and the actual order created. Given the nature of the elitist and weak democratic movement, the transition to political and social change identified with perestroika and glasnost the hope that the abolition of the CPSU will establish the democratic order was belied. The Yeltsin nomenclatura and the use of force against the Parliament was welcomed by the Western analysts, especially in the Clinton administration, since the introduction of the IMF reforms did not have to face the demands of rule of law. This related not only to the issue of introduction of the IMF strategies but also the implementation of policies with reference to the problems faced by the Russian Federation in terms of monetary crisis and the secessionist movements like the Chechnya revolt and the connected terrorism in Moscow. The democratic parties were splintering and had dubious linkages with the new oligarchy that was emerging in Russia. For a regime that rejected socialist pluralism, that had very weak liberal tradition of the Kerensky Government and the society in which traditionally the individual was more dependent on the state for entrepreneurial activity the Yeltsin era was a mark of continuity rather than change. The State bureaucracy had mattered. As a result the Yeltsin period, unlike the Gorbachev period, did not inspire the people to be active, one expert of the Chatham House says 'The Russian crises had one distinguishing feature compared with those of the 1980s- ordinary people have not been active in the political process....The ...public generally cares less and less about elections, politics and politicians. Individual prosperity or survival, the rapid acquisition of short-term material assets and rampant consumerism, rather than abstract ideas and wider undertaking, has become order of the day. Long term mobilisation not only for a political, but for any long term goal, be it career development or a pension scheme, is alien to a majority.'[76] In such a situation what are going to be the processes that will determine policy and its continuation on a reliable basis. Ad hocism combined with lack of institutional process and the indifference to the democratic procedure could provide the ground for short term domestic and foreign policy responses.

The third contradiction relates to the State formation itself. Owing to the economic crash the regions and their governors were asserting their sovereignty over the legitimacy of the regions. The Centre is unable to finance the regions. They fend for themselves. During the period 1996-98 regional autonomy had menacingly risen. They had buttressed their own legitimacy at the expense of stability within the Federation. There is regionalisation of the federal military structure. There is the replacement of the State owned financial industrial assets with private capital control. Owing to independent communication network there is fear of fragmentation. The implementation of the key initiatives by the key constituent parts of the Federation has further buttressed autonomy within the periphery. In 1998 Tatarstan ignored federal legislation on citizenship. Between 1996-98 Governors who were elected representatives replaced the previous system of Presidential appointees. Troops depended on the regions for basic amenities and salaries. The Governor's give gratis to them. This happened in the Pacific Fleet and in the Far East. Given the increasing Chinese interests and Chinese Diaspora in the region the country is bound to face not only internal pressures but also external pressures from China. Regional leaders are also signing agreements with foreign countries, e.g., Tatarstan with Ukraine.[77] Given a federal collapse, a secessionist movement in Chechnaya and terrorist incidents rocking Moscow the leadership will face the dilemma of the psyche of great Russian past and greater Russian marginalisation not only in the West but also with reference with China. This will only strengthen the Russian proclivity to admire the past and hope for the future in contrast to an unacceptable present.

Fourthly, as far as the military is concerned it is not even a patch work quilt. The General Staff of the Armed Forces reported on the psychological stress and low morale amongst troops caused by each cash starvation, regionalisation, and the growing criminalisation of the armed structures.[78] A later General Staff Report said that the Russian military was on the brink of being unable to fulfil its primary functions—the defense of the Federation.[79] Given the Russian commitments on the nuclear question and the decommissioning of the nuclear arsenal Russia is bound to slide from its current nuclear super power status as well as its traditional conventional military might. The recent incident involving the sinking of the submarine, Kursk, is a signal in that direction, according to many. Its knowledge, procurement and experience are its strength.

The Russian thinking on security is that it is being dragged into conflicts against its own interests and beliefs. The Presidential Decree of December 17, 1997 on National Security regarded NATO to be a threat; proliferation of WMD; potential and unauthorised use of weapons of mass destruction and destabilisation of internal security as a result of breaches of international agreements in the area of Russian control. The central theme of the paper is to protect Russia's special status as a strategic power vis-a-vis the USA. This is coloured by the perception that the USA is seeking to secure a strategic advantage while Russia is weakened, with reference to the US nuclear BMD.[80] Russia has little choice but to enter into counter moves, agreements and strategic understandings with who-so-ever is willing under the vision of achieving a multi-polar world. In that context the Russian-Chinese agreement on the BMD is understandable, despite the fact that the Chinese also accommodate the U.S. by de targeting the USA when Clinton made a visit to China.

Given these contradictions the Russian President was faced with quite a few paradoxes at the centre of which was how far will the concentric circles of Russian Federation remain from the State of Muscovy to which the Russian State is being threatened to be reduced as a result of the combination of economic, political and strategic reality? What is the nature of the Russian State today—some call it predatory, others call it shadow state and still others like to compare it with the Russian tradition.

In this broad analytic specific liberal themes emerged once the elections to the Russian Presidency were announced. Specific issues were raised. Crime was one major factor. According to Denis Dragunsky 'Crime is merging with capital, and capital is merging with power. Bureaucracy is swallowing, growing insolent and corrupt. Money is flowing abroad. The old infrastructure has worn out while the new one is not created....The national problem has not been solved. The economic situation depends on the fluctuation of world oil prices. Lastly there seems to be no end to the war in Chechnya.'[81]

Alexander Yakovlev said on Future of Russia "...if peoples of Russia want to be free citizens and their own masters (which I do not doubt for a moment) they must start an all out liberation struggle against the dictatorship of the officialdom, against the rule of nomenclature of the democrats, which I call 'Democrature'.[82] The liberal agenda had quite a few of its own contradictions. These related to their own support of Yeltsin and now a call for removing the legacy of that regime. Two, their opposition to the Democrature does not fit well with their own links with the plutocracy that emerged in the Yeltsin regime and the support they got from it during the elections.

Plutocracy has its crippling effect on the democratic communists as well. The liberals are a weak power with a weak mass and electoral base.

The Communists asked for a version of Welfarist State during the elections. The democratic Communist candidate for Presidential elections held on March 26,2000, Gennady Zhugyanov, made a case for a legal order at the political level and for State intervention to stop flight of capital from the country. His proposed measures in the political realm were: amend the constitution to limit President's absolute power; to create strong cabinet controlled by the Parliament; the restoration of the hierarchy of authority and the support of the local self government; creation of a Procurator-General's Office which had been destroyed and the support of courts that were paralysed by the criminal cases. Almost 10 million people had been subject to administrative punishment. At the economic level he suggested reduction of taxes, prevention of drain of hard currency since 1to 2 billion dollars leave the country each month. Some people were extracting people's wealth of natural resources to the tune of $ 80 billion per annum. He suggested a State monopoly on tobacco and vodka.[83]

In this context it is only natural that Putin and his views on Russia as they have emerged were focused. The Western Press and especially the right wing organisations in the US like the Heritage Foundation did not like his past. In a study it said this is the return of the Anti AmericanCzar.[84] At the time of publication of a book on Putin his secret service background was regarded as a critical point. Richard Pipes said that he was harassing media, e.g., NTV and licensing newspapers. He wants ejections of Governors from upper house so that he can prosecute them.[85] According to William Beer, who holds the Japan Chair, he will not move to look after Japanese relations.[86] Gorbachev said that 'He lacks sufficient experience to be able to lead a country such as this at a time such as this....He must distance himself from his past' and not revert to the Yeltsin era. The elections showed that Putin got 52.52 per cent of votes as against Zyuganov's 29.44 per cent, who was to get the second highest number of votes.[87]

There is enough in Putin's own words to construct his view of the State. He expressed a feeling of disquiet about the country's fate, about Russia's future.[88] In an article on the idea of Russia he views the Russian State to be playing a strong role. Like Lenin and Andropov he talked about the Russian backwardness and wants to bring order in Russia. He sees the war in Chechnya to cement the Russian society together. He is more worried about the lack of social harmony. In this context he upholds the values of modernist democracy values. He accepted the word Rossisskaya which did not carry any ethnic or nationalist undertones.[89] Leningrader, 47 year old President with Secret Service background, like Andropov here and Bush in the US, he is considered to be tough, cynical, and ambitious, has colossal capacity to work, fond of judo and alpine skiing and stands for technology and professionalism.[90]

Specifically on the State he says 'I am absolutely convinced that we will solve no problems—neither economic nor social-in the conditions where the state is falling apart. Therefore I believe that there is nothing unusual in the fact that we are now, currently, attaching such an importance and paying such attention to the problem of fighting terrorism. We must solve this problem once and for all. This is why I made the trip there.'[91] He asserted the primacy of the State in the context of the campaign in Grozny in order to normalize the social and economic situation in Chechnya. In fight against secession using terrorist-tactics States are known to use force in order to bring order in the region of turmoil. So, there is nothing dictatorial in this.

On the needs of Russia he announced during the elections:

1. We need a professional, dynamic and disciplined civil service (a point Lenin had made during his last days), not a bloated and out of hand bureaucratic world unto itself that is indifferent to people.
2. To achieve a compliance with the law and constitutional discipline relating to law and order.
3. 'We are a rich country for a poor people.'
4. 'Guarantees of property rights and reliable protection of the market from the official and criminal rackets.'
5. One cannot have a strong state without each citizen possessing personal dignity and the country possessing national dignity as a whole, and
6. Asked for a feedback from the people.[92]

The idea of a strong state did not have to give rise to fears of the Soviet/Russian/Marxist past since the State in the paradigm of Mills' writings was equally viewed by Marx as a strong state allowing for the full play of the market. More recently, from the perspective of the post modern the State in the West and the ones related to macro narratives are regarded as strong States. Putin's problems are related to a State which has jettisoned the welfarist programme without the market mechanism in its place and has a state structure that is difficult to hold together owing to centrifugal tendencies and the control of the plutocracy of the political and economic levers. The plutocracy has given rise to the theorisations of the shadowy States—neither liberal nor Marxist but predatory characterised by warlordism and Yeltsin's nomenclature and meltdown of the economy. In the classical sense of neo-liberal agenda what has to be seen is whether the nature of State that he creates would withstand the encirclement that Russian foreign policy is witnessing now. Going by his actions, we notice that Putin wants a stop to the secessionist based insurgencies and criminal aspects of the economy and polity. Given the fact that the Russian civil society is weak and fledgling Putin enjoyed a certain autonomy from the entrenched vested interests so that he could pursue his Russia's idea. In his path are domestic and external hurdles. In that context the remarks of Sergei Kovalev, who was Yeltsin's Commissioner of Human Rights until he resigned over the war in Chechnya, are made. He said 'we may look back on the Year 2000 as the twilight of Russian democracy'. This is an extreme critique borne of human rights concern in isolation. It should never be forgotten that Kerensky's Foreign Minister had said that Russia does not have a strong liberal tradition.

The members of the club freely looting the country were Boris Berezovsky, Mikhail Khodorskovsky, Roman Abramovich, Mikhail Fridma, and some others, who were largely coopted in the Government of Yeltsin and they caused systemic problem to Putin's idea of Russia to have a strong State and independent foreign policy. They dominate oil sector that accounts for 60 per cent of the market capitalisation of the Russian stock market and oil receipts amount to about 22 per cent of government's budget revenues. Though the oligarchs' assets were washed out by the 1998 meltdown of the economy, their influence continues to dominate the Russian political and economic life. The upswing in the economy in 1999 (e.g., 5 per cent increase in positive balance of profits and losses, be nearing doubling from $15.1 billion to 29 billion of the positive balance of trade and an additional R26 billion in budget income)[93] led to the availability of more cash with this group. This happened precisely because of the growth in oil prices.

The oligarchs began their career with the 'loans-for share' scheme leading to their control of the authorized banks, which appropriated billions of dollars from the government, and these funds vanished. The oligarchs like Khodorsky, Berezkovsky and Abramovich acquired control of oil business. They are holding assets with no operating business of their own. They sell oil to parent companies at prices lower than the international market prices. A portion of it is resold on world markets at the prevailing price. The oligarchs strip value from operating companies and their share holders, e.g., in a span of 26 weeks Khodorsky's Yukos managed to siphon off some $ 800 million.

These are unlawful activities engaged in by all the oligarchs. They engage in dilution of capital thus committing pillage. They loot their own companies directly by stealing valuable assets, including wells, equipment and anything else that can be found on the oil fields. International companies misuse these and since there is lack of rule of law benefit from these activities. Further there is capital flight. Boris is in trouble.

These oligarchs financed Yeltsin and captured him. They helped Zyuganov in the two successive elections. They helped the regional Governors. They prevent the initiation of criminal proceedings, e.g., against oil company offshore share transactions. They control the media, money and participate directly or indirectly in decision making at many levels of the Government. Through bribes, kickbacks and charitable contributions' officials are secured. The Russian judiciary faces similar situation. All of Russian political movements, including the pro-Western liberal movements are supported by them.[94] No capitalist class!

The rise of this group is made possible owing to weak democratic culture, the lack of party system, the presence of individual based factions, the weak civil society composed of mixed political persuasion, lack of independent sources of media, absence of small business, confusion and dispiritedness of civic organisations, absence of a business class and the inability of the new President to turn civic organisations into real lobbyists that he talked about during his election campaign, show up its weak democratic possibilities. Even if one acknowledges that capitalism was making some advance in the country, it has to be state capitalism and not plutocratic criminal elite creating a condition which in a different context Putin described as a situation of a rich country with poor people. As far as Russian State is concerned there is a siege from within with international linkages. His move to get rid of Governors who had charted an independent course in foreign policy is also coming under fire from the liberal commentators. Incumbent Governors were elected in the seven regions of Russia.

In the realm of foreign policy there are different levels at which it can be analysed. From the perspective of the current unipolarity, Russia wants multi polarity. From the perspective of European Union and Western financial institutions, Russia wants integration. From the perspective of Russian-German relations it wishes to move in the direction of a strategic understanding. On issues of nuclear proliferation and CTBT, Putin is with the USA and China. It wants to strengthen global security. It wants the prevention of regional conflicts. It wants to participate in international peace keeping efforts against international terrorism and drug trafficking.[95] It retains its nuclear status with 6500 nuclear weapons.

There is a siege from without that Russia cannot ignore. The features of the siege are: (a) growing trend towards a uni-polar world; (b) seeks democratisation of international relations; (c) in the Euro-Atlantic region there is threat of arbitrary interference in internal affairs; (d) expansion of NATO at the cost of Russian security interests including in Central Asia. (e) the handling of the Kosovo crisis; (e) the dedicated move by the West to get into the Caspian Sea Basin for oil and look for alternative pipelines; (f) create conditions of a new cold war in Central Asia and the Caucasia; (g) efforts for partition of Yugoslavia that might start a Balkan conflict; (h) the attempt on the part of USA to create a national missile defence system that will undermine the ABM treaty to which Russia is committed; (i) problems in Afghanistan which have a spill over effect on the CIS countries and Russian interests. (j) not much improvement has taken place since in the Russian-Japanese relations since the settlement of Kurile will not take place easily.[96]

In that context of encirclement, Russia would want a 'good neighbourly belt along the perimeter of Russian borders—a legitimate desire of minimal security in contrast to the maximalist security that took the former Soviet Union to the river Elbe. The post Yeltsin era in foreign policy indicates that the obssession with integration and cooperative relationship with the US may be on the wane.[97] A CRS study shows that the US looks at its relations with Russia negatively on the following issues, namely, Kosovo, Chechnya, Iraq, NATO expansion, Russian nuclear technology being given to Iran and military technology for Syria which have invited economic sanctions.[98]

If one applies the logic of neo-realism then one could ask a question if this is a change in the relational parameter wherein Russia is capable of asserting more against the unipolar hegemon. Given the nature of the internal siege and the social crisis that Russia is facing the stage may not have arrived for the Russian quitting the Sameness pattern of behaviour and performing the balancing act. It cannot yet perform that act. It wishes to continue with constructive foreign policy based on mutually advantageous pragmatism and promote its Eurasian identity. Putin's background is admirably suited for this. In that light one needs to see the Russian desire to have a perimeter of security, the urge to have a multipolar world and the camaradarie with India and China. In domestic terms Russia is not capable of challenging China. In fact it has moved in the direction of befriending it on strategic issues like the NMD of the USA. They have opposed Second Iraq War.

In that context its desire and move in the CIS is understandable. It has integrated with Belarus, Ukraine and Kazakhstan in 2003. It however may face suspicions in Georgia, Ukraine, Uzbekistan, Azerbaijan and Moldova. Peace is a must since Russia needs Statehood, consolidation of Civil Society and a rapid transition to stable economic growth. This is one commodity that it does not have. The CIS has not performed the way it could have in the face of the US proactive policy in Central Asia. Given the context of the US presence in its periphery of Central Asia Putin is attempting to assert the Statehood of Russia. This is evident in the manner in which he is dealing with various terrorist attacks, including in Bolshoi theatre in 2003, in Chechnya and other places in Russia. It is also evident in the manner of his moving against some of the plutocrats. Despite this the characterisation of the State cannot be democratic. In the ultimate analysis the system is nowhere near a liberal one or a capitalist one.

References

1. Yeltsin speech, Congress of People's Deputies, Summary of World Broadcasts, SU/1552
2. Richard Sakwa, edited, *Ruslan Khasbulatov, The Struggle for Russia, Power and Change in the Democratic Revolution,* London, New York, Routledge, 1993; Speech to the Congress of Peoples Deputies, SWB, SU/1553, December, 1992.
3. Vadim Madish, edited,Gennady Zyuganov, *My Russia, The Political Autobiography of Gennady Zyuganov,* M. E. Sharpe, Amonk, New York, London, England, 1997.
4. Stephen White, *Russia's new politics, The management of post Communist society,* Cambridge, Cambridge University Press, 2000.
5. Szleynic, 'The Rise of Managerialism: The 'New Class After The Fall of Communism',Discussion Papers No.16, *Collegium Budhapest,* October 18, 1995.
6. Francis Fukuyama, "End of History", *National Interest,* Winter, 1988-89; Samuel P. Huntington, "Clash of Civilization", Foreign Affairs, Summer, 1993.
7. Ralph Miliband and Leo Panitch, ed., "New World Order", *Socialist Register,* Merlin Press, 1992.
8. Benedict Anderson, *Imagined Communities, Reflections on the Origin and Spread of Nationalism,* London, New York, Verso, 1991.
9. Quoted in Lowell Dittmer and Samuel S. Kim, "In Search of a Theory of National Identity", in Lowell Dittmer and Samuel S. Kim, *China's Quest for National Identity,* Ithaca and London, Council University Press, 1993.
10. *Ibid.,* p.12.
11. *Ibid.,* p.13.
12. *Ibid.,* p.17.

13. Douglas W. Blum, ed., *Russia's Future, Consolidation or Disintegration,* Boulder, San Francisco, Oxford, Westview Press, 1994.
14. Andrew A. Michta, *Government and Politics of Post-Communist Europe,* Westport, Praeger, 1994.
15. Stephen D. Shenfild, "Post-Soviet Russia in search of identity", in Douglas W. Blum, *n. 8,* pp. 5-16.
16. Douglas W. Blum, "Disintegration and Russian foreign policy". In Douglas W. Blum, *Ibid.,* p.139.
17. Raymond Williams, "Culture", in David Mclellan, ed. *Marx, The First Hundred Years,* Great Britain, Fontana Paperbacks, 1983, p.17.
18. David Mclellan, *Marx Before Marxism,* Penguin, 1970, p.171.
19. Karl Marx, "On the Jewish question", in Marx and Engels, *Collected Works,* Vol. 3, Moscow, 1975, pp. 162, 163.
20. Quinton Hoare and Geoffrey Nowell Smith, ed, *Selections from the Prison Notebooks of Antonio Gramsci,* New York, International Publishers, 1971, p. 206.
21. David Mclellan, "Politics", in David Mclellan, n.12, pp.146-147.
22. Hegemony is defined as "an order in which a certain way of life and thought is dominant, in which one concept of reality is diffused throughout society in all its institutional and private manifestations, informing with its spirit all taste, morality, customs, religion and political principles, and all social relations, particularly in their intellectual and moral connotations." G.A. Williams, "Gramsci's concepts of egomania", in Journal of History of Ideas, 1960, Vol. 21, No. 4, p. 587, quoted in Ralph Miliband, *The State in Capitalist Society,* London, Melbourne, New York, Quartet Books, 1973, p.162.
23. Ralph Miliband , *Ibid.,* pp. 161-236.
24. C.B. Macpherson, Life and Times of Liberal Democracy, OUP, Oxford, 1977.
25. Marks, n. 14, p.163.
26. T.B. Bottomore, "Sociology," in David Mclellan, n. 12, pp. 135-36.
27. Tony Saich, " The search for civil society and democracy in China", *Current History,* September 1994, p. 262.

28. Albert Camus says, "All existence for a man turned away from the external is but a vast mime..." Albert Camus, *Myth of Sisyphus,* Penguin, 1977, p. 87.
29. Dostoevsky quoted in *ibid.* p.100 Dr. Rajendra Dengle of the German Centre, School of Languages drew my attention to this quote.
30. B.H. Summers, "Frontier", in Thomas Righa, ed., *Reading in Russian Civilisation,* University of Chicago and London, 1963, Vol. 1, pp. 1-19, hereafter referred to as RRC.
31. Dimitri Obolensky, "Russia's Byzantine heritage," in Thomas Righa, RRC, Vol. 2, *Ibid.,* p.202.
32. B.H. Summer, *n.28,* pp.10-11.
33. Derek Offord, *Portraits of Early Russian Liberals,* Cambridge, OUP, 1985, pp. 180-182.
34. It is held that Lenin had hardly any time for handling the issue of nationalities which formed the majority of the Czarist Empire. Implemention of self-determination, administration, political and territorial adjustments, cultural autonomy with a tinge of Russification without the binding thread of political participation. There have been multi-ethnic families cutting across religion, and Slav and non-Slav peoples' identities but owing to historical specificities, these came to be distorted by the problems of uneven development, ecological insecurities giant attempts to change geographical features, Stalinist distortions and many other problems that cropped up after the revolution, listed by the special conference on the nationalities question by the CPSU during the Gorbachev period.
35. Tom Bottomore, Lawrence Harris, V.G. Kiernan, Ralph Miliband, *A Dictionary of Marxist Thought,* Blackwell, 1983, p.77.
36. Paul Milyukov, "The Russian liberals", in Thomas Righa, *n. 28,* pp.421-424.
37. Cyrill Black, "The nature of imperial Russian society," in Thomas Righa, *ibid.,* p. 428.
38. Barington Moore, Jr., *Authority and Inequality Under Capitalism and Socialism: USA, USSR and China* Clarendon Press, Oxford , 1987 pp. 37-38.

39. Alexander Herzen, "The young Moscow," in Thomas Righa, *n. 28,* pp. 335-337.
40. Konstantin Pobedonostsev, "The falsehood of democracy", in Thomas Righa, *n. 28.,* pp. 401-420.
41. Neil Harding, 'Socialism, society, and the organic labour state" in Neil Harding, ed., *State in Socialist Society,* 1985.
42. Jerry F. Hough, "Political participation in Soviet Union", *Soviet Studies,* Vol. Xxviii, No. 1, January 1976, pp. 3-20.
43. Hedrick Smith, *New Russians,* Random House, New York 1990. Quasi-democratic institutions (themselves spectacular improvements on the old one) had stimulated the formation of the groups and movements that were anxious to go far beyond the limits envisaged by Gorbachev. Peter Frank, "Problem of democracy in post-Soviet Russia", in Ian Budge and David Mckay, ed., *Developing Democracy,* Thousand oaks, London, New Delhi, Sage, 1994.
44. Charles Fairbank, Jr., "After August coup", *Journal of Democracy,* Vol.2, No. 4, 1991.
45. Yeltsin observed at the Congress of People's Deputies that the body elected in spring of 1990 had stood for "genuine sovereignty for one country.... We are only just beginning to master the principle of division of powers, to master a democratic political culture, but it would still be describe for progress to be more rapid... Russia needs a reforming government," *Summary of World Broadcasts* SU/1553.2, December 1992, p. C1/6-7. At the meeting of the Federation Council, he said "For the first time in its thousand-year-old history, the multi-ethnic Russia—as an integral and a single state—has become a federation of free and equal peoples". *Summary of World Broadcasts* SU/1799, September 21, 1993, p.B/1. Introducing the draft new Constitution Yeltsin said, "....A dear price has to be paid for the lack of a democratic Constitution. With its adoption, a powerful tool will appear with which to solve the most acute problems of state and society...." "...Russia needs a durable order. Not an iron hand but a democratic state power will ensure progress towards a normal and worthy life for

citizens, towards prosperity for a single, integral Russia." *Summary of World Broadcasts* SU/1843. November 11, 1993, p. C/1. In his address to the UN General Assembly's special session on the occasion of the fiftieth anniversary of the UN, on October 22, 1995, Yeltsin described Russia as "democratic Russia", *Strategic Digest,* IDSA, New Delhi Vol. XXV. No. 12, December 1995, p. 1829.

46. Quoted in Barrington Moore, Jr., *n. 33,* p.47.
47. N.43, *Summary of World Broadcasts,* SU/1533, December 2, 1992, p.C1/7.
48. *Ibid., Summary of World Broadcasts* SU/1799, September 21, 1993, p. B/1.
49. N. Beliaeva, "Russian democracy: Crisis as progress" *Washington Quarterly,* Spring, 1993, pp. 5-17.
50. Regina A. Smith, "The Russian Parliament and political consolidation," in Douglas W. Blum, n.8, p.32.
51. Dev Murarka, "Russian elections: No exit from the labyrinth", *Economic and Political Weekly,* November 11, p. 2853. The fragility of the roots of democratic culture in Russia is evident by the following episode that was reported by a public relation firm: "One candidate walked into our office and said he wanted to be elected to the Duma. When we asked him which ticket he was planning to run on, he said that it was up to us to decide such questions," *Financial Times,* November 25, 1993.
52. *N.48,* p.23.
53. Barrington Moore, Jr., *n. 37,* pp. 62-68.
54. Peter Rutland, "Has democracy failed Russia" in Adrian Leftwich, *Democracy and Development,* New Delhi, J.K. Polity Press, 1996, p. 264.
55. *Ibid.,* p. 274.
56. Speech by Khasbulatov, Russian Congress of People's Deputies, *Summary of World Broadcasts,* SU/1554, December 3 1992, p.C1/3/.
57. Speech by Gaydar, Congress of People's Deputies, *Summary of World Broadcasts,* SU/1554, December 1992, p.C1/12-18.
58. Adrian Leftwich, "On the primary of politics", *Foreign Policy,* Washington, No. 89, Winter, 1992-93, p.21.

59. Ted Robert Gurr and Barabara Harff, *Ethnic Conflicts in World Politics,* Westview Press, Boulder, San Francisco/Oxford,1994.
60. *Ibid.,* p. 92.
61. *Ibid.,* pp.77-90.
62. Amitai Etzioni, "The evils of self determination", *Foreign Policy,* Washington, No. 89, Winter, 1992-93, p.21.
63. Democracies are vulnerable to terrorist violence. From the angle of the state it is an illegitimate and an unlawful force. Is definitions are mainly focussing on the commonality of means and ends. Scholars and the states in the West link it up with the Red network or the Islamic fundamentalist organisations. In India, terrorist activities are linked to both the extreme right and the left wing. It is, however, analytically more useful to look at terrorist violence from the perspective of means employed and effects intended that create fear, insecurity and anxiety in the people generally.
64. Shaposhnikov, Speech to the Congress of People's Deputies, *Summary of World Broadcasts,* SU/15.
65. Roland Dannreutter, *Creating new States in Central Asia,* Adelphi Paper, March 1994.
66. Momen Abdul Al Mashat, *National Security in the Third World* Westview, London, 1985; Edward E. Azar and Chung I. N. Moon, *National Security in the Third World,* Edward Elgar, Cambridge, 1988; Mohammad Ayub, *Regional Insecurity in the Third World,* 1989.
67. Interview of Foreign Minister of Russia, A. Kozyrev, Nezawisimaya Gazeta, Novemeber 24, 1993, as quoted in A. Raevsky and I. N. Vorobev, *Russian Approaches to Peace-keeping,* Research Paper No. 28, (UN, NY, Geneva, 1994).
68. "Detailed account of Russian Military Doctrine", Rossiyskiye Vesti (Moscow) in Russian, November 18, 1993, p. S1/1, transl, *SWB,* SU/1358, November 29 1963, p. S1/1
69. Thomas Goltz, "Letter from Eurasia: The Hidden Russian Hand", *Foreign Policy,* No. 92, Washington, Fall 1993, pp. 92-117.

70. Lilia Shevtsova, "The Two Sides of the new Russia", *Journal of Democracy,* Vol. 6, No. 3, July 1995.
71. Presidential Security Service Chief, headed by Major General Aleksandr Korzhakov, Main Administration for Protection of the Russian Federation, headed by Lt. Gen. Mikhail Barsukov, Federal Agency of Government communications and information, headed by Lt. Gen. Aleksandr Starovoitov and Ministry of Internal Affairs, headed by Col. Gen. Anatolii Kulikov, Korzhkov has been characterised as the key man.
72. Stephen White, *op.cit.,* Cambridge University Press, Cambridge, 2000, p. 67.
73. Peter Rutland, 'Mission Impossible? The IMF and market transition in Russia', *RIS,* Vol.25, December 1999, pp.186.
74. C. Dale Walton, The decline of the Third Rome: Russia's Prospects as a Great Power, *The Journal of Slavic Studies,* Vol. 12, No. 1 (March 1999, pp. 55-63.
75. William Reno, 'Shadowy States' in Mats Berdal and David M. Malone, ed., *Greed and Grievance, Economic Agendas in Civil Wars,* Lynne Rienner Publishers, International Development Research Development. Ottawa, 2000, p. 47.
76. Anna Matveeva, 'In Search Of Enthusiasts', *The World Today,* June 1999, p.19.
77. Graeme P. Herd, 'Russia: Systemic Transformation Or Federal Collapse', *Journal of Peace Research,* Vol. 36., May, 1999, Sag Prio.
78. *Summary of World Broadcasts,* SU 3343, S, 28 September,1998-Nezavisiomaya Gazeta, Moscow, 25 September, 1998.
79. *Summary of World Broadcasts,* SU/ 3346, S1/1, 1st October, 1998, Segodnya, Moscow, 26 September,1998.
80. Andrei Shoumikin, 'Current Perspectives on Arms Control and BMD', *Comparative Strategy, An International Journal,* Vol. 18, No.1 January- March 1999.
81. Denis Dragunsky, 'A New National Project', *New Times,* May 2000.
82. *Summary of World Broadcasts,* May 2000.
83. *Summary of World Broadcasts*, SU/3765, 16 February, 00, p. B/2.

84. *http://www.org//wgbh//pages//frontline//yeltsin/etc/synopsis.html).Commenting*
85. *http://www.intellectual* capital.com/issues391/item 10047.asp
86. *http.//www.csis.org/ruseura/exoo4.html.*
87. Summary of World Broadcasts, SU/3800 28 March, 2000. B/1
88. *Source:* ITAR-TASS news agency, Moscow, in Russian,1422 gmt 28 February, 2000, Summary of World Broadcasts, SU/3778.
89. Andreas Ruesch, 'Putin's vision of a strong Russia', NZZ Background on World Affairs, January, 2000, *http://www.nzz.ch/online/on* English background/2000/background 000108 russia htm
90. *Summary of World Broadcasts,* SU/3731, B/1 7 January, 2000.
91. *Summary of World Broadcasts,* SU/3730 b/1, 6 January, 2000.
92. *Source:* ITAR–TASS News agency. Moscow, in Russian,1422 gmt, 28 February,2000, *Summary of World Broadcasts,* SU/3778.
93. *Summary of World Broadcasts,* SU/0622, WA/1, 14 January,2000.
94. Lee S. Wolosky, 'Putin's Plutocratic Problem', *Foreign Affairs,* March/April, 2000, pp.18-31; For the view that all is not bad with Russian capitalism see Thane Gustafson, *Capitalism-Russian Style,* CUP, NY, 1999, 26 n.p.; Gail W. Lapidus, *The New Russia: Troubled Transformation,* Gail W. Lapidus and Edward W. Walker,ed. *Nationalism, Regionalism and Federalism: Centre-Periphery relations in Post Communist Russia,* Boulder, Co:Westview, 1995); On elites loot see also Anders Aslund, 'Russian Collapse', *Foreign Affairs,* September/October 1999. pp. 64-77; Graeme P. Herd, 'Russia: Systemic Transformation or Federal Collapse', *Journal of Peace Research,* Vol. 36, No. 3, May 1999. Sage/PIO.
95. Mission Statement of Putin, dated December 2000. *http./www.csis.org/rusera/ex oo4.html*

96. Foreign Policy Document, *http://www. mid. Ru/ mid/ eng/ econcept.htm*
97. Michael Pogorely, Putin Offers Another hint of His intentions, July 17, 2000.
98. CRS Study On Russia, *http://www.cnie.org/nle/inter-19.html*

4

State(s) in Central Asia

Independent Central Asian States have drawn focused attention from the Russian, Iranian, Arab, Pakistani, Indian, Western and Chinese elites for reasons of geo-politics and geo-strategy. It has drawn attention from scholars like Dilip Hiro to see how the road from Marx to Muhammad is traversed. Wishful thinking of its transition to One World Order have raised many an eyebrow in the Western world where the dream appeared first in the form of End of History and One World Order. Its natural resource has ignited the desires for extended accumulation in the guts of finance capital. This ancient land is marked by the nostalgia of its past history. This is signified by the Dari language, Iranian conquest of Islam, the land where the Zoarastrian classic religious text, called Avesta, was composed. Buddhism had its own version. Turkish elements spread among the people. These Turkic people with Iranian culture, remained peripheral in State terms to either the Turkish Empire or the Russian amalgamation or now western geo-strategy. They remained within the Soviet system. They are now currently the object of extended accumulation and this is laced with popularly elected autocratic governments at home and immiseration of the ordinary people. In Kyrghystan there has been a civil war raging and it has the distinction of both the Russian and US Air Force presence in Kant and Manas airports, respectively.

Nostalgia: *arts not democracy*

The images of backwardness and barbarism are a little off the mark about the region. The indigenous peoples are heirs to a culture of great richness and sophistication. With the Arabs they participated in the cultural flowering-a dynamic outcome of the expansion of Islam from the 9th to the 16th century. The successive rules patronised arts, painting and architecture. Persian epic poetry flowered during the Samanid dynasty based in Bukhara in the 10th century. Shahnama of Firdausi resonanced upto India. The works of al-Farabi and Sina (Avicena) considerably advanced medieval learning during the European Rennaisance. Its 14th century architecture was magnificent. Tamurelane and Ulugh Beg are famous for their rule. This tradition is not marked by any democratic traces of the ancient variety either.

Soviet Modernisation: *from semitribal to modernity with slavisation*

The Soviet experiment, preceded by the Czarist domination had its dynamics in transforming this region to Transoxiana from tribal and feudal into modern course of development with Soviet characteristics. Various regions of the territory that came to be identified with Soviet Central Asia and five republics have had different resource bases, different stages of development and similarity of Soviet cultural interaction with the indigenous people. The charge of Russification, and Slavisation even of the script and of the region has to be contextualised in the development strategy of Soviet Union that provided with Russian educational opportunities, Russian technical intelligentsia and administrator, Russian technical skill, Russian language and secular non-religious consciousness to a pre-capitalist people. It recognised Central Asian specificity and therefore did not break the traditional family structure and village ethos despite making available modern facilities and consciousness.

Nationalism: *Weak*

The declaration of independence by Russia started the announcement of independence by Central Asian States, despite the fact that their economies were interlinked with the Russian State. In other words, both the people and the elites were not articulating either the demand for independence or the desire to become Arabic, Turkic or Iranian. Therefore the highly invocative slogan of looking at the region in terms of transition from Muhammad Marx, or subsequently redividing the geographical lines of Central Asia were rather contrived. The obverse of this approach is the Western view that these peoples have languished in the Soviet prison house. They are looking for an escape from the cave of darkness into the world of liberal democracy. This Western approach aims to see Central Asia transit to Western civilization pattern through cultural nationalism. The argument has two parts to it. One, that the Soviet period denied to the region its cultural nationalism, work against the Soviet system and bring them closure to the democratic model of the Western world. Both these things have not happened in the region.

What has happened is that the new States have become authoritarian. There is personality cult. Old nomenklatura has continued in power. Periodic election till 2000 have brought back the old leadership to power in all the States. They have remained as Russia's "near abroad", expectations of greater Turkistan have not materialised[1]. In this context the USA has play a pro-active policy. Western oil cartels have coveted Caspian sea oil to offset the Russian influence in the region. The economic reform of big, medium and small enterprises had attracted Western forms to the largest enterprises and not others. The issue of polity and economy is raised by these developments of internal and external unexpectedness. If anything the military and political development taking place in the region since the War on Terror suggest a veritable cold war in which GUAM countries (Georgia, Uzbekistan, Azerbaijan and Moldoa) are competing with the US against the Russian influence. The two Central Asian countries therefor are not sufficiently strong to do so. Despite the independence euphoria, the Uzbek leader had very early said that Uzbekistan had never spent any money on its defence. It was the Soviet Union that was looking after its defence.

In order to understand the Post-Soviet State(s) in the five countries (Uzbekistan, Turkmenistan, Kazakhistan, Tadjikistan and Kyrgistan) we need to look at first the formation of the States. What follows is first the nature of new dispensation then the nature of the political economy, described as bureaucratic capitalism as it happened in other parts of the then existing socialist world,[2] and a discussion on the creation of CIS. Boris Rumer has called these States as ones dependent on Russia. He says,

"All across the territory of former Soviet Union there is still a single, Russian speaking elite, which shares a common set of old political elites (nomenklatura) and Mafia-like connections. These old ties still help to move goods spare parts, to make careers and fortunes to supply weapons, to create transnational corporation and to procure credits and the like. These networks, which transcend the bans and restriction of Government organs and penetrate customs barriers, encompass the entire territory of the Soviet Union... Thus the persistence of personal ties between Moscow and Central Asian bureaucrats, industrial executives, and business is as important factor serving to cement relations between ruling circles and active segments of the populations in Russia and Central Asia."[3]

Hunter suggests a close military dependence of the Central Asian States on Russia thus, "The central Asian countries' military are still highly dependent on Russia, and all of them have bilateral military agreements with Moscow. These arrangements assume that each country will have its own national armed forces. But the wide disparity in size and capability between Russia and its partners, along with the still undeveloped state of Central Asian Armies, inevitably restricts the Republics autonomy in forseable future"[4] . Russia, Ukraine and Kazakhstan are forming one economic zone.

The situation in "far abroad", in contrast to the 'near abroad' (terms used by Russia to describe the two regions under its influence and with it, respectively) is different for states like Poland, Hungary and the Czech Republic. This is so at the level of nationalism but not at the level of nature of elites. Nationalism is not for anti-states like in Bulgaria, Rumania, Belarus, Slovakia and Ukraine. They are close and dependent on Russia in economic terms like Central Asia. In most of these countries also there has been the return of the old elites (of the Soviet period) through the elections. These states defined themselves as viable polities, sustainable communities, market economies and modern day nation states[5] . As their reform effort fails Michta observes the continuity in these post-Communist states. There is the hold of former communists. Nationalism in these states has not yet resolved its old divisions[6] .

There is a discernible pattern that emerges for the former Soviet Central Asia and Eastern Europe in the post-Communist phase in terms of the nature of elites, nature of the state and pattern of political process. It is therefor possible to adopt the theorisation of Szelenyi on Eastern Europe and Russia for Central Asia as well. Central Asian States have been viewed as 'creaking states' or 'weak states' in weak societies after discussing the weakness of nationalism owing to marginal and overlapping identities. Dannmutter says "what did not emerge from these multiple and overlapping sources of identity was a clearly defined national consciousness on the European model of nation-state consolidation"[7].

The region therefore, like the Pakistani case, lacks nationalism for different reasons. In Pakistan, the situation was the product of British policies of thwarted development of the economy, lack of popular support to the Muslim League and the confusion whether Pakistan was a nation-state or part of the Muslim community, especially on its West. In case of Central Asia, the Soviet policies of developing the idea of a Soviet man and secular identities submerged identity formation in ethnic terms, especially in its revivalist form. The lack of spread of Islamic sectarianism and of rabid Islamic ideology, Soviet modernisation and urbanisation, even if within the mould of periphery[8], prevented the emergence of ethnicity based on religion, language, history, rituals, myths or previous national heroes. Even in Europe we notice that many countries even today have not been able to solve the national faultlines[9]. In Central Asia with post-communism the old faultlines are attempted to be resurrected, especially in irredentist fashion, e.g., among Turks and Uzbeks.

Managerial Class: *Trans Border Elites*

Szelenyi makes a distinction between State Socialism, Managerialism and Private Capitalism. In State socialism the economic coordinating mechanism is redistribution. The ownership relations are State ownership leading to property vacuum in which decision making power is appropriated by redistributors. In private capitalism market is the economic coordinating mechanism and ownership relations are based on identifiable owners or group of owners who legitimate economic decision by economic ownership. In managerialism economic coordinating mechanism is the market and the ownership relations are based on diffused ownership with no identifiable owner who makes decisions. The decision-making power is appropriated by managers. This managerialism is different from the managerialism of the 1960s. In the sixties managers had owners at the top. Now the new managers do not have owners. Despite the fact that it was then said that it seems capitalism is peoples and bureaucratic are socialist societies and organisation man has emerged in capitalist society. End of ideology had come about.

The political economy of the new post-communist managerialism has the following features. First, Diffused property relations, created by voucher system under privatisation, suggests that there is no capitalist class. This is true of the region under the then Warsaw Pact powers. Second, there are limits to diffusion of property ownership. Managerialism has generally been based on diffusion to exercise control. Managerialism, where a capitalist class operated, had its limits. In case of the managerialism in the present context there is no capitalist class to limit the power of the managers. Third, the managers themselves may have disincentives to become owners of property since they would then escape responsibility of negative performance if the ownership is shared among the banks, cooperatives, state and managers. Fourth, during the transition to privatisation, managers did acquire some property, but that remained in the name of wives or families as an adjunct to their new avenues of making money. Fifth, these managers do not want to become petty bourgeois when they can be part of a larger social governing compact. Six, the managerial elite is closely linked to the politocracy and so they become more dependent on politics than on the market. Seventh, the dominant ideology of the managerialism is monetarism. The experts on macro-economics, like Manmohan Singh of India, like Mahbub ul Haq, originally the private sector champion in Pakistan, the Russian shock-therapist, belong to the current era of globalisation. In Post-Communist societies he is not a minister or an economist but a manager of finances. Thus those who have grown in importence are managers of banks, investment funds, experts of the ministry of finance, advisors to IMF and the World Bank, experts working for foreign and international financial agencies. They are monopolistic owners of some very specialised knowledge—macro-economics.

Managing deficit budgets, negotiating international loans, setting exchange rates and the amount of money in circulation, the relationship of all these with the health of the economy and the living standards of the people seem to be part of their Platonic wisdom that others do not know. Monetarism is the new ideology replacing Marxism.

Class Structure

The class structure of the post-Communist society is based on the cultural capital. The political elite is recruited from the highly educated class of technocracy and politocracy. The professional types are the lawyers, economists, engineers, humanistic intellectuals. Still the most powerful segment is the manager. The other two segments are junior partners of the alliance structure. It is therefore a new class that has come to dominate Post-Communist States. In Pakistan the elite alliance was initially on equal footing between politicians, bureaucracy and the military brass. This constellation shifted in favour of the military. In India the class alliances are between the bourgeoisie, middle classes and the agrarian rich mediated by its bureaucracy and counter lites. The movement of this alliance indicates its broadening to include the middle castes and peasantry and cooptation of the dalits and scheduled tribes. In Central Asia, as also in other parts of post-Communist societies, except Russia, the military brass is completely absent. In Russia and India the military brass is subordinated from the beginning to the civilian rule.

In Central Asia, the dominant theory to bring about economic reform and accelerating the pace of development has been privatisation and marketisation. Hunter notes that the reform strategy and foreign aid has been disastrous for Central Asia. He says, "The process coupled with the growing involvement of foreign industrial and commercial concerns has deepened economic and social disparities and intensified the already existing culture of corruption and clientism"[10].

Central Asia is witnessing a phase of weak states and weak societies in an unprecedented process of transition, speaking both historically and theoretically. The transition in terms of primitive accumulation in erstwhile Soviet and East European societies is towards capitalism. There is a process of meltdown that is the characteristic of primitive accumulation in the region for further advancement of metropolitan capital in which the region and regional power structure will pass through profit and political meltdown with savage features of authoritarianism and clientism.

This meltdown has its constructive and destructive side. The constructive side is the formation of a new managerial elite that controls but not owns property internally. Externally, it will have trade and other economic linkages to allow the foreign capital to exploit the natural resources of the region like gold, oil, natural gas and large enterprises in the services sector. At the same time other industrial and human capacities are laid waste to rust and rest. At the social level it helps in the construction of traditional episteme instead of modern individual and secular solidarity. This may or may not lead to Islamocracy if the developments in Tadjikistan, supported by the USA, are an indication. The controllers of economic and political power in alliance with cultural and social capital may last till the time the social meltdown creates conditions of a political meltdown of either the current regimes or states leading to a power vacuum. Who takes over, no one can predict. The basic process is the same in all the five states even though the Kazakh, Uzbek, Turk, Tadjik and Kyrgiz States are at different levels of natural resource base, unequal capacities to exploit those resource bases—different demographic composition, different patterns of crop production, outdated infrastructure facilities combined with difference in speeds of privatization of properties of the small, medium and giant sizes firms, different orientation of domestic and foreign policy, regional alliance strategies, nature of political process and political set up, differences in degrees of the political role that Islam may be allowed to play. In this the contrast is of extremes between the Kazakh ruling group and kind of compromises that the USA may be interested in Tajjikistan between Islam and the ruling group. Given all these and other societal differences between urban and rural populations there is no denying the fact that internally controllers are at the centre of which modernity is identified with secular values and national entities. There is hardly anything that can help us to understand about the changes taking place from Soviet secular to regio-cultural consciousness among the people. The dawn of twenty first century may not be bright. It may be tainted with blackish grey mixed with crimson, i.e., the tragedy of the dying consciousness and genocide of a people enmasse owing to hunger and the market oriented greed that will turn the natural gas and oil into capital. The use of the concepts like State, Civil Society, primitive accumulation and socialist primitive accumulation and Islamocracy, given our inadequate vocabulary, are being retained. Briefly it will be the combination of the colour of oil and the blood of the immiserised people in the region that will mark the transition from 'command' to 'free' economy. Boris Rumer, regarded Central Asia as a Soviet periphery. He noted its richness in nature resource of oil and gas but only a small portion of it could be used. It is well endowed with rare and precious metals, but they used to go to the then USSR. It produced cotton for USSR, while a miniscule was processed in the region"[11].

The division of labour in the Soviet Union is now criticized as colonial and the place of the Central Asian region in it as that of "periphery". The proof of this description being a whole range of developments. Khruschev's virgin land's development strategy of Kazakhstan, development of cotton in Uzbekistan, laying of infrastructure facilities that took the resources –both raw materials and the goods—to the Soviet Union and/or its industrial belt, and Russification of the cultural ethos through Marxism, Russian language and the Slavic script, migration of ethnic Russians in these regions, strategies of nomenklatura in the Party and the Government that neglected representation to the local peoples. Imposition of Marxism even though Islam was used to create settled conditions for the rural populations by he Czarist Russian State. This relationship is now ruptured. The new condition is welcome to the West. The common economic political and military space is sought to be deconstructed despite the creation of the Commonwealth of Independence States (CIS), set up at the meetings at Minsk, Ashkabad and Alma Ata. This region came to described as 'Near Abroad' by the Russian elites but as an example of Russia's Eurasian hegemonic Monroe doctrine, the Western scholar alleges. In geo-strategic terms, Russia, China and the US are the important players. The dominance of Russia and China in the future[12] may have a question mark.

The common space got historically disrupted and new process of national formations came into action. National symbols, armies, recruitment thereto, military doctrines, scripts, software for computers, national currencies, change in post-communist leadership on the basis of new Constitutions and Electoral laws, renewal and creation of Islamic mosques, Islamic and other parties and religious practices accompanied the international recognition by other governments. Establishment of diplomatic missions, participation in the United Nations and foreign trips to Western countries led to the initial euphoria of the transformed old leaders and parties. These States are multinational in poly-ethnic societies where the territorial and cultural boundaries do not coincide. It is therefore difficult to analyze them from the perspective of looking at foreign policy roles that would provide cohesiveness to foreign policy as well as internal populations. States like Turkmenistan and Uzbekistan may look for carving out new states on the basis of irredentism and/or religious revival. In these states more than six crores of people are living under the fear of being deconstructed along ethnic lines of Russians, Ukrainians, Germans, Kazakhs (Kazakhastan); as Russians, Ukrainians and Uzbeks (Uzbekistan); Russians, Ukrainians, Tatars, Kirgiz and Tadjiks (Tadjikistan); as Russians, Uzbeks and titular nationalities (Turkmenistan). Islam is not enough to unite them though the ground reality is that most of them are of Sunni, Hannafi persuasion and the Muslim States surrounding them might want them to transit them from Marx to Muhammad in the mould of Persian or Wahabbi Islam. If that happens modern episteme world will be an endangered species from a modern and secular point of view unless a liberationist Islamic hermeneutic intervention offsets the kinds of interpretations found in current Islamic sponsors. The restoration of Tamerlane in Tashkent's central place(s) as national symbol in Tashkent is a reminder of the past. How far can myths, folk lore, religious symbols and national flags, national uniforms help to weld a modern consciousness of a people is difficult to answer. Would the creaking states provide an alternative to the earlier system and fill the vacuum? Calls for new definitions of Central Asia with Islam as the centre have their own cultural and strategic implications for the region. Disastorous, though.

Despite their interdependence in terms of critical networks of energy, fuel, transportation and communications linked with the Russian Federation, there is an attempt to link these regions alternatively to the fringe of the western market dynamic. The IMF studies on these states show the economic processes afoot. In Kazakhstan, which delinked from the rouble zone in November, 1993, following the introduction of Tenge inflation rate of 44 per cent was reduced to 32-34 per cent in May 1994; real wages declined between end of November 1993 and January 1994; a wide ranging 3 tier privatisation programme was adopted. Enterprise restructuring was low. State farms were sold to managers and workers. These farms were divided into three: large, small and medium to be sold (small) on privatised through a combined voucher investment scheme (medium and large). Special industrial facilities were sold on case by case basis. Out of 4,000 enterprises, 2,166 were sold by mid 1994. Land and apartments became privatised by 1994[13].

In Uzbekistan, petroleum, natural gas and coal, and resources for hydro electric power, gold, silver, copper, lead, zinc, wool farm and tungsten are available. It is fourth largest producer of cotton. Sum became its currency in 1993. It is the largest exporter of gas and major supplier of electricity to rest of Central Asia. It passed a law on privatisation in 1993. Joint stock companies were formed among large enterprises, with control of shares by managers and workers[14].

In Tadjikistan reforms began in 1991. Privatisation of twenty-nine enterprises took place. State's share of industry fell to 84 per cent from 98 per cent medium size enterprise were turned into joint stock companies, with a significant percentage sold to employees. Twelve per cent of small scale enterprises were privatised to employees collectives[15]. Similar economic review of Kyrgystan is noted by the IMF[16]. Except for states like Kazakhastan, Uzbekistan and Turkmenistan the other two states of Tadjikistan and Kyrgystan cannot survive on their own resources. A State like Uzbekistan does not have enough to finance its own Army. These regions depend on the Russian military for managing its regional security, under the CIS arrangements or bilateral military agreement. The former three are at the same time economically linked with the Russian Federation. These two groups of states can pull in opposite directions, if the latter come under a wholesome influence of the West or other regional players. Signs of opening up to the US and the West indicate this. If that happens then there is a possibility of these two making the first three vulnerable for they are dependent on the two Republics for the important natural resources of water. It is a scarce resource for cotton growing Uzbekistan and Kazakhastan also suffers owing to its scarcity. The source of water-the Amur and Darya rivers flow through the territories of the two more underdeveloped States of Kyrgystan and Tadjikistan. A political change in both Tadjikistan and Kyrgystan that is favourable to the West will mean trouble to the large three of the five states. If States like Kazakhstan and Uzbekistan do not turn hostile towards the Russian Federation then the Central Asian States will not be the buffer that may be the immediate aim of the Western countries. These States will continue to have internal hemorrage which is consequence of the destruction of the Soviet Union. The somber strategic reality and the geo-economic constraints in the path transition is more of a warp that is difficult to break out from. Influx of international finance, if it comes will not help establish the market as a system. It will only come in the regions of natural resources, in the region of the Caspian Sea. If that happens it will only benefit international market. Will that lead to alleviation of inhuman side effects? Perhaps not. Populations are suffering, labour is unemployed and divided on gender lines. Pipeline is West.

In a peculiar sense the State and the Civil Society show signs of slow but painful change, if not stagnation in the direction of economic well being and acquiring a new identity. The Civil Society is not the one that can be summed up in terms of individual ontos and episteme. Clusters of people are emerging. For the sake of specificity we look at the society in terms of urban and rural divide. The ratio is of 4:6 at the time of the beginning of the 1990s. The urbanised sector is more urbanised (Russianised/Westernised) and the rural sector more religious, restive, though not necessarily obscurantist in Islamic terms. The former controls the State. From this sector comes the managerial elite. The later is the more restive recipient of change. Except for Tadjikistan there is no movement worth the word to show that the alternative opinion has articulated itself through alternative institutionalization. There are human rights activists, artists and scholars who compose the weak cultural capital. The Islamists are as weak. Wherever they are there as in Tadjikistan, they are in alliance, ironic though this is, with democratic parties. This is no modernity. Civil war and not stability has been its products. In the other four states the civil society does not have an antagonistic relationship even though the hardships of the people are increasing and owing to the nature of political and economic change there may in the future be a different pattern of this relationship. As of now the state continues to be the vehicle of transition to the market with all its limitations.

History has witnessed two versions of economic change, viz., classical and socialist primitive accumulations for industrialization. Since the latter is rejected only the former could be used to prove an analysis. Marx makes the following points for the classical mode. The formation of capital take place when money and labour both get transformed and are out of the agricultural confines to be used for commodity production. This process, bloody and savage, frees the labour from the land and enclosures and the capital, existing earlier in the form of money, formed the economy of use values. The objective condition of capital also convert and transform the existing means of production as the wheel and the loom was transformed into the steam power. This process knew of no democracy[17]. Today, the labour, and the resources around the Caspian Sea and the other energy giving wealth is sought to be exploited by external technology. This means import of foreign technology. It is laying waste the internal infrastructure and industrial capacity that the people have created in the last seventy-five years but which do not serve the new technology that the West aims to introduce. The new technologies must destroy the old system if it must use the opportunity for creating wealth for advancement of technologies based on artificial intelligence that is the telegraphic message of the West to the rest. The properties, very large, that have come from the international corporation combine both capital and labour for its advantage. Whether this means local prosperity, except cheaply paid labour is easy to answer. No, it will destroy, however, secular solidarity and create traditional solidarity. The primitive accumulation will therefore accompany traditional epistemologies. In this it may be Islamic consciousness. Will this be helpful inputs as far as State power is concerned is doubtful. Is this the market society? Is this the telos of the heaven of freedom? Even if we do not look for the replication of the Western model, we find it very difficult to call this reality as a market with a human face. We also are not sure if it means creation of wealth for the region in the interest of its inhabitants apart from the small managerial class that has emerged instead of the traditional entrepreneurial class. It is a case of authoritarian rule and atrophied humanity.

The State(s) in Central Asia are part of the distorted conditions of primitive accumulation. In their domestic policy there is no sign of either independent capitalist development or democratic political life. By way of democracy there is no sign of a society of free and equal individuals that J. S. Mill had theorized about. The change in the small pattern of the property holdings has been triple layered i.e., privatization of the small scale enterprises (primarily in the service sector); privatization of the medium sized enterprises and the privatization of large state enterprises. The first is in the direction of the small property holder. The second on the basis of the voucher scheme and the third privatization, unlike the second privatization, is on a case by case basis and involves foreign capital. This process is accompanied by fall in real wages, tensions in the labour market, increase in unemployment both registered and otherwise, wage differentials in favour of the once managed by the States, particularly in the Kazakhstan's agriculture. In other States the progress towards privatization has been slower. In Uzbekistan, privatization has taken place in housing, retail trade , and consumer services. This country is one of the largest producing area of cotton and grain. If investment in this sector had increased there would have been real term benefits for the international finance. This did not happen. Instead the earlier cotton growing areas are now covered by drug cultivation that leads to smuggling to the Russian Federation through to the Baltic States and to China. In this country labour productivity declined by 26 per cent during 1991-1994; land under cotton cultivation decreased, wages declined and the living condition of the people became increasingly stressful. Privatization in Tadjikistan has found little scope for outside investors. Given the civil war condition it is difficult to talk about primitive accumulation. The results in Turkmenistan are chaotic, inflationary and predatory.

The class which has come into existence is not the owner of property but controllers of property with some members of the family of these elite group not owning property but controlling property through the voucher scheme and investment funds. This is not the traditional entrepreneurial class but the new manager who controls but does not own and whose stake is in keeping to himself large enterprises rather than own small-scale private property. This class establishes its links with the intellectuals and artist (culture capital) and bureaucracy (social capital) and the politocracy. This class has a homogenous nexus different from the traditional managerial elite. Unlike in the case of the traditional managerial class there is no class that is the owner of the private property enterprises in the country in case of the Central Asian States. They have no interest in owning property. The control of large enterprises brings in contact with personnel of multinational corporations and international funding institutions that gives them newer pasture ground for personal and family futures. This elite in these States also has Trans-border linkages that give it a homogenisation that cuts across the borders giving it a regional overview (inclusive of the Russian orientation). Their need of the West is underlined by the fact that they look for alternative markets for their resources. Western technology for their efficient exploitation and avenues for promoting their kith and kin in the international lending institutions and for education abroad of their children. In this sense it could be called an elite that is looking for interdependence or is Janus faced.

Their control over political power currently is unchallenged except in Tadjikistan. The new managers have manufactured consent for their regimes given the difficulties posed by internal instabilities and the challenge of Western geopolitics in competition with the Russian geopolitics. Initially the expression of it may be purely criminal terrorism to be followed by political terrorism. The two varieties are not far to seek. Russia and Afghanistan have these in abundance. The challenges could lead to either concentration or fragmentation of political power. That may not be conducive to stable democratic states pursuing capitalism with entrepreneurial capitalist class. To that extent the managerial class may be vulnerable particularly if the danger is from external powers. In that situation these states do not even have neither regular national armies, nor even money to finance them. The ones which do, like the Kazakh States, which has an army and a military doctrine, may find themselves overwhelmed by regional actors supported by the hegemonic state in the current unipolar power in military terms. The suasion may take the force of coercive diplomacy of the kind witnessed in Bosnia, Herzegovina, Kosovo and Iraq. This has amounted to increase in geographical reach of NATO.

The meltdown of the earlier situation may also reach a new *nadir*. The process of the meltdown could be viewed as a three stage one; first, began with the dissolution of the State and other structures of governance, second, dissolution of structures of economy and laying waste the industrial capacities save the huge enterprises taken over by the international finance; dissolution of the social life ; increase in social strife, increase mortality rates, shrinking of labour market for men preceded by women and third, incapacity of the elites to manage the economy and polity; the refusal of international finance and lending institutions to bail out these crises ridden polities; to the dissolution of the current structures of governance and economy and the incapability to manufacture consent.

International finance is on its way to benefiting from it all. Austrian, German, Turkish, Pakistani, Emirate of Oman, European Common Market, Japanese, the American, IMF, World Bank and other corporations from other countries like Italy and Norway have entered the field. Help has come to Kazakhstan, Kyrgystan, and Uzbekistan in oil, gas and gold from companies like Chevron (USA), Agip (Italy), British Gap (Britain), Lukoil(Russia), Statoil (Norway), Shell and Mobil oil(USA), Elfe-Aquitane (France), Newmont(USA), Lonhoro (UK), Cameo (Canada), Gold Bet Resources Limited (USA), Placer Dome and Gulf International Minerals Ltd.(Canada). In the service sector huge State enterprises have gone over to Philip Morris in Almaty. Yet neither the expected foreign capital nor technology came to this large region which is closer to the Russian Federation's economic orbit. The struggle in the Central Asia is how to delink this area economically from the Russian

Federation and link it up with the Western economic channels, One example being the exercise to lay pipelines in the opposite direction than was hitherto done. Given this exercise the Central Asian States have fragile existence, distorted process of accumulation of capital, social unrest, human genocide, an unhistorical managerial class dependent of foreign capital—a class that can be sniffed by coercive diplomacy that is the norm in the current unipolar moment where NATO is in command.

Modern Constitutions

Most of these States have adopted in their Constitutions principles of secularism, democracy, rule of law and republicanism.

Unitary and Presidential-type of government Uzbeks have created 'humane democratic state based on rule of law'. Turkmenistan established 'law based and secular state'. Tadjiks adopted the principles of 'sovereign democracy, law governed, secular and unitary state'. Sovereignty resides in the people among them. All of them have bi-cameral legislature. Economic liberalisation did not lead to scrapping of social rights like health care, education, housing and vacations. All States guarantee equality of rights and freedoms for their citizens, irrespective of race, religion, sex, language, nationality or social origin. Ethnic composition of each republic determines rights to minorities. The situation in Kazhakstan is delicately balanced between the Russian Kazakhs. As a result today Russian and Kazakhs language are at par. In Kyrgyzstan Russian language does not have a constitutional status. The Uzbeks do not refer to minority languages. In Turkmenistan the official language is Turkman.

Groups

In former Soviet territories, three kind of groups had emerged in the civil society, viz. Pro-Soviet, critical pro-Soviet groups and groups seeking independence[18] . Between 1987-1991 informal groups emerged in Central Asian States. By the end of 1990 many turned into political parties with the aim of seeking independence and participation in political activities. Many of these have not been registered after independence. Some have simply been banned. This has remained a fluid process with reference to Kazakh and Russian ethnic groups, Democratic movement of Kyrgystan, or, its Peoples Party, Communist Party or Agrarian Party. Birlikim Uzbekistan has strong nationalist and pan-Turkish trait. The Islamic Renaissance Party is banned.

Intellectuals founded a pan-Turkish group in Turkmenistan. Tadjiks had Hundered Flowers bloom in the period of Perestroika. People's Party of Tadjikstan was registered in 1994, whatever the institutions, democracy has not seen its dawn and the new managerial class shares in the spoils of freedom while the ordinary mortals struggle for ordinary bread. Political revolt is bound to be the agenda of future. This would be against local cities and their foreign patrons practising high finance.

CIS

The context of the formation of the commonwealth of independent states (CIS) casts its shadow on the prospectus of the political economic and military common space in the territories of Central Asia. There were some negative and some positive feature of the phenomenon in the dismantling of the Gorvachev regime and the Soviet Union. The ground reality was moving in the direction of fragmentation with a sentiment of continuance of a common entity; there was the movement for democratic reform without the political agency to do so; there was an emerging democratic polity in the Russian Federation without strong democratic structures and united democratic leadership. There was, on the one hand, a desire to achieve a rule of law and, on the other, a failed attempt at a constitutional coup that created its own problems in the security structures of the incipient States. All these paradoxes cast their shadow, in their own way, on the way the CIS emerged and the teething problems that it showed.

To be specific, there were stabilising and destabilishing factors that come to the fore in matters of achieving a common understanding about the supra-national policy that is sought to be achieved in that Eurasian land mass. We are not concerned here about the instability of the new regimes in the different Central Asian and Caucasian states. They are bound to reflect on the prospects of the CIS security perspectives.The concern here is with inter-state relations.

Stabilising Factors

Among the stabilising, factors were the following: geographical, historical, economical, political and military. Geographically, no one can ignore the significance of contiguity of the land mass, i.e., Eurasia. The compulsions of living together made the peoples here unite-fragment-unite while they were modernising themselves. This feature of Russian history and the history of the people living in the Eurasian land mass has been pretty consistent since the time of Peter the Great. Geographical reach had made this region unconquerable. Says Hans Morgenthau about the then Soviet Union's geographic impenetrability, "the Soviet Union constitutes an enormous land mass that extends over one-seventh of the land area of the earth and is two and one half times the territory of the United States... This territorial extension is a permanent source of great strength which has thus far frustrated all attempts at military conquests from the outside"[19]. If this is combined with the Mahan perspectives of forward deployment to deter a land power that Mackinder pointed to, then one realises the significance of geography to strategy. In the recent past, the euphoria of the dismemberment of the Soviet empire and the fragility of the new state structures and tenuous character of the new regimes cannot prevent people that matter from taking a hard and a long-term view of the security dimension of the changing world. History is replete with people wanting to become global leaders by controlling the seas as a counterpoint to this impregnability. In the last decade, global leadership was sought to be achieved through controlling of the space for battles on earth. Both violate the geographical advantage of the area. Today the confusion over what set of policies has to be adopted is sought to be halted in the US. The Clinton Administration was to be moving away from the ad hoc policy of the Bush Administration and adopting policies of caution even if marked by optimism[20], in the post-Soviet Union phase. Caution meant that Yeltsin was not given unconditional support. Bush is now present in Central Asia, with NATO.

The historical dimension is brought out by the common intermingling of the peoples of the region. The Slavs and the Muslims (Turkish-Persian) cut across a large part of the area and find sufficient representation in the past destinies even though some part and some groups of people have looked more to the Westerners. Some had told Peter once, "Russia has been an Asiatic land for too long, You fear the Europeans in this country..."[21]. The Baltic States have moved away from them over again. At the same time, the Asian of Central Asia, despite their hoary past, cultural heterogeneity and religious distinctness from the Slavs have continued to be steadfast in their desire to be with Russia after the fragmentation of the USSR. Even though the friendship among peoples that the erstwhile Soviet Union boasted of does not any more exist in fact or fiction, traditionally speaking, the racial intermingling of the people and the mixed families all over the CIS states proved stabilising potential even in the phase of ethnic blood letting and Turkish, Iranian and Pakistani overtures for a strategic symphony.

The political dimension is governed by their current Post-Communist perspectives to prevent authoritarianism, to live in freedom and to create new parameters of polity and political process. They have all been in a political culture that did not develop the instrumentalities of smooth transfer of power and today do not have them. That, of course, adds to the destabilisation of the region with disastrous potential, at the same time.

At the military level, the level of R&D, the production system of military hardware and weapons, the command, control, communication and intelligence assets, reconnaisance, space assets, the process of conversion of industries, the strategic nuclear forces, the anti-missile, anti-aircraft facilities and early warning systems impose a certain logic of unity that they cannot ignore even if the CIS countries want their independence, armed forces or have their own military doctrines or even foreign economic and military alliance systems. Recently situation has changed.

Destabilising Factors

Among the destabilising factors are the continuing crises that resulted from the disintegration of the USSR. Recently the Minister of Interior in the Russian Federation told the Russian Congress of People's Deputies that the security forces were not plotting against the government and such talk was empty. In his speech, Barranikov said, "State security determines, to a great extent, the national, ethnic and geo-political future." He warned against the external and internal threats to Russia. Among the external threats he emphasised, "This concerns the activities of certain intelligence communities which continue to treat Russia as the primary target in spite of the warning in the relation with a number of countries." The minister went on to narrate what these agencies do. He said, "We have at our disposal direct evidence that the effort of some special services are being increased by certain of the network of mobile residents around Russia's borders. This is only just taking place on the territories of yesterday's brothers in the socialist camp and in a number of former Soviet states... the priority tasks of many special services today include, on the one hand, more active regular recruiting of Russian citizens, and, on the other hand, further stifling and discrediting of the power structures in Russia." The attempt is to have porous border, trans-border smuggling in narcotics and conventional nuclear weapons and other items relevant for the manufacture of the nuclear weapons, i.e. help proliferation[22]. The overtures are hands of regional neighbours, the symphony with some identified powers.

The creation of porous borders impact on the weak structures of internal security; at the same time, they impinge on the problems of external security. The commander-in-chief of the CIS forces told the Russian Congress of People's Deputies in December 1992 that there is interference from the West-wittingly or unwittingly that will hasten the process of disintegration in the region and caste gloomy shadows over the prospects of collective security in the region. Marshall Ye. Shaposhnikov underlined the global extent of the damage that was to be caused if the West was allowed to interfere in the CIS countries. He said- "NATO is giving serious thought to establishment of peace-keeping force for use amongst other things in the CIS. Now that the USSR has collapsed-the influence of other States like Turkey-Iran-Pakistan and others is increasing. If this were to happen the prospect of a new axis of global confrontation between south and north would become a realistic one. That is preciously why – in addition to a number of other regions—the USA is stepping up its attempts to design a mono-polar system of world administration in which it would have a decisive role. All these – taken together—has to be borne in mind by CIS states and, above all, Russia-if, of course, it does have geo-strategic interest". This is a deftly worded warning and a nuanced stance without pinning down any single power as an enemy that was customarily done in the earlier times. The message, however, can not be ignored since what was at stake was not only the security of Russia but also the CIS countries.

Shaposhnikov was in line with the formulation of the then military doctrine that does not identify any single power as the enemy. That the situation was grim for the future of Russia and the CIS is brought out from the then hot spots on the territories of Georgia-Moldovia-Tajakistan-Armenia-Azerbaijan and Russian Federation itself. What was aflame was not just quest for identities for peoples in small areas. The survival of defined state boundaries was at stake in Chechnya, Karabakh, the Dnester region, Abhkazia, South Ossetia, Tatarstan and the Kulyabe region. Shaposhnikov did not mince words about the NATO approach. He says, "if NATO officials ever have spoken of close cooperation with certain CIS states, they did so-wittingly or unwittingly—in order to further intensify disintegration process within the commonwealth. Further more, by their own admission, they never even suspected how far these disintegration process might go"[23]. An impregnable land mass is attempted to be politically cracked up for strategic gains.

Given these processes, the magnitude of the problem can be gauged from the fact that the erstwhile Soviet Army had been in disarry. It had given way under the circumstances to a reality that can unfortunately be describe as a Slavo-Muslim (more Turkish than Persian) Army. After the August coup, it was little more than a patchwork quilt. The processes of societal and political disintegration had their echoes in it as also the lack of time the leaders of the Army had for a defence reform. After the coup, the then Defence Minister Shaposhnikov, said the defence reform had not taken off. The Chief of General Staff (CGS) of the USSR Armed Forces, Army General V. Lobov had said he "first thought about the need of the military reform long before 1985-somewhere in the second half of the 1970s"[24]. But the work in progress was disrupted by the dissolution of the USSR.

In the September 1991, the Defence Ministry said that reform will begin in the second half of 1992[25]. The Defence Minister of Russia said in December 1992 "... Now I would like to remind you of what Russia inherited from the might of the former Union's armed forces. Ruins and debris, basically"[26]. Worse was that the country's strategic nuclear forces were in territories outside the Russian Federation. As a result, the CIS States are having difficulties in arriving at a common understanding on the future of the nuclear emplacement and control. The row over the Black Sea Fleet and the control of the strategic nuclear weapons between Russia and Ukraine was the worst case scenario from the perspective of having military soyuz.[27]

Efforts to Achieve Unified Structures: *Collective Security Doctrine*

From December 1991 to December 1992, the efforts to formulate common structures and common defence policies along with collective security had been less than bright. There had been a lot more acrimony and less movement in this matter. One of the basic factors was the psychological problems of the new elites in that they were discovering new monsters amongst themselves, where they did not perhaps exist. For example, the position that Leonid Kravchuk had taken about foreign enemies only implied that he had in mind not any distant country nor even the ghost of Soviet authoritarianism; rather, he implied Russia to be the external threat despite the cultural difference between the Ukrainians and the Russians, which are more like those between the English and the Scots, there are many things in common between the Russian Federation and the Ukrainian State. It would be a tragedy for the Russians if Ukraine were to be in a different security orbit even if it is not in any military alliance, which it can not be since Ukrainian law prevents it from joining any military alliance. It is not very fantastic to imagine that strategicians in the West could think up of scenarios in which Ukraine is out of the Russian orbit of influence. The shrinking of democratic Russia may be regarded—rightly or wrongly—as good for the world of freedom. Going by the present perceptions of the democratic Russian leadership, such a scenario will not be welcome whether the CIS remains or not very early in 1991. Yeltsin first befriended Ukraine and Belarus in Minsk. Both the Russian Congress of People's Deputies and the Decree on the Establishment of the Russian Armed Forces underline the significance of the CIS military agreement. The Russian Congress of People's Deputies passed a resolution that among other things said, "To deem the following main areas of Russian activity within CIS: among others consistently follow the course of averting conflict situations within the CIS." The decree that established the Russian armed forces appealed to the member states of the Commonwealth of Independent States to conclude a collective security treaty[28].

That Yeltsin's Russia did underline this need is a sign of continuity rather than a break with the post-coup Gorbachev regime in the Soviet Union. The then sovereign republics and the union had agreed to have common defence structures and policies. An agreed text of the draft of the Union treaty that was hammered out on 23 July,1991 said, "The states forming the Union pledge not to resort to force or threat of force in relations between themselves; not to encroach one another's territorial integrity; not to conclude agreements running contrary to the Union goals or aimed against the states forming it"[29]. The draft that was prepared in November 1991 said that it was necessary to have unified armed forces with centralised control. The draft recognised that the "states party to the treaty are entitled to set up republican armed formations, whose functions and strength are defined by the said agreement"[30]. Both these documents were produced in order to stem the rot that had set in the USSR and the ethnic divide that had overtaken the erstwhile Red Army. These processes of alternative institutionalisation and the different concepts of defence reform were having their negative impact on the unity of the armed forces during the period of Perestroika. The festering conflicts in different regions of the republics were harming the combat readiness of the then Soviet troops. The confusion on the issue of conversion of military industries was dividing the leadership in and outside the armed forces. The increasing interplay of the civilian and the uniformed officer on issues of the defence budget and interpretations of the doctrine of reasonable sufficiency were creating tensions on the issue of civil-military relation as also the debate on the defence budget. It was, therefore, necessary for the Gorbachev leadership to show to the world that they could still manage to show. The Union treaty drafts are to be seen in that light of attempting to slow down if not halt the process of disintegration of the security structure of the state as also the armed forces.

Very much the same considerations must have been impressed upon Yeltsin to go in for multilateral arrangements of the CIS as also for separate bilateral understanding that he was achieving with the new leadership of the sovereign states. In order to control the process of dissolution of the multi-ethnic armed forces of the declining Soviet Union into the armed forces of sovereign states, he announced both the demise of the USSR and also the desire to continue with economic, political and military common space at the Minsk summit that developed into the Alma Ata summit. The Declaration on the formation of the CIS said, " The member states of the community intend to pursue a policy of strengthening international peace and security. The guarantee to honour international obligations ensuring for them from the treaties and agreement of the former USSR, and to ensure unified control over, and non-proliferation of, nuclear weapons"[31]. The Minsk agreement said, "The member states of the community will preserve and maintain under united command military strategic space, including unified control over nuclear weapons"[32].

The formation of the CIS was a hasty step and lot more work had to be done both in the direction of quadrilateral cooperation in the nuclear field and bilateral cooperation in the field of conventional area and weaponry. The need was to give up a maximalist approach to all round security and settle for minimalist consensus. The maximalist view that was identified by the USSR's security rationales levelled up identities for the defence of the Leviathan. The August coup gave rise to the miniscule perceptions of security on behalf of not only the sovereign republics like the Baltics and the Ukraine but also the local people in the Russian Federation like that of the people under Dudayev of Chechen-Ingushtia. In the latter case, the Russian enemy card was played as vociferously as it was by Leonid Kravcuk of Ukraine. Given these extreme perceptions, it is only natural to adopt an incremental approach towards security and to settle for a minimalist consensus. The instruments of arriving at this consensus have been to enter into multilateral and bilateral negotiations—the purpose of it not very clearly in harmony. As a result, while the official opinion veered to cautious optimism, the unofficial opinion cried failure whenever the CIS States did something worthwhile on the issue of having agreements on the military aspects.

Thinking on the need of collective security goes much more backwards in time than the agreement on it achieved in May 1992. After the coup, the discussion of the Union and Republics showed that some Republics wanted to withdraw from the military agreement while others wanted to have separate Armies. The CGS, Lobov, advocated the signing of an agreement between the republic for the collective defence, providing for single armed forces leadership[33] . He pleaded for a new military doctrine that ensured the nationwide security on the basis of single military-political space[34] . After the CIS was formed, the move towards the collective security doctrine was related to the efforts taken by the Central Asian republics. Before the CIS meeting at Tashkent that started on 15 May, 1992, and adopted the agreement on collective security, the Defence Ministers of the CIS met in Tashkent. There was a meeting of the Central Asian leaders at Ashkabad. The Uzbek President said that the Central Asian leaders wanted to sign a treaty on mutual security with the Russian Federation[35] . At the same time, the other members were not willing to sign such a treaty. The representatives of the Ukraine and Belarus had taken this position[36] . The main agenda for the Tashkent meeting was the military or the issue of joint armed forces. The Defence Ministers had said, "The CIS armed forces should consist of the Organisation of sovereign states and resemble NATO or Warsaw Treaty Organisation. We shall insist on preserving the allied forces of the Commonwealth"[37] . The issues that were to be discussed were the defence budget, conscription and strategic nuclear forces[38] . The Tashkent summit signed an agreement on collective security with six signatories. These were Russia, America, Kazakhstan, Kyrgistan, Uzbekistan, and Turkmenistan[39] . Subsequent to the signing of the treaty, the developments had not been very encouraging even though the summit was rated in positive terms by the Central Asian leaders. The Belarussian and Ukrainian leaders expressed their inability to sign the agreements since their hands were tied by their respective Supreme Soviet resolutions that prevented these republics from joining any military alliances. The meetings following these two enlarge the scope of the agreement floundered on some issue or other. For example, Azarbaijan and Moldovia who were members of the Defence Council setup for the purpose, failed to attend the meetings. Coordination could not take place. In late May, Georgia had participated as an observer. There were financial problems. It was reported before the agreement that the Central Asia, States were unable to fulfil their quota of conscription and the main burden feel on Russia. It was also true that Central Asian Republics like Uzbekistan and Turkmenistan had never paid for their security to the former Soviet Union. And as reported by the then C-in-C of CIS, even the Turks were not paying. As for he separate armies of the Sovereign states, they were merely nominal; so again, burden was on the Russian Federation. At the time of Tashkent meeting that adopted the agreement on collective security, the Uzbek leader, Karimov said, "our approach is that each Republic must have its own armed forces... nominal armed forces ... they will form part of the Joint Armed Force under Commander-in-Chief Shaposhnikov"[40].

Post-Tashkent: *Summit Developments*

Shaposhnikov assessed the prospects of the Union as bright since some agreement had been achieved. Despite the outburst of nationalism in state military policies among states like Georgia, Moldovia, Azerbaijan, Russia and Ukraine, some movement had taken place towards coordination. For example, even though Ukraine was not formally a part of the agreement, the country did participate in the Council of Defence Ministers at Minsk and had entered into an agreement with Russia on early warning, anti-missile defence, anti-aircraft defence, space communications, reconnaissance, navigation, aircraft identification, and so on. These concern the purely defensive aspects of military strategy. As for the strategic part of the problem between Ukraine and Russia, the Commander-in-Chief of the CIS strategic forces said, that the CIS nuclear potential cannot be split, and that the forces stationed in the four states of Belarus, Kazakhstan, Russia and Ukraine "are subject to centralised command and must be under the united command and control of the Commander-in-Chief of the strategic forces"[41]. This is a formal position since Ukraine had moved to create the conditions of double control. Taking under its jurisdiction and administrative control a group of strategic forces, the Ukraine leadership deprived Moscow the authority of the possibility of manning the troops, choosing and appointing officers of missile units, and making the officers of those troops take an oath to the Ukrainian people. The situation was further complicated by the fact that there was no hotline among the four leaders to coordinate a response in a crisis situation. The C-in-C of the strategic forces felt that till the time the strategic nuclear forces were not shifted to the Russian territory, the situation will cause anxiety and there should be every effort to prevent any possible confrontation between the two states.

Taking a cue from the diplomatic behaviour of the Ukraine that heeded the advise of the Western powers like the USA, France, Britain and Germany with regard to the removal of the conventional weapons, Maksimov, the C-in-C of CIS strategic missile forces, was hopeful that Ukraine will finally agree under international pressure to transfer the nuclear strategic forces to Russia. It was however not interesting to watch the evolution of the Ukraine-CIS relationship since Ukraine did chart its own political course. Ukraine has formed common economic space with Russia in 2003.

The other issue that was knocking on the doors of the CIS even at the time of its formation was the issue of peace-keeping and peace-making function in the region. Before the agreement on collective security, the President of Kazakhstan, Nursultan Nazarbayev, suggested the "immediate initiation of work on forming special peace-keeping and peace-making forces to serve in crisis regions of the CIS"[42]. The demands made by the situation in different parts of the CIS and the Russian Federation did require forces that were to help in defusing the crisis. Since in a number of places the conflicts were of multi-ethnic character, there was some point in having such a force. However, it is quite possible that in certain situations this may boomerang if the peace-keeping forces start taking sides, and the local leadership may ask for the withdrawal of these forces. It was suggested in some quarters that instead of having CIS peace-keeping and peace-making forces, it was better that the problem is attended to at the bilateral level on the basis of mutual agreement. This will also not entail the problem of sharing of financial burden since it may be found that CIS states are unable to pay for such forces as also are unable to provide for the requisite efficient troops to meet the situation. There has been talk of having either UN or NATO or European peace-keeping forces in the region. This would be a difficult situation for the ruling elites to handle because it will entail the presence of foreign troops. They are already facing the prospect of having soft borders, as in the case of the Tadjikistan-Afghanistan borders. This has happened to the CIS.

Comparative Assessment of Collective Security

Parallels were drawn between NATO and the CIS situation as noticed above. The specifies of each situation are dissimilar on the surface with similarities too. The model on which NATO developed is that of interdependence. Discussions of the model show that there are bound to be contradictions between power and interdependence. The former will involve conduit, coercive and cooperative aspects of power involving hierarchical relationship. It would essentially mean the existence of a hegemon[43]. In the case of the NATO alliance, such an overwhelming hegemon exists, i.e. the USA. In contrast to the buoyancy of the hegemon, there was the ruin and debris of the war-ravaged economies of Western Europe requiring what came to be called the Marshal Plan. The process of development showed that the hegemon's position had to be readjusted so as to allow for the greater autonomy of the other partners of the alliance. Therefore, the relationship had to be in constant flux involving the management of crises that were bound to arise. This did happen, as a study shows[44]. Therefore, interdependence had its own prospects and the paradoxes of cooperation and conflict, given the hegemon-subordinate relationship in a process of change. Change involved greater strength to the subordinate. Second Iraq war is an example.

In case one applies this to the situation that emerged at the time of the dismantling of the potential of the Russian Federation to play the role of the hegemon as also of the desire of the other States in the region to accept that role, to be more accurate, the Baltics showed the boot to the Russian domination. The Caucasian States were in no mood to listen to the tune of Russian supremacy. The attitude of Russia's Scottish neighbour may render the relationship between NATO and France under De Gaulle, if Ukraine goes on an uncompromising spree under some anti-Russian influence. This has not happened.

Secondly to be fair to Russia, it would be too much to label it a buoyant state on the lines of the USA after World War II. There is no denying the fact that Russia has the potential of a great power and that Yeltsin and Putin did try to retain the status of a Great power[45]. It is also true that Russia is still the strongest among the states in the region. Its power potential is therefor all to keep in mind while pursuing internal and external policies for the region. There are recent cultural and political similarities. All of them have moved out of the earlier authoritarian system in the direction of democratic reform and marketisation of the economy. The Russian Foreign Minister said, "the Russian Federation has been the centre of that configuration and is today economically, culturally and, in many other senses, certainly the locomotive which, by the direction and speed of its movement, determines willy- nilly the movement of other states"[46]. In the region of Asia and Pacific, it determines the course of politics. There are though some caveats to its strength since it needs to depend on the Western economic help and Japanese help to develop generally and to develop in its Siberian region. It is China's strategic partner.

Pragmatic Approach Needed in the Absence of External Enemy

Since interdependence is a process in which the hegemon must continuously adjust to the changing reality of the other partners either through self-adjustment or through direct or indirect influence, Russia will need to be pragmatic, to do so. It will have to correlate both the foreign and domestic policy to remove psychological barriers from among its neighbours. It will continue to have managed conflictual relations as exists with NATO. There is a difference, however. In the case of the formation of NATO, there was an external danger – Beneluex countries thought of Germany and this was transformed by American intervention when NATO identified the Soviet Union as the enemy country. In the case of Russia, it is very difficult to concretely identify the external enemy for itself and for the CIS and other states that have not signed the collective security agreement at Tashkent. In fact, the agreements subsequent to the Tashkent one, say it is NATO/US. The Defence Council met in November and concluded three documents viz. (a) to protect the victims of armed conflicts; (b) to coordinate the joint functioning of the Defence Ministries; (c) to change the list of Strategic forces to exclude many items that were included earlier[47]. This conference is reported to have discussed " the possibility of setting up an effective system of national and collective security suiting common interests for insurance of international stability and stability with the commonwealth... this applied to matters of eliminating and preventing armed conflicts within the CIS, the functioning and insurance of legal and social protection of servicemen, guarantees of the observance of their rights"[48]. What is, therefore, needed is not just a doctrine of deterrence at the nuclear level but to develop the capacities to have conventional deterrence for preventing armed conflicts in the CIS region. Therefore, what the military doctrine will have to develop is the provision for deterring small, local, short/ protracted violent conflicts apart from matching the dangers of soft borders and Western presence.

Nuclear Strategy

The other aspect of the NATO collective security was the development of a nuclear strategy. After the Truman and Eisenhower Years, the Kennedy and McNamara team formulated what was called the policy of flexible response to offset the Soviet preponderance that, according to the Europeans, may have led to a Soviet blitzkreig. In the 1950s, the United States had encouraged its European allies to believe that nuclear defence was just as good as, if not better than, conventional defence. The Kennedy-McNamara resolution meant the coupling of conventional deterrence with the use of nuclear weapons to deter a Soviet first strike. Kennedy thought that it was necessary to take two steps with respect to NATO, "...we must consider whether it is wise to maintain a situation in which information is denied to our friends which be no for certain is available to our potential enemies, and which places a premium on our allies developing at great expense nuclear capabilities which in themselves are of limited military significance."[49] Nuclear deterrence was combined with the doctrine of conventional deterrence and a massive programme of nukes was launched to bridge the "missile gap". The concept of limited war also found its expression as a response to the possible Soviet action outside the NATO theatre of security parameter. Kennedy mentioned the need of a limited war capacity of the USA. The evolution of the nuclear doctrine in the 1980s reached the stage in which limited nuclear war scenarios were developed. The USA officially adhered to a strategic doctrine in accordance with which a future nuclear war could be conducted in a limited manner[50].

As for the development of nuclear weapons and their control, the alliance showed that the French and the British were able to develop their nuclear arsenals; nuclear arsenals were placed in the then FRG but the control of those weapons was in the hand of the Sacuer i.e., in the hand of the NATO Commander and not in German hands. Any decision for renewing the nuclear arsenals or deploying new ones was debated within the alliance and a consensus was sought to be achieved in which the decisive say was that of hegemon. The Euro-missile crisis and the decisions with regard to the announcement of Strategic Defence Initiative (SDI) components were primarily those of the USA. The alliance partners were cajoled into these through various instrumentalities. The basic assumption in the alliance was the West European countries were not interested in decoupling their security from that of the USA. This rock bottom consensus was necessary for the alliance to countries. The intra-bloc relationship experienced conflict on the issues of financial burden sharing. In the 1980s the US Congress was insisting that the administration should make the partners pay more for their security. It is equally significant that these partners in collective security were unwilling to increase their share of the defence burden.

The CIS has, from the very beginning, been bugged by the nuclear issue. While the West has been talking of a possible first nuclear civil war, the Russians have been at pains to prove that the prospect of the same were remote since there was effective control of the nuclear weapons. There were two options left with the Russian leadership with regard to the nuclear weapon issue. Either it could have declared their existence on the territory of the erstwhile USSR, i.e. have four nuclear powers or it could have a successor to the USSR withdraw the nuclear weapons stationed in Ukraine, Belarus and Kazakhstan and emplaced them on its own territory. It opted for the latter. The situation is somewhat comparable with that of NATO since at its inception, apart from the USA, there were no nuclear powers. In the case of the CIS, apart from Russia, there is no nuclear weapons power though the Ukairne wanted to be one in future. Going by the present indictions, Ukraine may not have the technical know how to produce fissionable material even though it may have some parts of the production facility that were sprawling in the Soviet Union. The Union Defence Minister of Ukraine told the Ukraine Parliament in November 1992, "Ukraine believes that declaring Ukraine a nuclear state is not realistic and does not correspond to the economic possibility and the strategy interest of our state in the present period. The presence of nuclear ammunition only can not define the nuclear status"[51].

Legal Basis for Non-nuclear Ukraine

There was the legal basis for denuclearising the Ukrainian ammunition status since Ukraine had committed itself to the following; (a) that Russia was the successor to the USSR; (b) that Ukraine committed itself to own the international territory along with Belarus, Kazakhstan and Russia. They signed the protocol to the territory on limitation of offensive weapons. But the Ukrainian President has created condition by which there would develop a dual control over the strategic forces stationed on its territory till they are removed from there. Ukraine may not have its way since in Tashkent it is committed to reduced conventional weapons. It appeared by all evidence that the strategic offensive arms reduction treaties also be honoured by it. Commentators in Russia felt that the Ukrainian intrasigience was their since they wanted to confront the Ukrainian national security to that of the Russian[52].

Even if the Ukraine leadership aspired to the nuclear status in the future, it would go against the NATO experience where the French objected to the nuclear non-proliferation treaty (NPT) and went nuclear without offsetting the security parameters of the Alliance. Since the NPT is still regarded as discriminatory and ineffective, the Russian-Ukrainian relations will be strained since Russia wanted the NPT regime to be applied in its present form. It is not presented with a fait accompli in the next decade.

Re-coordinate Concept of Nuclear Deterrence

The CIS will, however, recoordinate the concept of nuclear deterrence and bring it in harmony with the doctrine of conventional deterrence in a situation where there is no defined external threat. This depended on the evolution of the Russian military doctrine that the Russian Defence Minister thought would be formulated for the first time. In absence of identification of an enemy or the nature of threat, the Russians proceeded to be ready to at least have minimal deterrence in the defensive mould and develop second strike capability. The defensive mould had evolved as a result of the writings of Nikolay Ogarkov, who wanted Russia/USSR not to rely on a single weapons system; on the WTO announcement on defensive defence and on the Gorbachev announcement on reasonable sufficiency. Common to all these developments was the fact that there would be new thrust on the development of high-technology weapons system emphasising on robotics, directed energy and manoeuverable weapons. The Deputy Defence Minister for Technology had said that the "new military technology policy of the Russian ministry of defence is the all around development of dual-purpose technology. So that we are self-sufficient in modern equipment in the Army and, at the same time, it can immediately go into parallel use in industry and in country's national economy as a whole"[53] . Further, he informed that the lag in robotics would be removed.

The changing parameters of the Russian defence doctrine and the emerging shape of the CIS collective security doctrine could not be adequately indicate till the stage of Moscow's Advanced Conventional Munitions (ACMs) is taken into account. This is also required by the ground reality of the CIS States where there is an increasing possibility of limited conventional conflict which would require the CIS intervention. Moscow, as we noted earlier, also proposed to develop a defensive doctrine that would require a second strike capacity. It has been argued that the Soviet theorists believed that a future war will be in the ACMs environment i.e., by 2010. Without going into the niceties of the emerging debate between defensive-offence and defensive-defence in the force structure in the Russian military doctrine, one must indicate that the new doctrine prepared for autonomous localised actions by highly mobile troops equipped with ACMs for battle-field purposes[54]. This is relevant for the localised action that the troops may have to take in order to defuse the localised conflict or engage in rapid action against forces that are involved in the instability on the orders. The emphasis would be on rapid responses and C^3I assets. Thus, it is obvious that the CIS forces will have to depend on ACMs and for this they will have to maintain common facilities across the borders, as the CIS C-in-C has often argued.

Finally, it must be noted that the CIS has been faced with a number of occasions to intervene in flash points. But it has been only Russian forces that have done so and, therefore, whatever be the basis for CIS forces, it is knocked off in reality[55]. Therefore, the accent is on bilateralism rather than on multilateralism that the CIS represents. At the given point, this was bound to happen. Most of the CIS states are in the process of forming their own armed forces that are at a very rudimentary stage, both in terms of structures and combat readiness. In the future, when the development of these forces takes place and when the leaderships come out of their present unsettled mould, the multilateral task forces may intervene. This is a very difficult objective to achieve if one again goes by experiences of other multilateral interventions like the allied one in the Gulf Wars. US/NATO presence, CIS States hve to deal with. A new peripheral status, once again!

References

1. Shireen T. Hunter, *Central Asia Since Independence,* The Washington Papers, The Center for Strategic Studies, Washington, D.C. Prager, Westport, Connecticut, London,1996, pp. xvii-xx.
2. Ivan Szelenyi, *The Rise of Managerialism, The New Class after the Fall of Communism,* Budapest Collegium, November,1995.
3. Boris Rumer, edited, *Central Asia In Transition, Dilemmas of Political and Economic Development,* M.E. Sharp, Armonk, London, New York, England,1996, pp. 36-37.
4. fn. 1, p. 117.
5. Andrew A. Michta, *The Government and Politics of Post-Communist Europe,* Prager, Westport, Connecticut, London, 1994, p. 6.

6. *Ibid.* p. 217.
7. Roland Danreutter, *Creaking New States in Central Asia,* Adelphi Papers, March 1994, p. 11.
8. Umirserik Kasenov, 'post-Soviet Modernization in Central Asia: Realities and Prospects', Boris Rumer, Stanislav Zhukov, edited by, *Central Asia: The Challenge of Independence,* M.E. Sharp, Armonk, New York, London, England, 1998, pp. 30-31.
9. Miroslav, Nationalism in Central Asia, in John Hutchinson and Anthony D. Smith, ed, Nationalism, London, NY, Routledge, Vol. 2, 2000.
10. Shireen T. Hunter, *op. cit.,* p. 168.
11. Boris Rumer, *Soviet Central Asia: A Tragic Experiment,* Boston, Unwin Hyman, 1989.
12. Boris Z. Rumer, 'Disintegration and Reintegration in Central Asia' in Boris Z. Rumer, ed., *Central Asia in Transition,* M. E. Sharp, Armong, NY, London, England, 1996, p. 31.
13. IMF, *Economic Review of Kazakhistan,* Washington D.C., 1995
14. IMF, *Economic Review of Uzbekistan,* Washington D.C., 1994
15. IMF, *Economic Review of Tadjikistan,* Washington D.C., 1994
16. IMF, *Economic Review of Kyrgystan,* Washington D.C., 1993
17. Howard Selsam, David Goldway, Harvey Martel, Selected and edited, *Dynamic of Social Change, A Reader in Marxist Social Science,* New World Paperbacks, NY, 1970.
18. H. Hodkins, edited, Post-Soviet Organisations, London, 1995.
19. Hans Morgenthau, *Politics Among Nations,* Calcutta, 1976, p. 113
20. *Times of India,* 14 February, 1993.
21. Alexy Tolstoy, *Peter the Great,* Moscow, 1985, Vol. 1, p. 226.
22. Speech by Barranikov to the Russian Congress of People's Deputies. *Summary of World Broadcasts,* SU/1563, 14 December, 1992.
23. Speech by Shaposhnikov to the Russian Congress of People's Deputies, *ibid.,* c 2/3-4.
24. Lobov, "Delay in transformation of armed forces would be worse than impermissible, "Krasnaya Zvezda, first-edition, Moscow, 23 October, 1991, trans. *Summary of World Broadcasts,* SU/1213, 26 October, 1991, p. B/3.
25. RIA report, "USSR Defence Ministry warns... Reform of USSR armed forces will begin in first half of 1992," Moscow Komosomolskaya Pravda in Russian, 24 September 1991, trans. *FBIS-SOV-91-186,* 25 September, 1991, p. 31.
26. Speech by Grachev at closed session on 5 December, 1992, Krasnaya Zvezda, Moscow, 8 December, 1992, *Summary of World Broadcasts,* SU/1562, 12 December, 1992, p. C1/1.

27. "Russian position within CIS," *Summary of World Broadcasts,* SU/1373, 6 May, 1992, p. C1/1.
28. "Yeltsin's decree establishes Russian armed forces, *Summary of World Broadcasts,* SU/1376, p. C2/1.
29. Treaty on the Union of Sovereign States, Agreed 23 July, 1991, trans. *FBIS-SOV-91-158,* 15 August, 1991.
30. Draft Treaty of Union of Sovereign States, *Summary of World Broadcasts*/Part 1, 27 November, 1991, Article 5.
31. Declaration on the Formation of the Commonwealth of Independent States. *Summary of World Broadcasts*/Part 1, 10 December, 1991.
32. The Minsk Agreement, Summary of World Broadcasts, Part 1, 11 December, 1991.
33. "Lobov advocates defence structure," Moscow Central Television First Programme Network in Russian, 17 October, 1991, trans. *FBIS-SOV-91-202,* 18 October, 1991, p. 33.
34. Lobov, n. 6.
35. *Summary of World Broadcasts,* SU/1378, 12 May, 1992, p. C3/1.
36. CIS military leaders discuss Tashkent summit, *Summary of World Broadcasts,* SU/1385, p. C3/1.
37. *FBIS-SOV-92-095,* 15 May, 1992, p. 7.
38. *Ibid.*
39. Assessment of collective security: Interview with Shaposhnikov. Moscow, Priorities and Prospects in English No. 3, September 1992, pp. 15-19. *FBIS-SOV-92-83,* 21 September, p. 2.
40. *FBIS-SOV-92-092,* 15 May, 1992, p. 7.
41. Interview with the Commander-in-Chief of the CIS strategic forces, General of the Army Yuri Manksimov, *FBIS-SOV-92-183,* p. 3.
42. "CIS crisis force proposed," Nezavisimaya Gazeta, in Russian, 5 March, 1992, p. 2. *Trans JPRS-UMA-92-010,* 18 March, 1992, p. 12.
43. Robert Keohane and Joseph S. Nye, Jr., *Power and Interdependence,* Boston, Little Brown, 1977.
44. "Power and interdependence revisited," *International Organisation,* 41, 4, Autumn 1987.
    Michiel S. de Vries, "Interdependence: cooperation and conflict: An empirical analysis," *Journal of Peace Research,* Vol. 27, No. 4, 1990, pp. 429-444.
45. Andrey Kozyrev outlines Russia's new foreign policy concept. Mayak Radio, Moscow, 14 December, 1992, *Summary of World Broadcasts,* SU/1557, p. A1/7.

46. *Ibid.*
47. CIS Defence Ministers met and conclude agreements, Russia's Radio, Moscow, 11 gmt, 6 November, 1992, *Summary of World Broadcasts,* SU/1514, p. C1/1.
48. Conference held on defence and security issues for CIS countries. Interfax news agency, Moscow, in English 1633 gmt 6 November, 1992, *Summary of World Broadcasts,* SU/1534, p.C1/1.
49. William W. Kaufmann, *The Mac Namara Strategy,* New York, Evantion and London, Harper and Row, 1964, p. 43.
50. Ian Clark, *Limited Nuclear war, political theory and war—Convention,* Princeton, Princeton University Press, 1982, p. 1.
51. Ukrainian Parliament fails to pass Draft Military Doctrine, Radio Ukraine World Services, Kiev 2000 gmt 28 October, 1992, *Summary of World Broadcasts,* SU/1527, 2 November, 1992, p. C/1/1.
52. Interview with Commander-in-chief of CIS Strategic forces, *n. 23,* p.4.
53. Deputy Defence Minister on Military Technology, Moscow Central Television First Programme on Orbita Networks, in Russian 1845gmt, 17 September, 1992, trans. *FBIS-SOV-92-184,* 23 September, 1992, p. 30.
54. Mary C. Fitzgerald, 'Advanced conventional munitions and Moscow's defensive posture', *Defence Analysis,* Vol. 6, No. 2, pp. 167-191,1990.
55. 'Prospects for military cooperation weighed', New Times International, in English, No. 36, September 1992, pp. 12-14, in *JPRS-UMA-2-138,* 21 October, 1992, pp. 7-9.

Bibliography

- Bengt Abrahamson, *Military Profession and Political Power, Grote borgs off settry ckeri,* 1987.
- Samuel Adamson, *The Military Establishment,* Beacon Press, 1964.
- Aijaz Ahmed, *Lineages of the Present,* Tulika, New Delhi, 1996.
- ——————, *Lineages of the Present, Ideology and Politics in Contemporary South Asia,* Verso, London, New York, 2000.
- M. J. Akbar, *The Siege Within, Challenges to a Nation's Unity,* Middlesex, Penguin Books, New Delhi, 1985.
- Tariq Ali, *Can Pakistan Survive, Death Of A State,* Penguin, New Delhi, 1983.
- Benedict Anderson, *Imagined Communities, Reflections on Origin and Spread of Nationalism,* Verso, London, New York, 1991.
- General K. M. Arif, *Working With Zia, Pakistan's Power Politics,* 1977-88, Karachi, Islamabad, New Delhi, Oxford, 1995.
- General K. M. Arif (Retired), *Khaki Shadows, Pakistan, 1947-1997,* Karachi, Oxford, 2001.
- Mohammad Ayub, *Regional Insecurity in The Third World,* 1989.
- Edward E. Azahar and Chung I. N. Moon, *National Security in The Third World,* Edward Elgar, Cambridge, 1988.
- Pranjali Bandhu, *Cinema in Focus, Black and White of Cinema in India,* Trivandrum, Odyssey, 1992.
- Paul Baran and Paul Sweezy, *Monopoly Capitalism,* Merlin Press, New York, 1966.
- Pranab Bardhan, *Political Economy of Development in India,* London, NY, Toronto, Delhi, Bombay, Calcutta, Madras, Karachi, OUP, 1984.

- Craig Baxter, edited, *Zia's Pakistan, Politics and Stability in a Frontline State,* Vanguard, 1985.
- Emile Benoit, *Defence and Economic Growth in Developing Countries,* London, Lexinton, 1974.
- Volker R. Berghahn, *Militarism: A History of International Debate, 1861-1979,* Cambridge, Cambrige University Press, 1981.
- Tom Bottomore, et. al, *A Dictionary of Marxist Thought,* Blackwell, Reference, 1983.
- Douglas W. Blum, edited, *Russia's Future, Consolidation or Disintegration,* Boulder, San Fransisco, Oxford, Westview Press, 1994.
- Rajeev Bhargava, edited, *Secularism and Its Critics,* Delhi, Oxford University Press, 1998; Sugata Bose, Ayesha Jalal, edited by, *Nationalism Democracy and Development, State and Politics in India,* Delhi, Calcutta, Madras, Mumbai, Oxford University Press, 1997.
- Paul Brass, *The Politics of India since Independence,* Cambridge, Cambridge University Press, 1996.
- Richard G. Braungart and Margaret M. Braungart, editors, *The Political Sociology of the State, Essays on Origin, Structure and Impact of the Modern State,* London, Jai Press Inc, 1990.
- Ian Budge and David Mckay, edited, *Developing Democracy,* New Delhi, Sage, 1994.
- Christiane Brosius and Melisa Butcher, edited, *Image Journeys, Audio-Visuals Media and Cultural Change in India,* New Delhi, Sage, 1999.
- Terence J. Byres, *The State, Class, Development Planning in India,* New Delhi, Oxford University Press, 1997.
- Albert Camus, *Myth of Sisypus,* Penguin, 1977.
- Sumita S. Chakravarty, *National Identity in Indian Popular Cinema,* Delhi, Madras, Calcutta, Oxford University Press, 1993.
- Bipan Chandra, *Communalism in Modern India,* Delhi, Vikas Publishing House, 1984.
- Partha Chatterjee, *The Nation and Its Fragments,* New Delhi, OUP, 1993.
- ———edited, *State and Politics in India,* Delhi, Oxford University Press, 1998.

- V. D. Chopra and Rakesh Gupta, *Nuclear Bomb and Pakistan, External and Internal Factors,* Patriot Publishers, New Delhi, 1986.
- Stephen Philip Cohen, *Civil Military Relations in India, Pakistan and Bangladesh,* mimeographed, 1973.
- ———, *The Pakistan Army,* ND, 1984.
- F. Cook, *The Warfare State,* New York, 1962.
- Colin Cooper, *Power and Politics in Soviet Union,* 1988.
- Rober A. Dahl, *Polyarchy,Participation and Opposition,* New Haven, Yale University, 1983, Roland Dannreutter, *Creaking New States in Central Asia,* Adelphi Paper, March, 1994.
- Jacques Van Doorn, edited, *Armed Forces and Society, Sociological Essays,* Mouton, The Hague, Paris, 1968.
- A. R. Desai, *Peasant Struggles in India,* Bombay, Oxford University Press, 1979.
- ————————, edited, *Repression and Resistance in India-Violation of Democratic Rights of the Working Class, Rural Poor, Adivasis and Dalits,* Bombay, Popular Prakashan, 1990.
- Lowell Dittmer and Samuel Kim, *China's Quest for National Identity,* Ithaca and London, Cornell University Press, 1993.
- Ashghar Ali Engineer, *Communal Riots in Post Independence India,* Hyderabad, Sangam Books, 1984.
- Peter Evans, Dietrich Reuschemeyer, Theda Skocpol, edited, *Bringing The State Back In,* Cambridge, Cambridge University Press, 1973.
- S. E. Finer, *The Man on Horseback, The Role of Military in Politics,* London, Dunmov, Pall Mall Press, 1962.
- Francine Frankel, *India's Political Economy, 1947-77, The Gradual Revolution,* Princeton, Princeton University Press, 1979.
- ————————and M. S. A. Rao, edited, *Dominance and State Power in India: Decline of a SocialOrder,* Delhi, Oxford University Press, 1990.
- C. J. Fuller and Veronique Benei, *State and Society in Modern India,* Social Science Press, 2000.
- Rajat Ganguly and Ian Macduff, edited by, *Ethnic Conflict and Secession In South, and South-east Asia, Causes, Dynamics, Solutions,* New Delhi, Thousand Oaks, and London, Westview Press, 2002.

- Sumit Ganguly, *Conflict Unending, India- Pakistan Tensions since 1947,* New Delhi, Oxford University Press, 2002.
- Madhav Gadgil and Ramchandra Guha, *Ecology and Equality,* New Delhi, Penguin, 1995; Mark Galeotti, *The Age of Anxiety, Security and Politics in Soviet and post Soviet Russia,* London and New York, Longman, 1995.
- Yu V. Gankovsky, *The Peoples Of Pakistan,* Moscow, Nauka Publishing House, 1971.
- Hasan Gardezi and Jamil Rashid, edited, *Pakistan: The Roots of Dictatorship, Political Economy of a Praetorian State,* London, Zed Press, 1983.
- Anthony Giddens, *The Class Structure of Advanced Societies,* London, 1973.
- *1998 Global Competitiveness Report of World Economic Forum.*
- *Government of India, White paper on Punjab,* New Delhi, GOI Publications, n.d.
- Asha Gupta, *Military Rule and Democratisation,* New Delhi, Deep and Deep, 2003.
- C. Das Gupta, *War and Diplomacy in Kashmir,* New Delhi, Sage, 2002.
- Dipankar Gupta, *Rivalry in Brotherhood, Politics in the Life of Farmers in Northern India,* New Delhi, Oxford University Press, 1997.
- N. L. Gupta, *Communal Riots,* Delhi,Gyan Publishers, 2000.
- Rakesh Gupta, *Soviet Policies in the Eighties,* New Delhi, Patriot Publishers, 1985.
- ————————, *Political Stability and Civil Military Relations under Gorbachev,* New Delhi, Lancers, 1992.
- ————————, *The Russian Military Doctrine,* New Delhi, Institute of Defense Studies and Analyses, 1996.
- Ted Robert Gurr and Barbara Harrf, *Ethnopolitical Conflicts in World Politics,* Oxford, Oxford University Press, 1994.
- Ted Robert Gurr, *Why Men Rebel,* Princeton, Princeton University Press, 1970.
- Mahbub-ul Haq, *Strategy of Economic Development : A Case Study of Pakistan,* Karachi, Oxford University Press, 1968.

- Mahbub-ul Haq, *Social Development in South Asia*, Karachi, Oxford University Press, 1998.
- Neil Harding, *State in Socialist Societies,* 1985.
- Selig Harrison, Paul H. Kriesberg and Dennis Kux, edited, *India and Pakistan, Fifty Years,* New York, Cambridge University Press, 1999.
- Rajen Harshe, *Twentieth Century Imperialism,* New Delhi, Sage, 1998.
- Sanjay Hazarika, *Strangers of the Mist, Tales of War and Peace from India's Northeast,* London, Viking, 1990.
- Donald A. Horowitz, *Deadly Ethnic Riot,* New Delhi, Oxford University Press, 2001.
- Samuel Huntington, *The Soldier and the State,* Cambridge, Harvard University Press, 1957.
- ——————————, edited, *Changing Patterns of Military Politics,* New Haven, The Free Press, 1962.
- ——————————, *Political Order in Changing Societies,* New Haven, Yale University Press, 1968.
- Mushahid Hussain and Akmal Hussain, *Pakistan, Problems of Governance,* Centre for Policy Research, New Delhi, Konark Publishers Ltd.
- John Hutchison and Anthony D. Smith, edited with introductions, *Nationalism, Critical Concepts in Political Science,* London and New York, Routledge, 2000.
- Morris Janowitz, *The Professional Soldier,* Glencoe, The Free Press, 1960.
- ——————————, *The Military in the Political Development of New Nations,* Chicago,University of Chicago, 1964.
- Owen Bennet Jones, *Pakistan, Eye of the Storm,* New Delhi, Viking, 2002.
- Chalmers Johnson, *Revolutionary Change,* Boston, Little Brown, 1966.
- Michael Kalecki, *Selected Essays on the Economic Growth of the Socialist and Mixed Economy,* Cambridge, Cambridge University Press, 1972.
- Pralay Kanungo, *RSS's Tryst with Politics, From Hedgewar to Sudershan,* New Delhi, Manohar, 2002.
- Afsir Karim, *Transnational Terrorism, The Danger in the South,* Lancer Papers, New Delhi, London, Hartford, Lancers International, 1995.

- Peggy Kauf, *A Derrida Reader, Between the Blinds,* New York, Columbia University Press, n.d.
- Narhari Kaviraj, *Farazi and Wahabi Movements,* New Delhi, People's Publishing House, 1982.
- Sudipto Kaviraj, edited, *Politics in India,* New Delhi, Oxford University Press, 1997.
- Fareed Kazmi, *The Politics of India's Conventional Cinema,* New Delhi, Sage, 1998.
- Nikhat Kazmi, *Ire in the Soul, Bollywood,* New Delhi, Harper Collins, 1996.
- Charles H. Kennedy, *Bureaucracy in Pakistan,* Karachi, Oxford, New York, Delhi, Oxford University Press, 1987.
- ————————, edited by, *Pakistan 1992,* Boulder, San Fransisco, Oxford, Westview Press, 1993
- Robert D. King, *Nehru and the Language Politics in India,* New Delhi, Oxford University Press, 1997.
- Atul Kohli, *India's Democracy,* New Delhi, Orient Longman, 1991.
- ————, *Democracy and Discontent, India's Growing Crisis of Governability,* New Delhi, Foundation Books,1991.
- Rajni Kothari, *State Against Democracy, In Search of Humane Governance,* New Delhi, Ajanta Publications, 1989
- Anne O. Krueger, *Economic Policy Reform,* Chicago, Chicago University Press, 2002.
- Veena Kukreja, *Civil Military Relations in South Asia, Pakistan, Bangladesh and India,* New Delhi, Newbury Park, London, Sage Publications, 1991.
- ————, *Contemporary Pakistan,* New Delhi, Sage, 2003.
- Ayesha Jayal, *Democracy and Authoritarianism in South Asia,* New Delhi, Cambridge University Press, Foundation Books, 1995.
- Arun Kumar Jana, Bhupen Sarma, edited by, *Class, Ideology and Political Parties in India,* South Asian Publishers Pvt. Limited, New Delhi, 2002.
- Anour Abdel-Malik, *Nations and Revolutions,* Social Dialectics, Albamy, 1981.
- Herman Kulke, edited, *The State in Modern India,* Delhi, Oxford University Press, 1997.

- Christina Lamb, *Waiting for Allah,* New Delhi, Viking, 1991.
- R. E. Lapp, *The Weapons Culture,* New York, 1968.
- Adrian Leftwitch, edited, *Democracy and Development,* London, J. K. Polity Press, 1996.
- V. I. Lenin, *State and Revolution,* Moscow, Progress Publishers, 1975.
- Seymour Martin Lipset, *Young New Nation.*
- David I. Lousher and Michael D. Salome, *Technology Transfers and US Security Interests: The Impact of Licensed Production,* Boulder and London, Westview press, 1987.
- D. A. Low, edited, *The Political Inheritance of Pakistan,* New Delhi, Macmillan, 1991.
- C. B. Macpherson, *Life and Times of Liberal Democracy,* Oxford, Oxford University Press, 1977
- Karl Mannheim, *Ideology and Utopia,* Routtedge and Paulkagan, London, 1947.
- Iftikhar H. Malik, *State and Civil Society in Pakistan,* Great Britain, St. Anthony's Press Ltd. 1997.
- Ved Marwah, *Uncivil Wars,* New Delhi, Harper Collins, 1995.
- Karl Marx and Frederich Engels, 'German Ideology', *Collected Works,* 1845-47, Moscow, 1985.
- Karl Marx, *Eighteenth Brumaire of Louis Bonaparte,* Moscow, Progress, 1974.
- ————————, 'On The Jewish Question', Marx and Engels, *Collected Works,* Vol. 3, Moscow, Progress, 1986.
- The Pickering Masters, *The Reception of John Locke's Politics,* Vol. iv, Pickering and Chatta, 1999.
- Allen Macgrath, *The Destruction of Pakistan's Democracy,* Karachi, Oxford University Press, 1996.
- George Mclenan, David Held, Stuart Hall, edited by, *The Idea of the Modern State,* Philadelphia, Open University Press, 1984.
- David Mclellan, *Marx before Marxism,* New Delhi, London, Penguin, 1972.
- ——————————, *Marx: The First Hundred Years,* Great Britain, Fontana paperback, 1983.
- John Mcguire, Peter Reeves and Howard Brasted, edited, Politics of Violence from *Ayodhya to Behrampada,* New Delhi, Thousand Oaks, London, 1996.

- S. Melman, *Pentagon Capitalism,* New York, 1970.
- Neil Melvin, *Russians Beyond Russia,* London, Chatham House, 1995
- Oliver Mendelson and Upendra Baxi, edited, *The Rights of the Subordinated People,* Delhi, OUP, 1994.
- Andrew D. Michta, *Government and Politics of Communist Europe,* Praeger, Westview Press, 1994.
- Joel S. Midgal, Atul Kohli and Viviene Shue, edited, *State Power and Social Forces: Domination and Transformation in the Third World,* New York, Cambridge University Press, 1994
- C. Wright Mills, *Power Elite,* New York, Oxford University Press, 1995
- Ralph Miliband and Leo Panitch, edited, 'New World Order', *Socialist Register,* New York, Merlin Press, 1992.
- B. B. Mishra, *The Indian Middle Class, Their Growth in Modern Times,* New Delhi, Oxford University Press, 1978.
- Barrington Moore, Jr. *Social Origins of Democracy and Dictatorship,* Boston, Beacon Press, 1966.
- ——————————, *Authority and Inequality under Capitalism and Socialism, USA, USSR and China,* United Kingdom, Polity Press, 1987.
- Gunnar Myrdal, *Asian Drama,* New York, Pantheon, 1968.
- Baldev Raj Nayyar, *India's Quest for Technological Self Independence, Policy Foundation and Policy Change,* Vols 2, New Delhi, Lancer, 1988.
- I. Natrajan, *India, Market Demographic Report, 1998,* CAER New Delhi, 1999.
- Bill Nichols, edited, *Movies and Methods,* Vols 2, Calcutta, Seagul Books, 1993.
- Amar Norman, *The Political Economy of Pakistan,* 1947-85, London, New York, 1988.
- Derek Offords, *Portraits of Early Russian Liberals,* Cambridge, OUP, 1985.
- Ola Tunander Pavel, Victoria Ingrid Einagel, *Geo-Politics in Post-Wall Europe, Security, Territory and Identity,* London, Thousand Oaks, London, PRIO, 1997.
- Amos Perlmutter and Valerie Plave Bennet, edited, *The Political Influence of the Military, A Comparative Reader,* New Haven, London, 1980.

- Gustav A Papanek, *Pakistan's Development: Social Goals and Private Interests,* Cambridge, Massachussets, 1967
- Nicos Poulantzas, *Political Power and Social Classes,* London, New Left Books, 1973.
- A. Raevsky and I. N. Vorobev, *Russian Approaches to Peace Keeping,* Research Paper No.28, UN, NY, Geneva, 1994.
- B. Raman, *A Terrorist State and as a Frontline Ally,* Lancer Paper and Publisher and Distributor, 2002.
- N. Ram, *Riding the Tiger,* New Delhi, Leftword Books, 1999.
- Tariq Rehman, *Language, Ideology and Power, Language Learning Among the Muslims of India and Pakistan,* Oxford, 2002.
- Thomas Righa, *Readings in Russian Civilization,* University of Chicago, 1963, vols. 2, London, 1962.
- Maroof Raza, edited, *Generals and Governments of India and Pakistan,* New Delhi, HR, Military Affairs series, 2001.
- Hasan-Askari Rizvi, *Military State and Society in Pakistan,* New Delhi, Macmillan Press, 2000.
- L. I. Rudolph, Susanne Rudolph, *In Pursuit of Lakshmi,* Chicago, Chicago University Press, 1987.
- Ranbir Samaddar, *A Biography of the Indian Nation, 1947-97,* New Delhi, Thusand Oaks, London, Sage, 2000.
- Ghanshyam Shah, edited, *Social Movements and the State,* New Delhi, Thousands Oaks, London, Sage Publications, 2002.
- ——————————, edited, *Capitalist Development, Critical Essays,* Bombay, Popular Prakashan, 1990.
- Swami Sahajanand Saraswati, *Mera Jeevan Sangharsh,* President, Sri Sitaram Ashram, Patna, 1952.
- Bhabani Sengupta, India, *Problems of Governance,* Centre of Policy Research, New Delhi, Konark Publications, 1996.
- K. Suresh Singh, *People of India,* National Series, Vols. 3, New Delhi, OUP, 1993.
- Edgar Snow, *Red Star Over China,* Pelican, 1973.
- R. S. Sharma, *The State and the Varna Formation in Mid-Ganga,* New Delhi, Manohar, 1996.
- T. V. Satyamurthy, edited, *Social Change and Political Discourse in India—Strutures of Power, Movements and Resistance,* Vols. 3, Delhi, OUP, 1994.
- Theda Skocpol, *States and Social Revolutions: A Comparative Analysis of France, Russia and China,* Cambridge University Press, Cambridge, 1979.

- Hederich Smith, *New Russians,* New York, 1990.
- Burton Stein and Sanjay Subramaniam, editors, *Institution and Economic Change in South Asia,* New Delhi, OUP, 1996.
- Ivan Szelenyi, *The Rise of Managerialism: The "New Class" After The Fall of Communism,* Institute of Advanced Study, Collegium Budhapest, Discussion Paper series No. 16, November 1995.
- Siara Suleri, *Meatless Days,* London, Collins, 1990.
- S. S. Thornburn, *Mussalmans and Moneylenders in The Punjab,* New Delhi, Mittal, 1983.
- Mao Tse tung, 'Hunan Report', Franz Schell and Orville Schruman, edited, *Republican China,* China Readings, New Delhi, Penguin, 1968.
- Alfred Vagts, *A History of Militarism,* Meridian Books, New York, 1959.
- M. S. Venkataramani, *The American Role in Pakistan,* 1947-58, New Delhi, Radiant, 1982.
- C. S. Venkataratnam, D. P. A. Naidu, *Privatisation and Labour,* SAAT and ILO, New Delhi, 2002.
- Pawan K. Verma, *The Great Indian Middle Class,* New Delhi, Penguin, 1998.
- Karl Von Vorys, *Political Development in Pakistan,* Princeton Centre of International Studies, Princeton, PUP, 1965.
- Mohammad Waseem, *Politics and the State in Pakistan,* National Institute of Historical and Cultural Research, Islamabad, 1994.
- Max Weber, *The Theory of Social and Economic Organisation,* New York, The Free Press, 1944.
- Stephen White, Alex Pravada, Zvigitelmann, edited by, *Developments in Russia and Post-Communist Politics,* New Delhi, Macmillan, 1995.
- Stephen White, *Russia's New Politics, The Management of a Postcommunist society,* Cambridge, Cambridge University Press, 2000.
- Rushbrooks L. F. Williams, *The State of Pakistan,* London, Faber and Faber, 1966 (Revised).
- Eric Wolf, *Peasant Wars in the Twentieth Century,* New Delhi, Penguin, 1976.
- Miles Wolpin, *Militarism and Social Revolution in The Third World,* Allenheld, Osmun, Landmark Studies, 1981.

- Lawrence Ziring, *Pakistan in The Twentieth Century, A Political History,* Karachi, Islamabad, London, New Delhi, Oxford University Press, 1997.

Articles

- John Adams, 'Pakistan's Economic Performance in the 1980s, Implications for Political Balance', Charles H. Kennedy, edited, *Pakistan 1992,* San Fransisco, Oxford, Westview Press, 1993.
- Hamza Alavi, 'Class and State', Hasan Gardezi and Jamil Rashid, edited, *Pakistan: Roots of Dictatorship, The Political Economy of a Praetorian State,* London, Zed, 1983.
- ———————, 'Peasants and Revolution', A. R. Desai, edited, *Peasant Struggles in India,* Oxford University Press, 1979 Bombay.
- Amiya Kumar Bagchi, 'Markets, Market Failures, And the Transformation of Authority, Property and Bondage in Colonial India' Burton Stein and Sanjay Subramaniam, edited, *Institutions and Economic Change in South Asia,* Delhi, Bombay, Madras, Oxford University Press, 1996.
- Pranab Bardhan, 'The State Against Society: The Great Divide in Indian Social Science Discourse', Sugata Bose and Ayesha Jalal, edited, *Nationalism, Democracy and Development, State and Politics in India,* Oxford University Press, Delhi, Calcutta, Madras, Mumbai, 1995.
- M. J. V. Bell, 'The Military in New States of Africa', Jacques Van Doorn, edited, *Army and Society, Sociological Essays,* Mouton, The Hague, Paris, 1968.
- N. Beliaeva, 'Russian democracy: Crisis as Progress', *Washington Quarterly,* Spring, 1993.
- Shaheed Javed Burki, ' Economic Policy After Zia-ul Haq' Charles H. Kennedy, edited, *Pakistan 1992,* San Fransisco, Oxford, Westview Press, 1993.
- Shaheed Javed Burki, 'Pakistan's Political Economy in 2000: Two Possible Scenarios' Henry Korson, edited, *Contemporary Problems of Pakistan,* in collaboration with American Institute of Pakistan Studies, Boulder, San Fransisco, Oxford; Lahore, Islamabad, Karachi, Pak Book Corporation, 1993.
- Brajadulal Chattopadhyaya, 'Political Process and Structure of Polity in Medieval India' Herman Kulke, edited, *The State*

in Modern India, 1000-1700, Delhi, Calcutta, Chennai, Mumbai, OUP, 1997.

- Stephen Philip Cohen,'The Nation and the State in Pakistan', *Washington Quarterly,* Summer 2002.
- Jean Louis Commot, Cinema, Ideology, Criticism' Bill Nichols, edited, *Movies and Methods,* Calcutta, Seagul Books, 1993.
- Radhika Desai, 'Culturalism and contemporary Right, Indian Bourgeoisie and Political Hindutva' *Economic and Political Weekly,* Vol. XXIV, No.12, March 20-26, 1999.
- 'Detailed Russian Military Doctrine', Rossisskiyee Vesti (Moscow) in Russian, transl. Courtesy, *Summary of World Broadcasts,* SU/ 1358, November 29, 1993.
- Amitai Etzioni, 'The evils of Self determination', *Foreign Policy,* Washington, No. 89, Winter 1992-93.
- Leela Fernandes, 'Restructuring the New Middle Class in Liberalising India' *Comparative Studies of South Asia, Africa, and the Middle East,* Vol. XXV, No.100, 2000.
- Peter Frank, 'Problems of Democracy in Post Soviet Russia', Ian Budge and David Mckay, *Democracy and Development,* New Delhi, Sage, 1995.
- Charles Fairbank, Jr. 'After August Coup', *Journal of Democracy,* Vol. 2., No.4, 1991.
- Francis Fukuyama, 'End of History', *National Interest,* Winter, 1998-99.
- Teesta Ghosh, 'Ethnic Conflict in Sindh and Its Impact on Pakistan', Rajat Ganguly and Ian Macduff, edited, *Ethnic Conflict and Secession in South and Southeast Asia,* Delhi, Thousand Oaks, London, Sage, 2003.
- Ye.T. Gaydar, Speech on December 2, 1992, *Summary of World Broadcasts,* SU/ 1554, December 3, 1992.
- Thomas Goltz, ' Letter from Eurasia: The hidden Russian hand' *Foreign Policy,* Fall, 1993.
- Kathleen Gough, 'Indian Peasant Uprising', *Economic and Political Weekly,* Special number, 1974.
- Afak Haydar, ' The Mohajirs in Sindh: A Critical Essay' J. Henry Korson, Jr. edited by, *Contemporary Problems of Pakistan,* Published in collaboration with American Institute of Pakistan Studies, Boulder, San Fransisco, Oxford, Westview Press, Lahore, Islamabad, Karachi, 1993.

- Jerry Hough, 'Political Participation in The Soviet Union' *Soviet Studies,* Vol. XXVIV, No.1, January 1976.
- Samuel P. Huntington, 'Clash of Civilization', *Foreign Affairs,* Summer, 1993.
- Ruslan Khasbulatov, Speech at the 7th Congress of Peoples Deputies' transl. Courtsey *Summary of World Broadcasts,* SU/ 1553, December1, 1992.
- Antol Lieven,' The Pressures on Pakistan', *Foreign Affairs,* January/ February 2002.
- Amithu Kothari, 'Whose Independence, The Social Impact of Economic Reform in India', *Journal of International Affairs,* Vol. 15, No.1.
- Veena Kukreja, 'Musharraf Style democracy in Pakistan', *World Focus,* April-May, 2002.
- Aftikhar H. Malik, 'Pakistan in 2001, The Afghan Crisis and the Rediscovery of the Frontline State', *Asian Survey,* Vol.42, No.1.
- Aditya Mukherjee, 'Indian Capitalist class and Foreign capital', *Studies in History,* No.1 January-June, 1979.
- I. N. Mukherjee, 'Economy and Democratisation of Pakistan', *World Focus,* 286-87, April-May, 2002.
- Dev Murarka, 'Russian elections: No Exit from Labrynth', *Economic and Political Weekly,* November 11, 1995.
- Eric A. Nordlinger, ' The Returm To The State: Critiques', *American Political Science Review,* Vol. 82, No. 3, September, 1988
- P. R. Panchmukhi, 'Social Impact of Economic Reforms in India, A Critical Analysis', *Economic and Political Weekly,* March 4, 2002.
- C. H. Hanumantha Rao, 'Agricultural Growth, Sustainability and Poverty Alleviation', *Economic and Political Weekly,* July 18-24/25-31, 1998.
- V. N. Rao, 'Economic Reforms and Poor: Emerging scenario', *Economic and Political Weekly,* July 18-24/25-31, 1998
- David C. Rapoport, 'A Comparative Theory of Military and Political Types', in Samuel P. Huntington, edited, Changing Pattern in Military Politics, New Haven, The Free Press, 1962.
- Hasan-Askari Rizvi, 'Civil-Military Relations in Contemporary Pakistan', *Survival,* Vol. 40, No. 2, Summer 1998.

- Tony Saichs, 'The Search for Civil Society and Democracy in China', *Current History,* September 1994.
- Khalid B. Sayeed, 'The role of Military in Pakistan', Jacques Van Doorn, *Armed Forces and Society, Sociological Essays,* Mouton, The Hague, Paris, 1968.
- Rajesh K. Singh, 'The nature of the state' M. P. Singh, edited, *Indian Political System,* Delhi, Jnanda, 1995.
- Shapashnikov, Speech to the Congress of Peoples Deputies, *Summary of World Broadcasts,* SU/ 1553 December 2, 2002.
- Lila Shvetsova,' The two sides of the new Russia', *Journal of Democracy,* Vol.6, No.3, July, 1995.
- Immanuel Wallerstein,' Collapse of Liberalism', Ralph Miliband, Leo Panitch, edited, *Socialist Register,* 1992.
- Eric R. Wolf, and Edward C. Hansen, 'Caudilla Politics: A Structural Analysis' in Amos Perlmutter and Valierie Plave Bennet, The Political Influence of the Military, Comparative Reader, New Haven and London,Yale University Press, 1980
- Yogendra Yadav, 'Theories of the Indian State' Seminar, 367 - March 1990.
- Speech by Yeltsin, *Summary of World Broadcasts,* SU/ 1553:2, December 1992.
- Speech by Yeltsin, *Summary of World Broadcasts,* SU/1799, September 1993.
- N. Vittal, 'Information Technology for Defence and Development', Talk Delivered at the National Defence College, March 2, 1993.
- S. Akbar Zaidi, 'Politics of Opportunism', *Economic and Political Weekly,* November 2-9, 2002, New Delhi.

Index

D

Y

Z